THE
MANCHESTER
BOOK
OF
DAYS

BEN MCGARR

First published 2013

The History Press
The Mill, Brimscombe Port
Stroud, Gloucestershire, GL5 2QG
www.thehistorypress.co.uk

British Library Cataloguing in Publication Data.
A catalogue record for this book is available from the British Library.

ISBN 978 0 7524 8308 5

Typesetting and origination by The History Press
Printed in India

JANUARY 1ST

1828: On this day, the first omnibus was launched – the forerunner of our present Metrolink. Passengers were taken to Pendleton for a fare of sixpence, or fourpence if they were willing to brave the elements and take their perch beside the driver. Locomotive power was provided by two sturdy horses. Others followed in the wake of the entrepreneur John Greenwood, so that 'commuting' was already in evidence by 1834.

1831: Temperance reformer, Joseph Livesey, noted on this day the great numbers of people 'crowded in every main street' who had turned out to greet both the New Year and a visit from Henry 'Orator' Hunt (*see* January 18th). He counted 162 people enter one dram-shop at New Cross in one half hour that evening – two thirds of which were women and girls. (W.H. Thomson, *History of Manchester to 1852*, John Sherratt & Son Ltd, Altrincham, 1967)

1894: Today saw the opening of the Manchester Ship Canal. The *Manchester Guardian* stated that, 'However far we may go back we shall not find a more epoch-making event in the history of Manchester.' Despite the 1884 construction estimates of £5,634,000, the final figure rose to £15,000,000. The *Guardian* then goes on to say, 'It is probable that never before have all classes of the population of a great industrial and commercial district so loyally and ungrudgingly supported a financial and commercial enterprise.' Four cotton ships from Galveston and New Orleans were the first to be unloaded.

JANUARY 2ND

1865: Richard Buxton, one of the greatest of Manchester's local self-taught artisan-botanists, died on this day aged seventy-nine. His chief monument is his *A Botanical Guide to the Flowering Plants, Ferns, Mosses, and Algæ, Found Indigenous Within Sixteen Miles of Manchester,* published in 1849, with a second edition published in 1859. Son of an Ancoats labourer, his official education amounted to three months of dame-school and two years of occasional attendance at Sunday school. Apprenticed to a shoemaker, he joined his master collecting herbs for medical purposes. He died at Limekiln Lane in Ardwick and was buried at St Mary's Church in Prestwich.

———— ◆ ————

1883: This day saw an unusual embassy arrive in the city. The Malagasy envoy from Madagascar was treated to a public soiree held by the mayor.

———— ◆ ————

1953: Seventy-eight-year-old Corporal Harry George Crandon died on this day. He had been awarded the Victoria Cross on the July 4th 1901, serving with Queen Mary's Own 18th Hussars at Springbok Laagte in the Second Boer War. His remains were laid to rest in Swinton Cemetery.

JANUARY 3RD

1942: Actor John Edward Thaw, best known for his portrayal of 'Inspector Morse', was born on this day in Longsight. His family moved to Gorton and then Burnage, where he attended the Ducie Technical High School for Boys. He left for London at the age of sixteen and gained a place at the Royal Academy of Dramatic Art.

———— • ◆ • ————

2011: On this evening, Manchester resident Craig Jones witnessed a UFO from his bedroom window. 'I saw a large orange light moving slowly towards the south for around ten to twenty seconds, then it extinguished itself and I saw what looked like a firework that didn't explode being fired from the ground towards where the light was.' In the words of 'Mike', posting on uk-ufo.co.uk, 'These orange glowing lights are being reported more and more and more. There *has* to be something going on!'

———— • ◆ • ————

2012: On this day, in the small hours of the morning, a 'mole gang' finally reached their target after digging a 100ft-long tunnel under a car park in Fallowfield to rob a cash machine. The tunnel had been made with laser guidance technology and was fully provided with lighting and buttressing. Once the gang were beneath the ATM, heavy machinery was used to cut through over 15in of solid concrete. According to police estimates the operation could well have taken six months to complete. Unfortunately for the ne'er-do-wells the machine's contents barely covered their expenses.

JANUARY 4TH

1609: Manchester was entering the modern age, and the seeds of its later wealth were already sprouting. On this day, according to a business contract signed by a local merchant, George Chetham, Manchester sent large batches of 'Stopport clothe, cotton yarne, or cotton wool, frizes, whites, ruggs, and bayes' to London. (William E.A. Axon, *Annals of Manchester*, John Heywood, Manchester, 1886)

—— ◆ ——

1872: Today saw St Mary's Church in Crumpsall hit by lightning and burn to the ground. The thunder storm was of unusual intensity, beginning with gale-force winds and heavy hail, followed by thunder and lightning – 'The flashes succeeded each other with great rapidity and were very vivid.' The church had been standing for thirty-three years, and its replacement was consecrated three years after this date by Dr Fraser, Manchester's first Bishop, becoming 'One of the finest ecclesiastical structures of the diocese'. (William E.A. Axon, *Annals of Manchester*, John Heywood, Manchester, 1886; William Arthur Shaw, *Manchester Old and New*, Cassell and Company, London, 1894)

—— ◆ ——

1956: Bernard Sumner, co-founder of the bands Joy Division and New Order, was born on this day. These two bands in particular did much to give Manchester's music scene its unique and successful distinctiveness through several decades.

JANUARY 5TH

1428: Today saw Reginald West become the first Baron of Manchester. His first act was to appoint three attorneys 'To receive seisin for him of and in the Manor of Manchester, with all and singular appurtenances'. His father, Thomas West, had married a woman named Joan. She was the sister of Baron Thomas la Warre who had established the Ecclesiastical College whose buildings are now occupied by Chetham's Library. (W. H. Thomson, *History of Manchester to 1852*, John Sherratt & Son Ltd, Altrincham, 1967)

———•◆•———

1719: The first ever Manchester newspaper, the *Manchester Weekly Journal*, containing 'the freshest advices, both foreign and domestic', was sold today for one pence. Over 300 issues were printed, until it was discontinued in 1726 (*see* January 7th). It was printed and sold by its proprietor, Roger Adams of Smithy Door, whose son, Orion, was to follow in his footsteps. Adams also printed Manchester's first book – *Mathematical Lectures* by John Jackson.

———•◆•———

2010: The unaccustomedly cold winter resulted in business losses of £24 million in Manchester for this January day. A foot of snow fell overnight, and the weather became so bad that *Coronation Street* was forced to cancel filming for the first time in fifteen years.

JANUARY 6TH

1708: Urmston-born dialect writer John Collier, better known as 'Tim Bobbin', was baptised at Flixton on this day. Moving around the wider Manchester area in his youth, he picked up the colloquial expressions of several districts before writing his most famous work, *A View of the Lancashire Dialect*. He has been described as, 'Coarse and sadly wanting in refinement', but his humour and love of caricature were well suited to the character of his subject. He was a schoolmaster for many years in Milnrow, where he died on July 14th 1786. (William E.A. Axon, *Annals of Manchester*, John Heywood, Manchester, 1886)

———— • • • ————

1847: On this day, James Crowther, one of Manchester's noted artisan naturalists, died. Born on June 24th 1768, this impoverished warehouse porter became a noted botanist, discovering the Lady's Slipper orchid and mudwort. It has been said that an eminent academic once went to Manchester in search of a particularly rare plant. He was quite surprised when he was referred to a porter working at a warehouse who knew exactly what he was looking for and told him exactly where to find it – a tale that was fictionalised in Elizabeth Gaskell's *Mary Barton*. (Percy, *Scientists in Humble Life*)

———— • • • ————

1854: Today saw all railway lines in Manchester shut down due to heavy blizzards, which resulted in the town being cut off to others.

JANUARY 7TH

1752: The first edition of the reincarnated *Manchester Weekly Journal* (*see* January 5th), published by Orion Adams, son of Roger Adams, was released today. The paper's existence was short, and Orion later died penniless in Chester in 1797, aged eighty. He had been reduced to posting playbills for a troupe of actors. At the age of seventy he 'Walked from London to Chester … with a heart as light as his pocket.' (William E.A. Axon, *Annals of Manchester*, John Heywood, Manchester, 1886)

———◆———

1837: This day saw the grand opening of the Corn Exchange (now known as The Triangle) at Hanging Ditch. The names of Shudehill and Long Millgate indicate a long involvement in agricultural matters and a specially built edifice in which the trade of grain and other goods could take place was built here. The main chamber is 600 square yards and the building cost £4,000 to construct.

January 8th

1835: Today saw the re-election of Manchester's first MPs of the modern age; Charles Paulett Thomson and Mark Philips. Joseph Brotherton was also re-elected as MP for Salford for a second term. All MPs stated here were Liberals.

———◆———

1840: Manchester's Police Commissioners relinquished their hold on civic power to the newly formed Borough Council on this day. It had been the organ of local government, which had presided over the town's growth as a world centre of industry since its formation in 1792. They were granted the 'use of such room or rooms in the Town Hall as may be necessary for holding the meetings of the Council or any Committee thereof.' The remaining administrative structures of the old Police Commission were then absorbed into the machinery of the new Municipal Corporation. (W.H. Thomson, *History of Manchester to 1852*, John Sherratt & Son Ltd, Altrincham, 1967)

———◆———

1868: An application was posted on this day from Manchester City Council to Parliament, which marked the amalgamation of the Manchester and Salford Courts of Records.

JANUARY 9TH

1782: On this day, philanthropist Dr Thomas Barnes proposed the founding of a scientific institute. In a paper he read to the Manchester Literary and Philosophical Society, Dr Barnes recommended attaching a museum to a textile factory in order to demonstrate the workings and benefits of the various machines and processes involved in manufacture. Aside from the clear benefit such a body would provide the town, one of the more practical motives behind the plan was an attempt to highlight to the workers the advantages of mechanisation – a vital matter in the times of Ludditism, when many old-style weavers, discontented with the changes happening in their industry, were intent on destroying the machines that threatened their livelihoods.

———— ◆ ————

1846: Manchester's captains of industry, trade and finance gathered today to discuss the furtherance of the Anti-Corn Law League (*see* January 10th). As a result, a committee of gentlemen intent on increasing the fund of the League to £250,000 by gathering contributions in person was formed.

JANUARY 10TH

1839: Manchester businessmen met today to lay the foundations of the Anti-Corn Law League, which would impress upon the nation the newfound political will of the town; it would also go down in history as the first true ancestor of the organised modern single-issue lobbying group. Motivated by a healthy mixture of philanthropy and self-interest, they sought to influence Parliament against the crushing tax on corn importation, which impoverished their workers and indirectly damaged their trade. Mr J.B. Smith, who would later become Secretary of the League, promised to donate £100 to the movement, a start that would soon see its funds grow to tens of thousands of pounds.

———•◆•———

1844: Today's *Manchester Guardian* printed the obituary of J.E. Taylor, its founder, owner and principal editor since it was established in 1821 (*see* May 5th). A dissenting clergyman's son, he rose to prominence in the political pamphleteering of the early 1810s, decrying the Peterloo Massacre and successfully defending himself against the libel charges of his reactionary enemies. His many innovative editorials for the old *Manchester Gazette* are said to have quadrupled the newspaper's circulation. These unpaid services to liberal politics ended in 1821, when the *Guardian* ushered in a new era of provincial reporting, characterising previous local papers as being 'little better than compilations from the London journals'.

January 11th

1749: On this day, the remainder of the rebels who had formed Bonnie Prince Charlie's Manchester Regiment were removed from Southwark Gaol and transported to the Americas after three years' imprisonment.

◆

1845: The German-born Manchester-silk manufacturer Louis Schwabe was poisoned to death today. He had produced Queen Victoria's wedding dress and items for the French King, Louis Phillippe. He had been married to the cousin of author W.M. Thackeray, and sat on the Council of Art which was promoting the Royal Manchester Institution. However, the news of his father's death at his birthplace of Dessau is thought to have driven him temporarily insane from grief. As a result, he took his own life at the age of forty-seven.

◆

1859: Mr Owen's toyshop on Oldham Street burnt down today, which saw £4,000 worth of playthings go up in smoke! (*see* November 19th.)

January 12th

1643: It was on this day that Civil War General Sir Thomas Fairfax set up his Roundhead headquarters in Manchester. Fairfax left to relieve Northwich in Cheshire on the 21st, accompanied by 2,500 infantry and 28 cavalry. He was succeeded by Sir John Seaton, who took part of the local garrison to retake the town of Preston for the Parliamentarians (*see* February 10th).

1878: Local hero Mark Addy was summoned to Salford Town Hall today. MP W.T. Charley presented him with an illumined address and a bag of 200 guineas, which were the result of a subscription, started in his honour among the public, grateful for his many rescues of people who had fallen into the River Irwell.

2003: Bee Gee superstar Maurice Gibb died today in Florida. Born on the Isle of Man, he and his brothers grew up in Manchester, the native city of their mother Barbara. Maurice had suffered from a serious alcohol addiction, partly initiated by his early years as a drinking buddy of Ringo Starr, though he managed to pull himself together after a stint in rehab. He was awarded a CBE alongside his brothers in 2002, but passed away before the ceremony. His son, Adam, collected the honour on his behalf. (*BBC News*, May 27th 2004)

JANUARY 13TH

1840: On this day, 4,000 supporters of the Anti-Corn Law League attended a banquet – the first event to be held in the new Free Trade Hall on Peter Street. Irish MP Daniel O'Connell was among the attendees.

◆

1890: Metal engineer and boiler manufacturer Daniel Adamson, of Daniel Adamson & Co., died on this day. Born in Durham in 1820, he was the thirteenth child of fifteen. He was employed as an apprentice to the engineers of the Stockton and Darlington Railway and was the manager of Heaton Foundry in Stockport by 1850. He established the Newton Moor Iron Works near Hyde and made his fortune by manufacturing Manchester Boilers. Exporting these all over the world, he found himself with the means to engage in successful experimentation to improve the understanding of engineering with steam and metal, and to promote the Manchester Ship Canal project (*see* June 27th).

◆

1906: The *Manchester Guardian* reported the following on today's General Election: 'The outstanding features of Saturday's polls are: the magnificent victories of Liberalism and Labour; the defeat of the ex-Premier [Balfour]; the triumph of Mr Winston Churchill; the utter rout of the Unionist party in the great constituencies of Manchester, Salford, Bradford and Plymouth; Manchester, Liberal, labour and free-trade triumph.' Four Liberal MPs (including Churchill) and two Labour MPs (Clynes and Kelley) replaced four Conservative (including Balfour) and two Liberal MPs. Salford elected three Liberals, including the writer Hilaire Belloc, replacing three Conservatives.

JANUARY 14TH

1832: On this day, violinist Niccolo Paganini played a concert in Manchester. The *Manchester Guardian* reported: 'Reader, you have seen some of the portraits of Paganini ... caricatures of his person and his countenance. You have probably thought that, even for caricatures, his peculiarities were grossly exaggerated. Reader, you were under a mistake ... His smile on receiving the applauses of the audience is the most extraordinary, the most unearthly expression that ever marked the countenance of a human being; but to form the most remote conception of it, he must be seen. We shall certainly not attempt to describe it. Then his performance! It is almost as little amenable to the powers of description as his countenance ... his tones were the most extraordinary that we ever heard from any musical instrument ... susceptible of all the varied intonation of the human voice; to be capable of expressing all the varieties of human passions; in short, they wanted nothing but articulation to form a complete language.'

———— • ◆ • ————

1881: Today, a bomb exploded at the Salford Barracks, injuring a boy named Richard Clark; he died two day later. The bomb was believed to have been the work of Fenian terrorists, and a £500 reward was offered by the government for the capture of the perpetrators by the 22nd. On the 26th, the coroners returned a verdict of 'wilful murder' but nobody was ever charged.

January 15th

1581: On this day, it was recorded that 'Margret Wilson, a Kendall woman, was slain with a tree in the churchyard.' As to the precise nature of this accident, the reader's guess is as good as anyone's. (Richard Wright Procter, *Memorials of Manchester Streets*, T. Sutcliffe, Manchester, 1874)

———◆———

1601: It was on this day that Alice Hodghead, the daughter of Richard, was 'borne in the dungion' – another laconic communication from the old town records. Mrs Hodghead remains unnamed, and there is no information to suggest why a heavily pregnant woman was incarcerated in the town dungeon. It is most likely that when mentioning the dungeon, it is referring to the unpleasant small chamber built into the base of the old stone bridge across the Irwell (which was demolished in 1776).

———◆———

1867: Thirteen-year-old Richard Hughes was killed at Bradford Colliery today. His head was 'crushed between the roof and an empty coal tub when it started moving up the jig brow', as recorded on his death certificate. (pittdixon.go-plus.net)

———◆———

1884: Today, the Japanese Ambassador Jushi-i-Mori and his wife visited Manchester. They were shown around the Sir Elkanah Armitage and Sons Mills and the Hoyle and Sons Printworks, before being entertained by the mayor at a luncheon in the Town Hall.

January 16th

1807: Julius Leuchte, leader of the band at the Manchester Gentleman's Concert, died at the age of twenty-five following a short illness. An early member of Manchester's German community, Leuchte was the the chief source of the local forays into classical music.

———◆———

1844: Colonel John Drinkwater-Bethune, almost the last survivor of the heroic 72nd Regiment of Manchester Volunteers, died on this day at the age of eighty-one. Born in Salford, he studied at Manchester Grammar before entering the army at fifteen, just as the 72nd was being raised in the town. As captain of the regiment, he kept a detailed journal of the bold defence of the Rock of Gibraltar, which, at almost four years, was the longest siege withstood by the British Army. From these notes he later went on to write the military classic, *A History of the Siege of Gibraltar*.

———◆———

1939: Today saw the IRA let off three bombs in Manchester; one at Mosley Street, one a Princess Street and a third on Hilton Street. The Hilton Street bomb fatally injured a market trader who was on his way to Smithfield Market. Over the next twenty-four hours the police carried out major raids, in which ten members of the IRA were captured, along with six barrels of explosives and forty sticks of gelignite. One of the captured men was later sentenced to seven years in prison.

JANUARY 17TH

1833: Robert Stephenson of Worsley died at the age of seventy-nine on this day. He had defended Gibraltar as part of the 72nd Manchester Volunteers Regiment, and had been the first man to begin mining into the Rock of Gibraltar, which is now riddled with tunnels.

———•◆•———

1863: On this day in Chorlton-on-Medlock, a baby boy was born to William George and his wife Elizabeth; they named him David. Two months later, William returned to his native Pembrokeshire to die and Elizabeth (*née* Lloyd) took the children to her native village of Llanystumdwy in Gwynedd. This is how the great Liberal Prime Minister, war leader and founder of old-age pensions, David Lloyd George, is known to be from Gwynedd and not Manchester.

———•◆•———

1948: Today saw Manchester United chalk up their top 'home attendance' figure, with a crowd of 83,260 watching the 1–1 draw against Arsenal – the second highest turnout of all time in English football (for the first, *see* March 3rd). Oddly enough, damage suffered at the hands of the Luftwaffe at Old Trafford meant that this match took place at the ground of their rivals, Manchester City, at Maine Road. Adding injury to insult, United were paying City £5,000 a year for the privilege and were £15,000 in debt by the time Old Trafford finally reopened in 1949. Old Trafford's own record attendance figure didn't involve Manchester United either; the record figure of 76,962 in 1939 was for an FA Cup semi-final between Wolverhampton and Grimsby.

JANUARY 18TH

1819: Hero of the Radical movement, Henry 'Orator' Hunt, arrived in town on this day. His provocative speeches would strike fear into the hearts of the local Reactionary party and Magistrates, and set in motion the chain of events that was to culminate in the bloody tragedy of the Peterloo Massacre in August that year (*see* August 16th).

———◆———

1846: Today saw the King Street's York Hotel buildings host the first annual meeting of the Manchester Commercial Association, chaired by the president of the association, James Aspinall Turner.

———◆———

1960: Manchester-born Henry Kelly died today in Prestwich. Kelly served as a major in the 10th battalion the Duke of Wellington's (West Riding) Regiment, and his feats of bravery in the Somme on October 25th 1916 won him this most prestigious of all military medals, the Victoria Cross. His grave is at the Southern Cemetery in Manchester.

JANUARY 19TH

1863: On this day, Manchester cotton workers showed their support for Abraham Lincoln. The workers were suffering from the Cotton Famine caused by the American Civil War, nevertheless they supported the Union against the cotton-growing Confederacy (*see* December 31st), for which Abraham Lincoln was particularly thankful today: 'I know and deeply deplore the sufferings which the working people of Manchester and in all Europe are called to endure in this crisis ... I cannot but regard your decisive utterances ... as an instance of sublime Christian heroism which has not been surpassed in any age or in any country. It is indeed an energetic and re-inspiring assurance of the inherent truth and of the ultimate and universal triumph of justice, humanity and freedom.'

1951: Today, the *Manchester Guardian* reported an unlikely notice in a shop window: 'Gentlemen's hair permanently waved, from 21s.' Perms for men were apparently becoming a lucrative business and this same article stated that many erstwhile barber shops were becoming 'ladies' and gents' hairdressers'. It is also stated that the average 'masculine perm' would take one and a half hours, with the more elaborate requiring two or three hours and costing three guineas.

JANUARY 20TH

1806: The Portico Library opened its doors for the first time today. Located in Mosley Street, this combined newsroom and library was built at a cost of £7,000. Its archived newspaper collection was later regarded as the most complete of any outside the capital.

———◆———

1845: Evan Price was arrested today for stealing £3,500 from his employer, Mr Percival, a woollen draper on King Street. Price was later found guilty and transported to Australia.

———◆———

1887: John Prettyjohn died in Manchester on this day. He was a colour-sergeant of the Royal Marines, and was awarded the Victoria Cross for his involvement in the Battle of Inkerman on November 5th 1854, during the Crimean War.

January 21st

1526: Thomas West, the eighth Lord la Warre and fifteenth Lord of Mamcestre, died today. Thomas had been a great favourite of Henry VII, who had amply rewarded him for his support of the Lancastrian side in the Wars of the Roses. Thomas' exploits took him far from his manor, seeing him serve in arms in Flanders in 1491 and against Cornish rebels in 1496. He was made a Knight of the Garter in 1510 and a Knight Banneret for his valour at the 1513 Battle of the Spurs. Lord Mamcestre had escorted Holy Roman Emperor Charles V from the Channel port of Gravelines over the sea to Dover.

1802: A terrible hurricane struck Manchester on this day, and a whole cotton mill was blown down at Pendleton, while one of the clock faces of St Ann's clock tower was blown out.

1867: Today saw Manchester prohibitionists celebrate being one step closer to their goal of making the town a 'dry borough', as Mayor Neill presided over a town meeting which introduced a ban on Sunday trading in intoxicating liquors.

JANUARY 22ND

1554: The trial of Mancunian Protestant proselytiser John Bradford, charged with heresy and sedition, took place on this day. Occurring during the reign of 'Bloody' Queen Mary, champion of the Roman Catholic cause, the guilty verdict would have come as little surprise. Bradford would mount the scaffold and suffer martyrdom for the reformed faith over a year later, on June 30th 1555.

———◆———

1875: The Marquis of Salisbury, on a visit to Manchester with his wife the marchioness, had a hectic day of formal visits and receptions. Beginning at the Town Hall to receive the address of the Corporation, the marquis and marchioness – along with the Lord Chief Justice, Sir A.E. Cockburn, and several local MPs – then went on to the Athenaeum to inspect the artworks on display, as well as celebrate the institution's refurbishment after a devastating fire (*see* September 24th). Both Salisbury and Cockburn gave speeches to members at the Free Trade Hall, before they rounded off the day's programme with a visit to the Exchange to see the financial heart of the city. The party took luncheon at the Queen's Hotel as guests of the Manchester Chamber of Commerce.

JANUARY 23RD

1749: The heads of Manchester Jacobite heroes Deacon, Syddall, and Chadwick were stolen from the top of the Exchange today. Their heads had been placed there several years earlier by the victorious Hanoverian forces, who decreed that the heads be displayed. Rumour has it that they were secretly buried by loyal followers of the Stuarts in the gardens of a nearby house.

———— • ◆ • ————

1819: On this day, Radical politician Henry Hunt and his party were involved in a political scuffle against Earl of Uxbridge and several officers of the 7th Light Dragoons at Manchester's Theatre Royal.

———— • ◆ • ————

1848: On this day, the first ever Bishop of Manchester, James Prince Lee, was consecrated at Whitehall by the Archbishop of York, and the Bishops of Chester and Worcester.

JANUARY 24TH

1834: Manchester showed itself as being well ahead of its time in political matters, as well as those of trade and industry, arguing for the public ownership of utilities. Today's *Manchester Times* reported that it was 'In Manchester alone that people could be found who advocated the municipal provision of public utilities as a consciously held and fully articulate doctrine of social ownership.' That this was no minor matter was well illustrated by the recent contribution of the Gas Commissioners of £10,191 7s 5d to the Improvement Fund, which demonstrably indicated the scale and prosperity of the undertakings concerned.

1840: Manchester's chief of police Captain Sleigh was awarded a medal by the Royal Humane Society on this day. He received the honour for constructing a makeshift raft from a pair of gates in order to save the lives of the inhabitants of several cottages by the River Irwell, which had swollen to a remarkable height.

1864: Fifteen-year-old Martin Judson was charged today with stealing several pounds of cheese from the shop of Mr John Markendale on Berkeley Street in Strangeways. The boy's father said that his son had been led into 'bad company of late', and begged for the case to be dismissed. The Magistrate replied that 'The prisoner had already been convicted of [picking pockets] and the offence could not be overlooked.' Martin was sentenced to one month's imprisonment and five years in reformatory. (*Manchester Guardian*)

JANUARY 25TH

1796: Today saw the publication of Thomas Battye's *A Disclosure of Parochial Abuse, Artifice & Peculation in the Town of Manchester*. The town's administrative provisions – which were still medieval in manner – were clearly in need of some reform, but it would take several generations before the matter would be satisfactorily dealt with. His publication of the next year bore the even more inflammatory title of *The Bed Basil Book, or Parish Registers for the Maintenance of the Offspring of Illicit Amours*, which can hardly have been welcome to the local bigwigs for the revelations contained within.

1915: James Miller, better known as folk musician 'Ewan MacColl', was born in Broughton today. Shadowed by MI5 for his Communist activism, he took part in many political actions during the Great Depression, including the Peak District mass trespass in 1932 (*see* April 24th). His song 'Dirty Old Town' (often mislabelled as a traditional Irish song) commemorates the Salford of his youth. He did not hesitate to use his song writing for political purposes, sometimes rather shockingly, as in 'The Ballard of Stalin': 'Joe Stalin was a mighty man and a mighty man was he! He led the Soviet people on the road to victory.' MacColl died on October 22nd 1989.

January 26th

1796: Veteran soldier John Shaw died on this day, aged eighty. He was the master of Shaw's Punch House – home to a club of 'Church and King' Tories, where convivial local chatter was combined with serious discussion of nationwide politics. An advocate of early closing hours, at 8 p.m. he would crack a horsewhip and cry out that the time had come to drink up. Protesters were met with little mercy, treated to a bucket-full of cold water by the sturdy maid Molly Owen. Even the county MP was not immune: 'Colonel Stanley, you are a law-maker, and should not be a law-breaker; and if you and your friends don't leave this room in five minutes, you will find your shoes full of water.' (Richard Wright Procter, *Memorials of Manchester Streets*, T. Sutcliffe, Manchester, 1874)

1869: On this day, Chartist leader Ernest Jones died. Despite his aristocratic birth and having the King of Hannover as godfather, he joined the radical cause – a decision that would eventually result in him spending two years in prison. Occasional violent outbursts got him into trouble, especially his ominous prediction of June 6th 1848 in which he said, 'The green flag of Chartism will soon be flying over Downing Street.' He was intending to run for election in Manchester, but died before he had the chance. One hundred thousand people lined the streets to watch his funeral procession. (William E.A. Axon, *Annals of Manchester*, John Heywood, Manchester, 1886)

January 27th

1801: On this day, twenty-three people perished as Littlewood and Kirby's cotton mill, by the River Medlock, caught fire.

———◆———

1808: A meeting was held at the Bull's Head Tavern today, which discussed buying the manorial rights of the town from the Mosley family, as part of a general Local Act to promote urban improvements. The suggested sum of £90,000 was mentioned, and a veritable war of pamphlets for and against broke out over the issue. Failure to reach a positive resolution saw the matter postponed for a further forty years, when the newly formed Town Council would be forced to cough up over twice that amount.

———◆———

1984: Madonna made her first UK appearance in Manchester tonight, at the Haçienda. Televised by Channel 4 for the programme *The Tube*, the performance was a one-off performance of her hit song 'Holiday'. Fatboy Slim (DJ Norman Cook) was in the club that night and stated that the 'Queen of Pop' 'mesmerised the crowd'. (The *Guardian*, November 23rd 2005)

JANUARY 28TH

1845: A locomotive boiler at the Manchester and Leeds Railway engine house in Miles Platting exploded today, killing three men instantly and destroying a considerable part of the building. The jury at the inquest requested a *deodand* (an inanimate object or beast found 'guilty' of causing death) of £500 for the engine.

———◆———

2010: Ben Holden, local man and frequent drinker at The Castle public house on Oldham Street, had a eureka moment today – the Manchester Egg; a pickled egg (a traditional pub favourite) wrapped in Lancastrian black pudding and deep fried in breadcrumbs. To date, several venues across Manchester stock them and this pub snack has crept into the stadium fayre's old meat pie monopoly (*see* November 3rd).

JANUARY 29TH

1800: A young woman lost her life today when Salisbury's factory at Knott Mill burnt down. Such fires were commonplace at this time, before adequate measures were taken to fireproof the new mills and warehouses. A further blaze occurred five days later at Pollard's factory in Ancoats and in 1799 Robinsons' Mill on the River Irwell had suffered some £12,000 worth of fire damage.

· ◆ ·

1818: The last living witness of the Jacobite occupation of Manchester in 1745, Mrs Sarah Bowden, died on this day. At the age of ninety-two, she possessed a clear recollection of the tumultuous events of that year. And it seems her family had a remarkable disposition to longevity; living with her sister and two brothers, their combined age was some 320 years.

· ◆ ·

1839: Prince Louis Napoleon Bonaparte, who later became Emporer Napoleon III, arrived in Manchester today to visit its mills and public buildings.

· ◆ ·

1868: The final meeting of the Manchester Natural History Society was held on this day. For over fifty years it had amassed a museum collection worth some £20,000, which it left to the Manchester Museum allied with Owens College (now the University). It also left a generous endowment, specifying that the future museum must be free entry.

January 30th

1713: Edmond Harrold, local wigmaker and Manchester's answer to Samuel Pepys, pens a rather typical entry in his diary: 'Went none to church, but drank all day. Thus I ended the month of Jan. with loss, grief, shame and pain.'

————— • ◆ • —————

1858: Sir Charles Hallé conducted the first performance of the Hallé Orchestra this Saturday evening at the Free Trade Hall. Beethoven, Mozart, Auber, Rossini, Berlioz and Weber occupied a full programme. The *Manchester Guardian*'s review remarked that, 'No provincial town except Manchester, we venture to think, is in a position to make such an experiment; partly from the fact that no other town has so large a body of resident instrumental musicians, but more, perhaps, from the fact that no other town possesses a resident musician of Mr Hallé's calibre.' Hallé would prove a Manchester institution for the rest of his long life, his funeral procession bringing the bustling metropolis to a respectful standstill thirty-seven years later, in 1895.

————— • ◆ • —————

2007: The government announced today that East Manchester would be the site for a new regional super casino. It would have a minimum floor area of 5,000sq m and up to 1,250 slot machines, as provided for in the 2005 Gambling Act. It was to have been built near the Sport City complex, and would have helped to provide jobs and attract further private investment to the area. Plans for development were scrapped when Gordon Brown became Prime Minister later that summer.

January 31st

1792: On this day, George III signed an Act for the 'cleansing, watching and regulating the streets, lanes, passages, and places within Manchester and Salford, and for widening and rendering more commodious several of the said streets, lanes and passages, and for other purposes therein mentioned.'

———◆———

1818: The Manchester and Salford Savings Bank in Marsden Square (now a corner of the Arndale Centre) was established on this day.

———◆———

1835: Today saw Collier and Co.'s works at Church Bank in Salford totally destroyed. An 'immense' wall of masonry collapsed on the other side of the River Irwell, which had held up the new road at Hunt's Bank. Luckily, there were no fatalities. (William E.A. Axon, *Annals of Manchester*, John Heywood, Manchester, 1886; W.H. Thomson, *History of Manchester to 1852*, John Sherratt & Son Ltd, Altrincham, 1967)

———◆———

1842: On this day, the Theatre Royal played host to an Anti-Corn Law bazaar, where a staggering £9,000 was raised – a truly remarkable flexing of the new civic muscle of Manchester.

———◆———

1849: A great banquet at the Free Trade Hall today celebrated the final repeal of the Corn Law. George Wilson presided, and the number of people thought to have been at the gathering was some 3,000, including 20 MPs and 200 merchants.

FEBRUARY 1ST

1643: Gamaliel Whitaker, vicar of Kirk Burton in Yorkshire, died at Widow Birch's on this day. A staunch Royalist, Revd Whitaker had been captured by vengeful Parliamentarians after the attack of the Duke of Newcastle in Holmfirth. An assault on his parsonage on January 12th resulted in his wife, Hester, being shot and the Revd being carried off in custody to Manchester, where he met his end 'from grief and ill usage'. (Richard Wright Procter, *Memorials of Manchester Streets*, T. Sutcliffe, Manchester, 1874)

———— ◆ ————

1788: Sir Ashton Lever died at the Bull's Head Inn today. It is thought that he committed suicide, possibly from drinking poison. This Alkrington character had been a compulsive collector of zoological and archaeological curiosities, ever since having shot a 'white sparrow' as a boy. His 'Leverian Museum' was auctioned in 1806, taking a remarkable sixty-five days. Francis Looney was later to resmark that the 'operative naturalists' so common in the region had played a great part in increasing his fossil collection – working men with an interest in palaeontology that Sir Ashton had encouraged by allowing them to borrow his books and inspect his own pieces. ('Percy, Scientists in Humble Life: The Artisan Naturalists of South Lancashire' in the *Manchester Region History Review*, Vol. V, No. 1, 1991)

———— ◆ ————

1913: Manchester City played Sunderland in the second round of the FA Cup today. Their ground, Hyde Road, recorded its highest official attendance – that of 41,709.

February 2nd

1769: Roger Aytoun, better known as 'Spanking Roger', came to town. Ninth Laird of Inchdairnie in Fife, he married the rich elderly widow Barbara Mynshull of Chorlton Hall on this day. She had been married to Thomas Minshull, a successful apothecary who owned a shop on Creaton Street, which still stands there today. Roger turned up to the wedding service blind drunk and had to be supported by two comrades. Showing a stiffer nerve on the battlefield, he served as captain when the 72nd Manchester Volunteers withstood the Siege of Gibraltar. Aytoun Street and Harpurhey's Spanking Roger pub commemorate him. Mrs Aytoun died in 1783, though Roger had long since squandered her fortune.

———•◆•———

1879: Ulster-born fifty-seven-year-old Robert Hawthorne died in Manchester on this day. He was awarded the Victoria Cross for his bravery during the Indian Mutiny. The *London Gazette* described his achievements thus, 'Bugler Hawthorn … not only performed the dangerous duty on which he was employed, but [also] bound up [the] wounds [of Lieutenant Salkeld] under a heavy musketry fire, and had him removed without further injury.'

———•◆•———

1931: Today saw the birth of the comedian Les Dawson in Collyhurst. He injected a great deal of local flavour into his comic routines, particularly while playing Ada Shufflebottom, whose mouthing of risqué matters mimicked the way mill workers communicated by exaggerated 'meemawing' amid the din of the machines.

FEBRUARY 3RD

1728: Another laconic parish register entry on the fate of a nameless vagrant: 'A strange man found dead in John Oldham barne in Cheetham.' (Richard Wright Procter, *Memorials of Manchester Streets*, T. Sutcliffe, Manchester, 1874)

1833: The Scotch Kirk at St Peter's Square was opened on this day. It was designed by Johnson, and built at a cost of £7,500. Its first minister was Dr Muir of Edinburgh.

1885: On this day, Roman Catholics of the area gathered in great numbers at the New Islington Hall in Ancoats. They had assembled to show their support for the Catholic Voluntary School Association. The meeting was supported by several clergymen – including the association's chairman, Canon Liptrott – and resolutions were passed to campaign for their denomination's educational institutions, perceived at the time to be disadvantaged in comparison with the Anglican Board Schools.

FEBRUARY 4TH

1805: Prolific historical novelist William Harrison Ainsworth – best remembered for his work, *The Lancashire Witches* – was born on this day. He published around forty novels before he died on January 3rd 1882. From a well-to-do family of dissenters, he attended Manchester Grammar School and spent much of his youth at his parent's second home on Smedley Lane in Cheetham Hill. Play-acting with his brother Thomas in the wooded and hilly surroundings would inspire his young imagination. (S.M. Ellis, *William Harrison Ainsworth and His Friends*, John Lane, London, 1911)

———•◆•———

1832: Today's *Manchester Guardian* reported on stirrings of sectarian antipathies in the Irish neighbourhood of Angel Meadow: 'St George's [Rochdale] Road was the scene of two or three wanton assaults', pistols were brandished, a man was attacked in his home and police had to intervene with cutlasses. The victim and his friends were Protestants and it was stated that they had been upbraided by their more numerous Catholic neighbours for being 'bloody heretics and Orangemen'.

———•◆•———

1870: The *City News* of today reported on the death of the Salford Fire Brigade's dog, Lion. Having attended 332 fires, he had saved several lives and in December 1863 had been presented with a special collar, inscribed: 'When duty calls I must obey, so onward let me jog; For my name is Lion, the Salford firemen's dog.' (William E.A. Axon, *Annals of Manchester*, John Heywood, Manchester, 1886)

FEBRUARY 5TH

1838: The Night Asylum for the Destitute Poor opened in Smithfield on this day.

———◆●———

1852: On this day, heavy rains caused the rivers and streams of Manchester to overflow their banks. The River Irwell was so swollen that the majority of Peel Park was under water 4ft deep. Those living beyond Strangeways and Salford were forced to find alternative ways to travel home; some sailed up the flooded Great Clowes Street, Lower Broughton Road and Hough Lane. Great damage was also done in the lower reaches of the rivers Medlock, Irk, Mersey Goyt, and Black Brook.

———◆●———

1869: Archbishop Lycurgus of Syra, Tenos and Milos (islands in the Aegean Sea) visited Manchester on this day. He was preaching the next day in the Greek Orthodox Church in Higher Broughton.

FEBRUARY 6TH

1649: Today, following Cromwell's orders to sequester most of the Church's property, soldiers burst into the parish church and arrested Warden Heyrick. He held his ground, though, unwilling to back down without at least a show of defiance. Sadly, the soldiers then took many old documents from the Chapter House to London, where they would ultimately perish in the Great Fire. Heyrick himself was perilously close to meeting his end there too, but he rode out the political storms and held onto his wardenship into the Restoration.

1958: A tragic day for Manchester football, as 'Busby Babes' Bent, Byrne, Colman, Jones, Pegg, Taylor and Whelan died in the Munich Air Disaster. Their team mate Edwards was injured in the disaster and died a fortnight later. Nine players survived, but Berry and Blanchflower would never play again. Sir Matt Busby himself seemed near death, but pulled through in time to see the 1958 FA Cup Final. Several club personnel were also killed in the crash, as well as twelve other passengers and crew members, including *News of the World* correspondent Frank Swift, who had been goalkeeper for both England and Manchester City. The tragedy was not limited to the Red side of the city, though; Busby himself had played for the Blues. City fans have been accordingly respectful of the memorial gestures, notably holding a minute's silence at the fifty-year anniversary derby match in 2008. United played in a replica of the 1958 kit and both teams wore black armbands. Sir Alex Ferguson himself applauded the City fans for their decorum.

1216: On this day, King John appointed Adam de Yeland as the new Baron of Manchester, in place of the disgraced Robert Grelley. Writing to the Sheriff of Lancaster, John ordered that 'The castle of Mamecestre, withall appurtenances and all the land of the same Robert (de Greslé), which he held under the Lyme, to be ... committed to our beloved and faithful Adam de Yeland.' This was a direct contravention of the terms of the Magna Carta, which Grelley and others had compelled King John to sign only eight months previously. Coincidentally, while staying at Swineshead Abbey, a monastery founded by and long-maintained by the Grelleys, King John fell suddenly ill (food poisoning from the renowned surfeit of lampreys) and died several days later. Robert would receive all his lands and titles once more in 1217. (W.H. Thomson, *History of Manchester to 1852*, John Sherratt & Son Ltd, Altrincham, 1967)

—— • ◆ • ——

1820: In Manchester today, Mr Thomas Sharpe announced George IV as King, who succeeded his long-debilitated father. Upon hearing the news, the mass of the populace found little to cheer about, remembering how as Prince Regent he had congratulated the magistrates on their bloody suppression of the peaceful protest at Peterloo (*see* August 16th). Nevertheless, powerful elements ensured that a procession took place, as well as a *feu de joie* at Ardwick Green by the 15th Hussars and Manchester Yeomanry.

FEBRUARY 8TH

1814: On this day, the body of the 'Manchester Ophelia' was discovered after two months of being frozen deep under the ice of the River Irwell (*see* December 6th).

———— •◆• ————

1983: The British Waterways Act was passed on this day. This would see Benjamin Outram's 1797 Ashton canal upgraded to Cruising Waterway Standard, as well as the completion of the Cheshire Ring, following years of neglect, and the canal's 1961 closure and reopening in 1974. At Shooters Brook the canal crosses Store Street Aqueduct – Grade II listed and the first such structure known with a skew in it, i.e. with the road beneath being not at right angles to the canal above, but a full 45 degrees in this case, presenting considerable engineering challenges for Outram and his workmen.

FEBRUARY 9TH

1838: On this day, a meeting was held at the Town Hall, concerning the incorporation of the town as a borough, and was attended by around 2,000 people amid heightened partisan feelings. The opposition had organised a major campaign of 'violent and inflammatory' posters against the proposition, many fearing that the unwelcome intrusion of a new power in local administration would rob industrialists of their earlier freedoms in the unofficial city that wasn't a city. Despite the concerted opposition, the motion was carried and a petition was drawn up for submission to the Privy Council. (W.H. Thomson, *History of Manchester to 1852*, John Sherratt & Son Ltd, Altrincham, 1967)

———•◆•———

1862: Sailing from the Union port and metropolis of New York, the USS *George Griswold* arrived in the Mersey today. It was stocked with many tons of provisions sent by the Northern Yankee forces to alleviate the distress in Lancashire caused by the Cotton Famine during the American Civil War. Despite their suffering at the stoppage of the cotton supply, the cotton workers were largely supportive of the Union's anti-slavery stance and President Lincoln's intransigence on these issues. The ship was received in the port of Liverpool with a royal salute.

FEBRUARY 10TH

1643: On this day, Major General Sir John Seaton led three troops of Manchester's Parliamentarian forces against Royalist forces in Preston. The Royalists within the town walls surrendered after two hours. Manchester's Captain Booth had been the first to climb the walls, crying 'Follow me, or give me up forever!' Following their victory they then took possession of the King's supplies which had been washed ashore as a Royalist ship foundered on the nearby sands. (William E.A. Axon, *Annals of Manchester*, John Heywood, Manchester, 1886)

———•◆•———

1996: Today saw the 400th anniversary of Queen Elizabeth I's confidante and one time King of Bohemia, Dr John Dee's arrival in Manchester. In honour of the occasion, the Manchester Area Psychogeographic Society organised an 'action' in which they walked around the Corn Exchange anticlockwise (or 'widdershins' in such occult circles), and made a public declaration, in order to temporarily levitate the building. Apparently, a slight movement was registered by the staff in the ground-floor fish and chip shop. (MAP, uncarved.org)

FEBRUARY 11TH

1225: On this day, the Baron of Manchester, Robert Grelley, witnesses the signing of the Magna Carta at the field of Runnymede in Surrey. The careful eye can distinguish the name 'Mancestre' deep in the spidery Latin scrawl of this epoch-making document, among those of the other barons putting their names to the document. The Magna Carta forced King John to grant the liberties and rights that would form the keystone in the later development of representational democracy in England.

1589: Sir John Radcliffe of Ordsall Hall was buried in the graveyard of the parish church on this day. Five of his sons had died during battle, and one of his two daughters passed away due to grief. It is said that Sir John and his daughter haunt the ancient timber-framed building to this day.

1716: Four Jacobites were hanged on this day at Knott Mill for their involvement in the recent Rebellion. The ringleader, Syddall, had his head unceremoniously lopped from his body, whereupon it was taken to the Market Cross and displayed as a warning to any Mancunians who might dare to raise arms against the incumbent monarch. Lancaster's High Sheriff recorded the executioner's fee for the hangings and beheading as £8 10s.

FEBRUARY 12TH

1617: On this day, an indenture recorded in the papers of the Court Leet of the Manor assigned the rents accrued to the Lord of the Manor from his holdings at Collyhurst to a fund for the relief of the town's poor folk, to be dispensed by the burgesses of Manchester.

———◆———

1835: On this day, Namick Pasha, the ambassador of the Sublime Porte and Ottoman Turkish envoy, visited Manchester. He came to take in the sights of the city's industrial heritage.

———◆———

1837: An actor named Campbell was accidentally shot today by the props man, whilst he was performing in the drama *Lillian, the Show Girl* at the Queen's Theatre. Local theatre goers raised £120 10*s* 6*d* for his widow.

FEBRUARY 13TH

1789: Today, special constables were instructed by the Boroughreeve to patrol the town throughout Shrovetide, in order to prevent the 'unlawful practices of cockfighting and throwing at cocks'. (Richard Wright Procter, *Memorials of Manchester Streets*, T. Sutcliffe, Manchester, 1874)

———◆———

1868: The Hiberno-Italian Deansgate-born Jerome Caminada joined the Manchester Police Force today. Assaulted on his very first night in John Dalton Street, he gave chase and, after a struggle, apprehended the perpetrator. Caminada's career brought him up against many a devious criminal, and his resourcefulness saw him rise to the head of the Criminal Investigation Department as the first ever detective superintendent (*see* March 10th).

———◆———

1956: Peter Hook, co-founder of the band Joy Division, was born on this day. Along with Bernard Sumner they recruited Ian Curtis to complete the line-up. After Curtis's suicide they re-formed as New Order and helped Tony Wilson establish the Haçienda, to which they contributed the proceeds of their hit, 'Blue Monday' (the top selling 12-inch of all time). Primarily a bass guitarist, he played on and off with New Order until 2007. His memoirs of the Haçienda period can be found in his book, *How Not To Run A Club*. He was at one point married to Bury-born comic Caroline Ahearne, and now plays with The Light.

FEBRUARY 14TH

1825: Today saw the opening of Manchester's first Infant School in Buxton Street near London Road, on the initiative of the local Society of Friends (the Quakers).

1862: As the Cotton Famine wore on, some turned to illegal means to improve their financial condition. As such, the Bank of Manchester Ltd was broken into on this day; the culprits managed to get away with £1,000 in cash.

1955: On this day, following the Manchester derby match, the *Guardian* reported, 'MANCHESTER CITY IN FORM'. The newspaper then went on to say, 'The Blues triumphed over the Reds 5–0 at Old Trafford itself. United's reliance on an attacking strategy was foiled by City's midfield schemer Don Revie, with the two centre forwards, Hayes and Hart, proving more than capable of incisive bursts in response to Revie's perfect passes. Trautmann kept the visitors' own goal safe, while United proved uncertain on the frozen turf, and deceived by the commendable simplicity of City's attacks.' The Busby Babes learnt a harsh lesson that wintry day!

FEBRUARY 15TH

1792: On this day, Boroughreeve Thomas Walker published the first ever written account of the accumulated charities, which the benevolent had entrusted to the town authorities. The by now considerable sums of money under his official management and distribution amounted to some £4,887 16s 1½d per year.

————•◆•————

1988: The first series of the sci-fi comedy *Red Dwarf* aired today. Though they made the lead character a chirpy irrepressible Scouser, the creators – Rob Grant and Doug Naylor – were from a respectable distance inland; Grant heralding from Salford, and Naylor from near the River Irwell. The duo created the series as 'Grant Naylor' – their self-described Gestalt entity – and had previously been involved in writing for *Spitting Image*, including penning the lyrics for the unforgettable 'Throw a chicken in the air …' song, which reached number one in both Britain and Ireland in 1986. *Red Dwarf* has since reached more than fifty episodes, with yet more reportedly in the pipeline.

FEBRUARY 16TH

1753: Dr Thomas Deacon died on this day. According to his epitaph, 'Here lie interred the remains (which through mortality are at present corrupt, but which shall one day surely be raised again to immortality and put on incorruption) of Thomas Deacon, the greatest of sinners and most unworthy of primitive bishops, who died ... in the 56th year of his age.' Though he had founded a chapel in town for his small sect of Nonjurors that he termed 'The True British Catholic Church', of which he was a 'bishop', he was buried in St Ann's Anglican churchyard. A fervent Jacobite, he had lost his sons to that cause, seeing the head of one mounted on a spike over the Old Exchange. Rioting mobs trashed his house when he refused to join in the celebrations of the victory of the Hanoverians. He had been a successful medic in the town, enjoying a prominence wider than just his small sect. (William E.A. Axon, *Annals of Manchester*, John Heywood, Manchester, 1886)

───────●◆●───────

1993: The last episode of Cosgrove Hall's internationally successful animated series *Count Duckula* was aired on this day. Using the voice talent of David Jason, the cartoon had been made at the studios in Chorlton since before the first episode, which aired on September 6th 1988.

FEBRUARY 17TH

1840: The newly formed Borough Council met this day for the first time in the Town Hall, following over a year's struggle against the intransigence of the Police Commissioners, the town's previous government.

———◆·———

1876: Jacob Bright was elected MP for Manchester on this day. Due to the new universal householder suffrage, the 22,770 votes cast in his favour broke the record for any English candidate hitherto. A Liberal Quaker, he spoke up in Parliament for international peace and women's rights.

———◆·———

1882: On this day, labourer Thomas Gillmore was seriously injured while working on the Victoria Station extension. Two of his comrades were also killed when a great load of earth collapsed into the pit they were digging, and Gillmore was crushed.

———◆·———

1993: Today, at a Downing Street press conference, Prime Minister John Major backed the Manchester Olympic bid. He stated that, 'The Manchester bid is more than just a superb technical achievement. It is a vision that the citizens of Manchester have for the city's future and for their region. I share that vision. The Manchester bid is the British bid.' Large sums of government money were already being lavished on the infrastructure, with the stadium, velodrome and arena construction already underway. On top of the direct investment of £75 million a further £40 million would be channelled into the regeneration of East Manchester generally.

FEBRUARY 18TH

1879: Joseph Rayner Stephens, a Chartist leader, died today. Educated at the town's grammar school, he was ordained before he left to study in Stockholm at the age of twenty. In 1830, once he had returned home, he was imprisoned for eighteenth months for sedition, and suspended from the Methodist Conference. A great orator, he was actively involved in the Ten Hours Movement and during the Cotton Famine he was remembered in an anecdote of the Failsworth Chartists rushing up to Oldham at rumours of an uprising. Their spirits fell when they saw a picture of Stephens in a shop window, accidentally placed upside down: 'It's no use gooin' any fur'r, Brayly [Brierley],' said Phil; 'they'n turned Stephens th' wrong side up. It's domino wi' th' strike.' (Ben Brierley, *Home Memories and Recollections of a Life 1886*, Heywood, Manchester)

1889: On this day, Manchester was shocked by a 'horrific gas explosion in the Hyde Lane Coal Pit, which killed twenty-three men and seriously injured five more victims … Twenty survived, but many with serious burns.' The survivors found their way out in total darkness, assisted only by their sense of smell and following the currents of air. The youngest killed was Frank Ashton, aged fourteen, whose mother Jane had to identify his body. The oldest victim was James Hall, who, at sixty-five, had fifty-two years of experience down the pit. Three ponies working in the seam survived the blast.

FEBRUARY 19TH

1904: Today's *Times* reported on Winston Churchill's speech at the Free Trade Hall, describing it as 'One of the most powerful and brilliant he has made'. At its climax, he flattered the civic pride of the crowd, saying, 'It is the fashion nowadays to sneer at the Manchester school; and no abuse, however ribald, is considered bad enough for Mr Cobden. But I dare say there are some people tonight who will think that it is about time that the philanthropic, peaceful, progressive, socialising doctrines which were prescribed by Mr Cobden and Mr Bright [cheers] were a little more considered by the statesmen who govern our land.'

◆

1910: Old Trafford held its first match today. Club chairman since 1902, brewery magnate John Henry Davies had deemed the previous ground, Bank Street in Clayton, a polluted and unfit site for the First Division and FA Cup-winning side. Enlisting the services of Scottish architect Archibald Leitch (noted for designing Anfield, Goodison Park and Ibrox stadiums), work began beside the Manchester Ship Canal, just south west of the city, in 1909. £90,000 later, and a slight modification from Leitch's initial 100,000 capacity design, United were left with a state-of-the-art ground which holds around 80,000 spectators, reinforcing their nickname of 'Moneybags United'. Today's match was against Liverpool, who won 3–4.

FEBRUARY 20TH

1785: Charles White, co-founder of the Manchester Royal Infirmary, passed away in Sale on this day. Born in Manchester in 1728, White was made a Fellow of the Royal Society in recognition of his contributions to the treatment of broken bones. His textbook on midwifery advocated a less interventionist approach to childbirth and paid greater attention to hygiene and ventilation during labour – all very modern notions.

Manchester may have lost a great physician today, but it gained a mummy! Around fifty-five year's before, White had been present at a funeral where the corpse was found (in the nick of time) to be merely comatose. John Beswick subsequently made a full recovery, but a deep impression had been made upon White's sister, Hannah. She then insisted that White keep her above ground until fully certain of her death. Somewhat overstepping his charge, he had her embalmed and stored in at his home – for fifty-five years. On his death, the 'Manchester Mummy' found its way to the Museum of Manchester Natural History Society, where she would remain until 1868 (*see* July 22nd).

———•◆•———

1984: On this day, Manchester band The Smiths released their first (eponymous) album. Morrisey was not pleased with the quality, as it had been recorded in a very piecemeal fashion due to touring commitments, but the £6,000 overheads demanded that it be released. *Rolling Stones* magazine placed it 22nd in the top 100 albums of the 1980s.

FEBRUARY 21ST

1752: On this day, Samuel Peploe, Bishop of Chester and former Warden of Manchester's Old Church and College, died. Having lived in constant antagonism with the local Tory clergy, his removal to take up the mitre at Chester brought them no relief, as he used his position to place his own son as his successor over them. The results of an inspection of the college's affairs in 1718, highlights the bishop's temperament: 'He denounced the fellows and chaplains as void of honour, void of common honesty and void of grace, and charged them with a wilful intention to wrong the college.' (William E.A. Axon, *Annals of Manchester*, John Heywood, Manchester, 1886)

1877: Today, a meeting was held at the Old Town Hall on King Street to decide its future use. The Council were moving operations to the present Town Hall, and it was proposed that the old classical colonnaded structure be turned into a Central Free Reference Library, a motion that was carried. Structural dangers at the free Library in Campfield (the former Hall of Science) saw all of its collection moved into the Town Hall that March, until a more fitting building could be constructed.

FEBRUARY 22ND

1631: Mention is first made on this day of post horses being in the employ of the town. The sum of *2s 2d* was entered in the town's accounts for their upkeep: 'Paid Richard Halliwell's man for meals for three post horses for Mr Cotton. 00.02.02' (W.H. Thomson, *History of Manchester to 1852*, John Sherratt & Son Ltd, Altrincham, 1967)

———◆———

1804: At the age of sixty-six, Thomas Furnival, the last governor of the archaic House of Correction at Hunt's Bank, died. The medieval gaol was pulled down in 1790 and was replaced with the New Bailey in Salford. There was no doubt that the New Bailey was far more efficient, but it lacked in the humanity and picturesque nature of its predecessor, where it had been a common sight to see the prisoners dangling little pouches on strings for the alms of the generous passers-by. Much of said alms were reportedly spent on strong liquor, readily provided by the businesslike gaoler.

———◆———

1815: On this day, the Mancunian Wesleyan Methodists established Manchester's first Missionary Society. The Established Church soon followed suit on April 10th, as did the New Church (Swedenborgians) in August.

FEBRUARY 23RD

1852: A five-day Musical Festival began in the old wooden Free Trade Hall today, after which the temporary structure was closed to be demolished. On the cleared space, the stone Free Trade Hall of today was soon erected.

———◆———

1926: On this day, Sir Henry Slesser spoke in Parliament of the risks to English heritage presented by rich American Anglophiles. He warned that the sixteenth-century timber-framed Agecroft Hall in Pendlebury would be snapped up by the wealthy Americans, just as Gainsborough Hall had been. He warned that, 'Absolutely invaluable heritages for the understanding of the history of this country – and every patriot should have the greatest pride in their conservation – are being sold to the highest bidder.' Slesser was not able to save Agecroft Hall and it now stands beside the River James in the Blue Ridge Mountains of Richmond in Virginia, 3,500 miles from the 'ruined landscape' of coal pits and railway lines it left in 1923. (Hansard)

———◆———

1976: Today, Mancunian industrial landscape painter L.S. Lowry died aged eighty-eight. In the words of Brian & Michael, who wrote a tribute song to the painter (*see* April 8th), 'The fever came and the Good Lord mopped his brow.' Lowry passed away at his home, The Elms, in Mottram in Longdendale. A statue of the painter stands, or rather sits, on a park bench in Mottram.

FEBRUARY 24TH

1847: On this day, Lydia Ernestine Becker, a tireless Mancunian suffragist, was born on Cooper Street. The eldest of fifteen children, she came from a family that had long been resident in the town; one her ancestors had been a vitriol manufacturer in Pool Fold in the 1700s. One of Miss Becker's particular triumphs was her election to the newly formed Manchester School Board in November 1870. Committed to the improvement of public life, she herself lamented that 'perpetual contention for a bare right' (i.e. votes for women), had kept her from devoting more of her energies elsewhere. As the writer William Shaw wrote, 'In every sense Miss Becker was a Manchester woman. Strong – over-strong some of her women's right colleagues thought her – over-masterful, terse in speech, resolute and prompt in act, and yet withal a woman, and an out-and-out defender of corsets, as she declared herself at the Newcastle meeting of the British Association.' She died from exposure while on holiday in the Swiss Alps in 1890. (William Arthur Shaw, *Manchester Old and New*, Cassell and Company, London, 1894)

1875: Today saw the Manchester Royal Institution hold an exhibition of the paintings of Frederick James Shields, to mark the Pre-Raphaelite artist's departure from Manchester. He had been resident in rooms at the then rather decrepit Ordsall Hall, and before he left he was treated to dinner at the Queen's Hotel.

FEBRUARY 25TH

1565: Elias, the 'Manchester Prophet', died in a London prison on this day. Born Elias Hall to a carpenter in 1502, he had prospered in trade until he began to see visions, the content of which he recorded in verse in *A Book of Visions*. Two years before his death he had travelled to London in order to seek an audience with the Queen, but was arrested and flogged.

———◆———

1917: On this day, writer Anthony Burgess was born in Moss Side. Of his five dozen or so works, *A Clockwork Orange* will be most familiar to most. A former English literature lecturer at Manchester University and Malaysian expatriate, his books show interesting experimentation with language, as in the Russified slang of the 'Droogs' in the above work, or his use of Elizabethan English in his Shakespeare biography, *Nothing Like the Sun*.

———◆———

1994: Today saw the opening Friday night of the Frog and Bucket Comedy Club, then on Newton Street. Dave Perkin had taken on the lease of the old Britannia Tavern, and entry was £2 including a bit of supper thrown in. Perkin acted as compère (and likes to encourage the rumour that the *Phoenix Nights* character Den Perry was based on him), with Ian Baskerville and Matt Seber performing. The club flourished and currently occupies the corner of Oldham Street.

FEBRUARY 26TH

1649: Hundreds of people in the Market Place observed a peculiar celestial phenomenon on this day. Contemporary chronicler Hollinworth recorded that, 'At 10 a.m., three perheli (mock suns) [were seen] ... which vanished away one after another, so that at eleven none were seen. I saw two of them myself.' (William E.A. Axon, *Annals of Manchester*, John Heywood, Manchester, 1886)

* ◆ *

1889: Manchester City and Manchester United predecessors, Ardwick and Newton Heath, played a match at Belle Vue Athletic Ground today. It was in aid of the Hyde Coal Mine disaster, in which twenty-three miners lost their lives, with others receiving horrific burns (*see* February 18th). Ten thousand fans saw Newton Heath win 3–2. This was also the first floodlit Manchester derby match.

* ◆ *

1902: In New York today, George W. Garret died from tuberculosis. A penniless submarine pioneer, as a child he moved from London to Manchester, where he attended the town's grammar school and Owens College. It was here, while studying chemistry, that he damaged his lungs in experiments removing the carbon dioxide from stale air, trying to discover if it might last longer in a confined space. He travelled the South Seas before becoming a curate in Hulme, forming the Garrett Submarine Navigation and Pneumataphore Company Ltd. It was with this company he created the 'Resurgam', his most famous invention (*see* November 26th).

FEBRUARY 27TH

1653: On this day, bookseller and binder Thomas Smith died. He had moved to Manchester from Barnstaple during the reign of Charles I, and had petitioned the Lords of the Privy Council for the right to 'Furnish the place with all sorts of Latin and English bookes allowed by authority to be sold'. He would later print and sell the Puritan version of the *Siege of Manchester* and *Lancashire's Valley of Achor is England's Doore of Hope*. (Richard Wright Procter, *Memorials of Manchester Streets*, T. Sutcliffe, Manchester, 1874)

1855: As war weariness kicked in, the earlier Jingoism of 1853 (*see* November 16th) gave way to a desire to withdraw from the blood-soaked Crimean war, and a meeting was held in Newall's Buildings today to urge for peace with Russia. Others took place in the near future, given further impetus following the death of Tsar Nikolai in March.

1858: Today, Joseph Dickinson Esq. of the Geological Society and Inspector of Mines, produced his annual report for Manchester. It indicated that the immediate environs of Manchester constituted the richest points in the Lancashire/Cheshire coalfields, with Oldham, Ashton-under-Lyne, Dukinfield, St Helen's and Wigan being the zones where the beds of coal and ironstone, as well as building stone, were of the greatest value.

FEBRUARY 28TH

1642: On this day, 1,200 townsfolk signed the protestation against the arbitrary absolutist rule of the monarch. Though soon overtaken by events, the tone of this document was still quite moderate; pledging to defend the King and the Church of England, while simultaneously demanding that Members of Parliament speak freely without hindrance or fear of prosecution, and that traditional rights of the individual be upheld. The petition was originated by the Long Parliament, and Warden Heyrick – a man whose loyalty to the crown would almost see him lose his own head during the coming period of republican rule – took the lead in gathering signatures. The petition was handed to Charles I at York, and a reply was returned on June 6th (*see* June 6th).

———◆———

1781: The Manchester Literary and Philosophical Society, the oldest such civic institution still in existence, was formed today. Its nucleus had been a circle of private individuals of scientific bent, who gathered at Dr Thomas Percival's house on King Street. But the popularity and quality of the papers submitted informally there soon demanded a more organised approach. As with many institutions of old Manchester, subsequent meetings were held in local taverns until permanent premises were obtained in 1804.

FEBRUARY 29TH

1736: Ann Lee, founder of the American sect known to the world as the 'Shakers' was born in Manchester today. Born to a Quaker family, she encouraged celibacy, speaking in tongues and expression of religious ecstasy through dance in Quaker worship. She left with eight followers to found religious settlements in New York in 1774.

1828: On this leap day, thirty-eight revellers were drowned in the River Irwell. On its maiden voyage the vessel called *Emma*, of the town's New Quay Company, was swamped. The disaster caused great public consternation and a subscription fund was soon set up to reward the brave rescuers, and to bring some material relief to the bereaved relatives of those who did not survive.

2012: Openshaw-born Davy Jones, former Monkee, Artful Dodger and teen heart-throb, died at the age of sixty-six on this day. He had just managed to squeeze in a celebratory reunion, touring Britain and North America to great success, in a hectic schedule during mid-2011. The tour consisted of more than forty performances from Manchester to the Albert Hall, and Niagara Falls to Los Angeles.

MARCH 1ST

1753: On this day, the ostler of the Swan and Saracen's Head on Market Stead Lane was found hanging in the stable. It was ordered that the body be 'Drawn upon a sledge and buried at four lane-ends, with all his clothes on, and to have a stake driven through his body; which was executed on Tuesday forenoon, in the presence of a numerous concourse of spectators.' In 1846, two coffins were unearthed at New Cross, containing the remains of similarly treated suicides who had been buried superstitiously at the crossroads in a former age. One was named as the bootcloser Smith, unlucky in love, and the other a young woman who had taken poison in September 1808. (Richard Wright Procter, *Memorials of Manchester Streets*, T. Sutcliffe, Manchester, 1874)

---◆---

1841: Today saw the Manchester and Leeds Railway finally open to passengers.

MARCH 2ND

1581: Manchester makes an early appearance in literature, as the *Ballad of Fair Em, the Miller's Daughter of Manchester* was entered into the Stationers' Register, an early form of copyright. Around a decade later a play appeared with the same name, occasionally attributed to Shakespeare, though this is now dismissed. It was often performed by the troupe of Lord Strange, later Earl Ferdinando of Derby, who had strong links with Manchester and may himself have been the author.

———◆———

1795: James McConnel and John Kennedy, canny young Scotsmen seeking their fortune in the budding Cottonopolis, set out together in a joint partnership today – their venture soon became the biggest textile empire in the world; overtaking earlier pioneers Arkwright and Murray, their six Ancoats mills soon employed 2,000 people. Their heirs would later erect the Paragon Mill, which, in 1912, was the tallest cast-iron building to date.

———◆———

1852: The celebrations of the Anti-Corn Law League (*see* September 4th) in 1846 seemed in vain, as rumours circulated of a return to the old days of protectionism. It was on this day that the Council of the Anti-Corn Law League was resurrected to fight against this; George Wilson presided over a hasty reunion of all the old faces, and within half an hour the funds promised to finance the renewed attack were £27,520!

MARCH 3RD

1752: Today saw the first copies of the *Manchester Mercury* released for the growing reading public of the town: 'Four pages of twenty narrow columns for threepence halfpenny ... for current information, these old Manchester newspapers compare favourably with the ordinary French journal of today.' The paper survived several name changes and printed 3,672 issues up until its closure on December 28th 1830. (W.H. Thomson, *History of Manchester to 1852*, John Sherratt & Son Ltd, Altrincham, 1967)

———•◆•———

1817: Ever more heavy-handed in their bid to uproot 'conspiracy', the government temporarily suspended habeas corpus – the right to freedom from imprisonment without charge or trial – today. A dozen men were then seized at Ardwick, including the weaver-poet Samuel Bamford, before they were unceremoniously clapped in irons and sent to London, much to their, and others, astonishment. They were later released and dismissed, as the suspicions of a great 'plot' proved to be unfounded.

———•◆•———

1934: Manchester City breaks records for English home ground attendance today. They beat Stoke City 1–0, but this FA Cup quarter-final is remembered more for the astronomical crowd figure of 84,569. Queuing began four hours beforehand, and Maine Road's concerned stewards closed the turnstiles early, without which the numbers might well have exceeded 85,000. The record remained unbroken in the sixty years before the terraces were consigned to oblivion. United holds second place, a full thousand behind (*see* January 17th).

MARCH 4TH

1810: Thomas Henshaw died on this day. The businessman and hatter from Oldham left vast sums of his fortune to Manchester charities – £20,000 for a Blind Asylum, £1,000 for the Infirmary, and £500 to the newly opened Ladies' Jubilee School.

———— •◆• ————

1875: A delegation from the Manchester Chamber of Commerce met with the Chancellor of the Exchequer today. They hoped to highlight the increasingly inadequate postal provisions for the city, particularly the manner in which the Post Office in Brown Street had massively outgrown its 1840 premises. From 1861 staff numbers had doubled in order to keep up with numbers of letters delivered there, which had more than doubled in the same time. In 1861, 401,000 letters were delivered compared to the 927,000 which were delivered in 1875, and in 1861, 485,000 letters were posted; in 1875 it was 1,134,000! (William E.A. Axon, *Annals of Manchester*, John Heywood, Manchester, 1886)

MARCH 5TH

1862: On this day, John Ivon Mosley was invited to visit the capital of the Isle of Man, Douglas. After having been fêted in the *Mona's Herald* on September 19th 1861 as, 'a remarkable man who has a genius for language, and who has made Manx his special study', he was invited to meet with the Manx Society, so that they might purchase from him his English-Manx dictionary. An entirely self-taught man and a wood turner by trade, he became master of most major languages of Europe, and many from further afield. Having learnt the other Celtic tongues, he noted that Manx lacked a printed dictionary and set to work. Sadly, his work of 40,000 definitions was used merely to supplement that of another. (*Yn Lioar Manninagh*, Vol. 3)

———— •◆• ————

1958: Andy Gibb was born in Manchester; he was the only Gibb brother to be born in the city, and the only one not in the Bee Gees. The family moved to Queensland within the year but Andy returned to England in 1967, and even became a singer in Ibiza when he was a young teenager. He left for the USA in 1976, where he found considerable success. At one point, the number one slot was successively held by the three older Gibbs, then Andy with his '(Love Is) Thicker Than Water', before the Bee Gees once again held the position. He dated the glamorous *Dallas* actress Victoria Principal, but drug abuse began to take its toll on his health. He died at the age of thirty, in England on March 10th 1988.

MARCH 6TH

1351: On this day, Manchester became the last town to become a part of Lancashire. This followed the conclusive establishment of the county palatine of Lancaster, the youngest of England's historic counties. As such, Manchester's Northern credentials were reaffirmed, but the town was to remain ecclesiastically subservient to Lichfield and Chester until well into the Victorian age.

1752: On this day, Manchester received a new Market Cross designed by Oliver Nab. Several stone crosses once graced the town's thoroughfares, including one at Hyde Cross (the end of Withy Grove), New Cross, and the one in the Market Place. One is preserved in the grounds of Chetham's College.

1862: James Rigby of Salford died today, aged fifty-six. He had contributed much effort to the cause of the Ten Hours Bill (that women and children might be protected from grueling and exploitive hours), and had been a close friend, as well as secretary, to the social reformer Robert Owen. Salford was, at this period, a hotbed of politically active vegetarian radicals, and Rigby claims to have 'never tasted animal food'. (William E.A. Axon, *Annals of Manchester*, John Heywood, Manchester, 1886)

MARCH 7TH

1796: A riot broke out in the Theatre Royal during the singing of the National Anthem today. The next day, in response to this, the playbills were printed with the headline '"God Save the King" will be sung at the end of the farce, to give the Non-Conformists time to retire.' (William E.A. Axon, *Annals of Manchester*, John Heywood, Manchester, 1886)

—•◆•—

1826: Heiress Miss Ellen Turner was brought clandestinely to Manchester by Edward Gibbon Wakefield today. After an elopement from her school in Liverpool by means of a forged letter, the two stayed at the Albion Hotel in town, before hurrying on to Gretna Green. From there the newlyweds fled to Calais, but were intercepted by Ellen's uncle. The rash Edward was then sentenced to three years in Newgate Prison. Despite these early setbacks, he was a prominent figure in later life and did much to promote British settlement in the antipodes, New Zealand in particular.

—•◆•—

1837: On this day, a blaze at the Oxford Road Twist Company factory of Cook and Hyde caused an estimated £6,000 worth of damage; nearly double the usual figure for a contemporary mill fire.

MARCH 8TH

1824: Matthew Falkner, aged eighty-six, die on this day. Once a well-to-do Manchester stationer, bookseller and newspaper printer, he was, according to his friend Joseph Aston, 'Seduced into political opposition ... one of the kindest-hearted of mankind was driven from his country, and his fortunes, till then prosperous, entirely ruined.' In 1793, the Market Place offices of his newspaper, the *Manchester Herald*, were attacked by a violent mob of reactionaries who smashed up his presses and threw his type into the street. He fled England for the USA, prudently remaining there until 1806. Despite his best efforts, he failed to recover his property and former station, dying in obscurity in Burnley.

❖

1916: Today, on the dusty plains of Mesopotamia, Manchester-born Private George Stringer won himself a Victoria Cross at Es Sinn, fighting in the 1st Battalion Manchester Regiment against the Ottomans. Born in 1889, he died in Oldham on November 10th 1957, and was buried in Philips Park Cemetery.

❖

1917: Exactly one year after the last awarded Victoria Cross in Mesopotamia, Lance-Corporal Jack White won his. He was awarded the prestigious honour for fighting with the 6th Battalion King's Own Royal Lancaster Regiment at the River Dialah. White died on November 27th 1949, and was buried in the Jewish Cemetery in Blackley.

MARCH 9TH

1818: Growing fears of violent rebellion prompted the local magistrates to take ever more intrusive measures against the unsanctioned political activity of some of the weavers of the region. Their agents were not above infiltration of workers' associations and gatherings, even going so far as to become agent provocateurs and deliberately stirring up strife and violence to justify their own wages. Today, one of their many spies was identified and received his just deserts at a Reform meeting in the town – a good hiding being his recompense for actions that might have led to imprisonment or worse for those he betrayed. A Withy Grove confectioner, this hapless James Murray had gone to the meeting disguised as a weaver, but his true identity was soon uncovered and he had to be taken home in a carriage, thanks to his beating. After being unmasked as an informer, his customers stopped visiting his shop and he was forced to close it and leave town.

1853: On this day, the town was shocked to hear that Ollivant's jeweller's on Exchange Street had been robbed. Such incidents were scarce during that period, so much so that it was noted in *Axon's Annals of Manchester* some thirty-plus years later! (William E.A. Axon, *Annals of Manchester*, John Heywood, Manchester, 1886)

March 10th

1829: Today saw the death by dysentery of Manchester-born John Ferriar at Pasto, Carthagenia, Columbia. He was Military Governor of la Provincia de Coro and brother to Thomas Ilderton Ferriar, from whom he inherited command of the British volunteers in the newly independent country. He was a member of the honorary Orden del Libertador.

1848: The first coining of the term 'the School of Manchester' was heard today in the House of Commons, as future Prime Minister Benjamin Disraeli included it in a speech. He would expressly claim the honour of having christened this ideology in a further speech on June 6th the following year.

1914: Jerome Caminada, Manchester's 'Sherlock Holmes', died at his Moss Side home on this day, aged sixty-nine. His colourful exploits included him hiding inside pianos, wearing disguises, and carrying a pistol against the numerous felons who had threatened his life. There are rumours that his story may soon reach the small screen – he even enjoyed some celebrity in his lifetime, releasing his memoirs *Twenty-Five Years of Detective Life* in 1895. Local author Judge Parry called him 'The Garibaldi of detectives ... never stultified by a petty adherence to regulations.' The present Greater Manchester Police (GMP) veteran club is named in his honour. (Ancoatslittleitaly.com, gmpsportsclub.com)

MARCH 11TH

1835: On this day, Deputy Constable Henry Bailey drowned in the River Irwell while attempting to save a boy named Trees. Bailey's body was not found until September 12th, near Barton Bridge, and a subscription was begun for his family which reached £1,641 8s 7d.

———— • ————

1868: Today, the treasurer of the Manchester Operative House Painters' Association, William Dodd, was sentenced to five years' imprisonment. He had been found guilty of embezzling funds to the value of £800.

———— • ————

1941: On this day, in a repeat of the bombings of December 22nd, Old Trafford football ground was put completely out of action by direct hits from the Luftwaffe. The damage included the destruction of the main (now South) stand, and United were forced to relocate to the premises of their chairman James W. Gibson at Cornbrook Cold Storage. Rental of Manchester City's Maine Road ground was then arranged, but at the annual cost of £5,000 and a cut of the proceeds from ticket sales. The War Damage Commission would later grant United the sum of £4,800 to clear the wreckage of the bombed-out stadium, and a further £17,478 to rebuild. By the time Old Trafford was to see a match again, on August 24th 1949, almost a decade had passed since the German raid.

MARCH 12TH

1706: The earliest preserved Manchester post mark was stamped on a letter posted in the town on this day.

------ ◆ ------

1817: Cotton spinner and radical campaigner Elijah Dixon was arrested out of the blue on this day. He was charged with High Treason, clapped in irons and sent to London, where he was questioned before the Home Secretary, Lord Sidmouth himself. Dixon kept his cool, insisting, 'I am not guilty, and I don't know who is.' He was kept in jail for eight weeks, after which he was returned to freedom and went back to Houldsworth's Mill in Manchester. He was later present at the Peterloo Massacre, and continued to promote the cause of reform.

------ ◆ ------

1851: Owen's College opened its doors for the first time today, to admit hopeful young engineers, chemists and physicists of the time. Christened in honour of its benefactor, the late John Owens, who had bequeathed it the sum of £100,000, it was originally located at Quay Street. Under its first principal, Professor A.J. Scott, it would continue to be housed at Quay Street, until its transfer to the present Oxford Road campus in 1873.

MARCH 13TH

1382: Thomas la Warre, the younger son of the aristocratic dynasty who had assumed lordship of the town in 1313, was today made Rector of Manchester. At the unexpected death of his elder brother in 1398, he would become Lord of Manchester as well. Thomas used his combined powers to re-form the parish church as an ecclesiastical college with Warden and Fellows, which would last until Manchester became a Bishopric the 1800s. Thomas's uncle and cousin were proponents of the semi-heretical Lollard doctrines of Wycliffe, of which he too may have been a sympathiser. His statue was placed on the Town Hall façade, showing him in full clerical dress holding a model of his church.

———•◆•———

1848: Being the 'year of Revolutions' in Europe, local Chartists assembled before Salford Town Hall today to make a public statement of congratulations to the French people on their uprising to topple King Louis Phillippe and reinstitute la Republique.

———•◆•———

1896: Corporal William Norman, of the 7th Regiment of Royal Fusiliers, died in Salford on this day. He was awarded the Victoria Cross for his courage in the Crimean War on December 19th 1854. His remains lie in an unmarked common grave in Weaste Cemetery.

MARCH 14TH

1831: Several Manchester related hangings took place at Lancaster today. Ashton and William Worrall were hanged for the murder of Sarah M'Lellon in Failsworth, while Moses Ferneley took the plunge for killing his stepson at Hulme. The latter's cadaver was then shipped to a dissection class at the Manchester Infirmary.

———◆———

2004: Today, the first Manchester derby match to be held at Manchester City's new stadium – the City of Manchester Stadium – was played. The home side won 4–1, and the crowd of 47,284 was almost 13,000 stronger than the last Derby hosted by City at their old ground, Maine Road, where attendance had been 34,649 (*see* November 9th).

———◆———

2010: Today saw the culmination of a programme of several days to celebrate the centenary of Manchester United Football Club. In a match against Fulham, the half-time was used to assemble the descendants of the players who had played in the first game on February 19th 1910, as well as those of the chairman and stadium architect, in order to bury a time capsule of memorabilia in the centre tunnel. Fans attending were given replicas of the first ever match programme.

MARCH 15TH

1215: Robert Grelley, Baron of Manchester, attended the conference of Stamford on this day. The meeting was held to discuss the terms that he and the other rebellious freedom-loving Barons of the Realm would put to their defeated monarch, King John. Robert, a 'Presumptuous and fiery baron', then marched to London with his fellow barons to submit their demands to their sovereign in a great charter – the Magna Carta. (W.H. Thomson, *History of Manchester to 1852*, John Sherratt & Son Ltd, Altrincham, 1967)

• ◆ •

1785: Today witnessed the end of an extremely cold winter. Only 26 of the 128 days that had passed since October 18th had seen the thermometers register a positive value in the Centigrade system. The extreme of -18.5 degrees centigrade had even been reached on some days.

• ◆ •

2010: Manchester band The Hollies were officially inducted into the Rock and Roll Hall of Fame on this day, alongside Abba, Genesis and Iggy Pop. A full sixty years had passed since some band members had started out together, and they took the opportunity to sing 'Bus Stop', 'Carrie Anne', and 'Long Cool Woman in a Black Dress' in celebration.

MARCH 16TH

1820: The Radical leaders arrested at Peterloo (*see* August 16th) received their sentences today at the Lancaster Assizes. Justice Bayley determined that, for protesting the unfair and unrepresentative nature of the contemporary parliamentary system, the defendants should all receive custodial sentences. Henry 'Orator' Hunt, who had done himself few favours in his overly inflammatory and violent rhetoric, was to serve two and a half years. His comrades, Joseph Johnson, Joseph Healey and Samuel Bamford, each received a year apiece. Both Hunt and Bamford published widely read accounts of the injustices they suffered while in prison, in *Letters from Manchester Gaol* and *Life of a Radical*.

1839: Chartist MP Fergus O'Connor was arrested today in Manchester, accused of publishing seditious libel in his *Northern Star* publication (the Chartist newspaper). He had printed the speeches of several of his fellows, including one given in the town by William Dean Taylor. He was sentenced to eighteen months' imprisonment at York Castle.

1858: On this day, Watt's Warehouse on Portland Street opened. A striking building, which combines a flamboyant mixture of architectural styles in a not too displeasing whole, it is probably a fair bet that no single edifice before or since has combined Ancient Egyptian, Elizabethan and Venetian architecture! Since 1982 it has been in business as the Britannia Hotel.

MARCH 17TH

1830: St Patrick's Day, and the 87th Regiment of Irish Fusiliers marched from Salford barracks to St Augustine's Roman Catholic Church on Granby Row today. They were accompanied there and back by the regimental band who were playing 'Saint Patrick's Day in the Morning', as well as 'great numbers of their countrymen wearing the shamrock in their hats'. (*Manchester Guardian*)

———— • ◆ • ————

1882: Today, smoke-blackened Manchester hosted the exhibition of smoke prevention devices and fuel economy in the Campfield Market. The exhibition was organised by the Manchester Noxious Vapours Abatement Association, and was opened by Mayor Thomas Baker.

———— • ◆ • ————

1885: Sir Thomas Bazley, aged eighty-seven, died today. He was know for being the greatest cotton spinner in the world, as well as the Salford Boroughreeve, a Manchester Councillor, president of the Manchester Chamber of Commerce, Royal Commissioner for the 1851 Great Exhibition and the 1855 Paris International Exhibition and, from 1858, Manchester's Liberal MP. Inducted into the French Légion d'Honneur in 1867, he was made a baronet in 1869. He retired in 1880 as the oldest member of the House.

MARCH 18TH

1855: The Niagara Suspension Bridge over the famous falls was opened today. The wires used to construct the bridge were made at Bradford Wire Works in Manchester, and the firm of Richard Johnson and Nephew.

———— • ✦ • ————

1875: On this day, unmarried Margaret McVickett, aged twenty-six, died. On the 13th, she had received a botched abortion administered by Alfred Thomas Heap at his shop in West Gorton. Margaret's mother had paid a pound for the highly illegal operation. Heap was arrested, and it was found that he had almost killed another in the same fashion several years previous, for which he had served five years in prison. This time he was sentenced to the noose and was hanged in Liverpool on the 19th.

———— • ✦ • ————

1879: Alderman Paul Ferdinand Willert, who had come to Manchester from his native Mecklenburg-Strelitz, Germany, at the age of twenty-five in 1821, died on this day. By 1828 he had already been elected Commissioner of Police (the old organ of local government before the Corporation was established), and was elected councillor for Ardwick in 1838, being made alderman in 1841. He was a successful merchant and financier, and like many other German Mancunians, was a lover of music, playing the fiddle in the band of the Foreign Library (of which he was treasurer).

MARCH 19TH

1788: Aulay Macaulay, notable for inventing a system of shorthand, died on this day. Although better known for his work with shorthand, he was in business as a tea dealer on St Ann's Square. His system has not stood the test of time however, and his Mancunian predecessor John Byrom's version is closer in relation to today's system.

———◆———

1832: Today, as the country mulled over the coming Great Reform Act, a radical Mancunian, signing himself 'One of the oppressed', penned his own cynical analysis in the *Poor Man's Guardian*. He stated that, 'The influence of those men who impose those rents and profits is to be increased in making the laws, and that your influence is to be diminished by this Bill … You will be starved to death by thousands, if this Bill is passed, and thrown on to the dung hill, or on to the ground, naked, like dogs. … Of all the Bills, or plots (for it is nothing else), that ever was proposed on earth, this is the most deceptive and the most mischievous … your influence will not be more than a one-twentieth part of that which will be exercised by those who live on the fruits of your labour.' Such feeling would later fuel the more violent side of Chartism and Marxist-inspired Socialism in the town.

MARCH 20TH

1772: This day saw Mrs Elizabeth Raffald's first Manchester Directory – an alphabetical list of the town's chief inhabitants – released. A renowned cook, she had previously authored *The Experienced English Housekeeper*, which is considered a masterwork of its genre. Her directory lists such curiosities as a Welsh father and son who combined banking and tea dealing, and a multi-tasking tallow chandler and governor of the House of Correction. Somehow, Edmund Kelsal was still managing to get by as a bow and arrow maker on Long Milngate, and outlying districts such as Ardwick, Collyhurst and Smedley are listed as 'country' still. Mrs Raffald's cookbook was advertised at 6s, and was a resounding success. (John Harland, *Collectanea Relating to Manchester and its Neighbourhood at Various Periods*, Chetham Society, Manchester, 1866)

———◆◆———

1845: The first Mayor of Manchester, Sir Thomas Potter, died today after serving two terms from 1838 to 1840. Born to a farming family in 1774, he had followed his brothers into business in Manchester. His greatest triumphs lie in his 'most arduous struggle' to ensure a Charter of Incorporation for the town. Around 1820, he established a day school at Irlams-o'th'Height for seventy boys and girls. His family initially turned down a public funeral, but in the end gave way to the request of the Corporations of Manchester and Salford. Ninety carriages made up his cortège to Ardwick Cemetery on March 27th.

MARCH 21ST

867: On this day, Aelle, the last independent English King of Northumbria, fell in battle against the Danes, alongside his former rival and brief ally in national desperation, Osberht. Their Kingdom died with them as a new age dawned in the North, and Manchester fell under the control of the Scandinavian Kingdom of Jorvik.

1783: An argument over two dogs broke out in Spencer's Tavern in the Market Place today, between two officers of the 79th Regiment. A duel was then fought in which Cornet Hamilton killed Captain Mouncey. He was buried at a public funeral in St John's, and Hamilton was acquitted by a coroner's jury.

1839: Hugh Hornby Birley – better known for having led troops with drawn swords against unarmed protesters at Peterloo (*see* August 16th) – chaired a meeting at the York Hotel today, to discuss founding an institution to present public demonstrations of scientific interest, fostering the development of science and its application in the town. The Royal Victoria Gallery for the Encouragement of Practical Science was eventually formed in June 1840, allowing James Prescott Joule to give his first public lecture. Unfortunately, by 1842 funds had dried up and the institution was forced to close.

MARCH 22ND

1156: The feast day of the boy-saint William of Norwich was celebrated today. According to his credulous monkish biographer, one of his miracles involved Albert Gresley, a future Baron of Manchester. As a boy, Albert had a favourite falcon, which fell sick. Having prayed to St William, the falcon was miraculously cured, despite the mockery of his father and other knights who 'deemed it ridiculous to pray to the saints or make vows to them for such trivial matters.'

1526: On this day, James Stanley, Bishop of Ely and Warden of Manchester College, died. As the younger son of the Earl of Derby (Henry VII's stepfather), he had had ecclesiastical dignities thrust upon him. An amusing episode in Jortin's *Life of Erasmus* describes how the continental scholar had been offered 'A large pension, and larger promises, from a young illiterate Englishman, who was to be made a bishop and who wanted him for a preceptor.' Erasmus refused, but Stanley sat upon the throne at Ely in 1509 regardless. The would-be scholar spent his summers in Manchester throughout the rest of his life, founding the Derby Chapel in the town's present cathedral, in which he is buried. He was reputed to have spent his winters at Somersham with his mistress, their bastard son later being knighted at Flodden Field.

MARCH 23RD

1596: On this day, London mercer, John Lacye, sold the Manor of Manchester to Sir Nicholas Mosley. The Wests had sold it to Layce for £3,000, before he sold it on to Mosley (Sheriff and Lord Mayor of London) for £3,500. Mosley's descendants were linked to Manchester until well into the nineteenth century, and are commemorated in Mosley Street.

1839: After an eventful construction, beset by floods, hurricanes and broken legs, the Victoria Bridge over the River Irwell finally had its keystone set today. Its medieval predecessor had once contained a small chapel, later used as a dungeon, in which several had lost their lives in times of flood. One might wonder if there had been something a little more than 'natural' at work against those intent on replacing it!

1846: Charles Ewert, aged seventy-seven, died on this day. At the Battle of Waterloo he had taken a French Imperial Eagle (found on staffs carried into battle) from one of the most renowned French divisions, a gallantry for which he was made Ensign in the Royal Veteran Battalion. He was buried in Salford's Bolton Street Graveyard.

1909: Today saw Manchester's Dog Show at Belle Vue Gardens celebrate a record number of entries, as well as enjoying royal patronage. Two thousand six hundred and fifty-five animals participated, including pets of both the King and Queen. His Majesty was unlucky but his Consort's pets won three prizes.

MARCH 24TH

1760: On this day, the act is passed for 'The most noble Francis Duke of Bridgewater to make a navigable cut or canal from or near Worsley Mill, over the River Irwell, to the town of Manchester, and to or near Longford bridge, in the township of Stretford.'

1816: Reverend William Cowherd, who had served as Anglican, Swedenborgian and Bible Christian pastor in rapid succession, and was an early pioneer of vegetarianism, died today. Cowherd expected full temperance from his flock and is said, albeit by a partisan, to have claimed personal revelation from God and regarded himself as 'The greatest and most extraordinary man living'. (William E.A. Axon, *Annals of Manchester*, John Heywood, Manchester, 1886)

1990: On this night, at the Longdendale reservoirs, many local residents went up into the hills to observe the Hale-Bopp comet. They got a little more than they bargained for, though, as a large military aircraft seemingly flew into the hillside. This is not an isolated case and many reports have been made of such craft flying over the area, often at dangerously low heights and on apparent collision courses. Tales of ghost planes are even accompanied by those of phantom airmen appearing at the crash sites – it is no wonder, given the fifty or so crashes that have taken place in the surrounding moors.

MARCH 25TH

1851: A boiler exploded at Thomas Williamson's steam sawmills in Riga Street on this day. The explosion killed nine people, and the jury subsequently returned a verdict of manslaughter against Thomas Egerton, the engineer and owner of the faulty device.

———— • ◆ • ————

1860: Fife-born Dr James Braid died on this day. He started his medical career in Manchester, deserving most of the credit for demystifying hypnosis. Dismissing it as fanciful notions of 'animal magnetism,' he linked the phenomenon to sleepwalking, advocating medical use.

———— • ◆ • ————

1939: Today witnessed Old Trafford host its record-breaking attendance figure of 76,962, but United were nowhere in sight. The match was an FA Cup Final between Wolverhampton Wanderers and Grimsby Town, in which the Wolves were victorious over the Mariners 5–0, in a most unlucky game for the latter; goalie Moulson was replaced by an outfield player and the team were down to ten men.

MARCH 26TH

1572: The records of Manchester's Court Leet, the body that oversaw the running of the town, contain some interesting entries for this day: 'All that keep, or hereafter shall keep alehouses in Manchester, shall not suffer any unlawful gaming in their houses, gardens or back sides, 20s' – the latter being the fine payable upon breaking of this by-law. The next entry was regarding the number of alehouses in the town: 'The most part of the jury do think thirty alehouses and inns to be sufficient in Manchester.' Notwithstanding this sober calculation, in 1863 there were 484 hotels, inns, taverns, and 1824 beer-shops in town. Another entry stated: 'The jury doth present John Skillieborne, plumber, to be a common easing-dropper, a naughty person, such a one as doth abound in all misorders; therefore we desire that he may be avoided the town, and have such punishment as unto such doth apertain. Whereas there is great misorder in wearing of unlawful weapons, as daggers and such like, and also in wearing a hat upon Sundays and holidays.'

1921: Unofficially, thanks to fans having smashed down the gates to gain admittance, Manchester City's Hyde Road stadium saw its largest crowd of all time today, in a First Division match against Burnley. Contemporary estimates bandied around figures from 50,000 to 55,000, and photographs show dangerous numbers of spectators perched on the roofs of the stands.

MARCH 27TH

1877: Rochdale plasterer John McKenna was hanged at Strangeways today, for the brutal murder of his pregnant wife Annie. They had been drinking at a neighbour's, and McKenna had repeatedly sent his wife out for more liquor. Turning violent later on, he beat her to death. He was soon caught on the run in Liverpool, after which he was brought to the gallows in Manchester.

———◆———

1920: On this day, King George V makes a rare appearance in Manchester, and became the first reigning monarch to go to a provincial football ground – Manchester City's Hyde Road. City were playing Liverpool, and a makeshift royal box had been lavishly plastered with scarlet upholstery. On his appearance, the 'noise swelled to a roar and burst in three rumbling cheers' according to the *Manchester Guardian*. The King then stepped onto the pitch and shook the hands of all players. Football historian Gary James claims that the King chose this ground because he knew it would be 'a great way to meet a large number of Mancunians as City remained Manchester's number one club, despite United's move to Old Trafford in 1910.' (Gary James, *Manchester City FC: 125 Years of Football*)

MARCH 28TH

1836: James Bohanna, one of the last remaining veterans of the Manchester Volunteers' gallant and record-breaking defence of Gibraltar, died today. On each anniversary of the British victory, Bohanna visited the college to see the 72nd Regiment's colours where they were kept. In honour of his seniority and valour, he had headed the King's birthday procession in Manchester for many years prior to his death.

———◆———

1856: The first game of chess by telegraph was played today between the Manchester and Liverpool Chess Clubs; some may call it a breakthrough in online gaming.

———◆———

1857: Manchester's John Bright loses his seat in the General Election, part of a general defeat of the old Manchester School. Bright's exit from the Commons was regretted by all parties, as he had done much to elevate the quality of debate. His place was taken by Sir John Potter, son of the first mayor, and benefactor of the Free Library, an 'Advanced Liberal' in favour of extending the franchise, but of a different faction to the old guard.

MARCH 29TH

1788: On this day, a York carrier named Mr Worthington was shot dead leaving an inn in Miles Platting, despite having begged for his life. The culprit took his watch and purse. A suspect was arrested but later released for want of evidence. (*Gentleman's Magazine*, Vol. LVII)

———◆•◆———

1819: Liberal pamphleteer and future *Manchester Guardian* editor, John Edward Taylor, defended himself personally in court today at the Lancaster Assizes. The case was cooked up against him during the high tide of reaction in the town (Peterloo would follow in only a few months' time – *see* August 16th). He was acquitted thanks to his own eloquent and earnest defence.

———◆•◆———

1843: John Young died at the age of seventy-nine on this day. He was 'believed to be the oldest Sunday school teacher and visitor in the kingdom'. He had joined the profession in its earliest days in Manchester in 1786, dedicating fifty-seven years of his life to the cause. (William E.A. Axon, *Annals of Manchester*, John Heywood, Manchester, 1886)

———◆•◆———

1852: Manchester finally received its long sought 'City' status today, being granted its Royal Charter.

MARCH 30TH

1781: Manchester's second Methodist chapel, an unassuming brick structure on Oldham Street, was opened by John Wesley on this day. In his own words, 'At the communion was such a sight as I am persuaded was never seen in Manchester before-eleven to twelve hundred communicants at once, and all of them fearing God.' Oldham Street Chapel was to play a great role in the town, as well as in the history of Methodism as a whole, hosting many conferences and attracting many powerful preachers. (William Arthur Shaw, *Manchester Old and New*, Cassell and Company, London, 1894)

———•◆•———

1825: The Manchester Mechanics Institute was opened today. The brainchild of Benjamin Heywood, it did great work to democratise learning and 'Instruct the working classes in the principles of the arts they practise, and in other branches of useful knowledge, excluding party politics and controversial theology'. Subscription was only 5s a quarter. (W.H. Thomson, *History of Manchester to 1852*, John Sherratt & Son Ltd, Altrincham, 1967)

———•◆•———

1851: The second full modern census showed a growth in Manchester's population from 235,162 in 1841 to 303,382 in 1851. 16.6 per cent of the population were Irish born, and 2,995 were living in cellar dwellings. Due to flood damage, the records of 217,717 individuals were once thought lost beyond hope. Thankfully, the archives were still kept, though in a perilously tattered condition, and a team led by Jack Reese of ancestry. co.uk – a forensic photography expert – has been able to recover many 'lost souls' from the 3,000 damaged pages. (BBC)

MARCH 31ST

1863: The first Armenian Mass was celebrated in Manchester today, at a rented chapel on Romford Street. The mass was performed by Father Karapet Shahnazarian, who would later print the first Armenian periodical in the country, *Yercragound*. His flock would later build their own church in Ardwick.

------◆------

1952: Alan Turing's OBE for his services in breaking the German Enigma code was not enough to save him today from being convicted of 'Gross Indecency' on this day. He was given the grim choice of going to prison or receiving a programme of hormone treatment to 'cure' him of his sexuality. Perhaps wishing to continue his work at Manchester University, he chose the latter, which may have contributed to his suicide two years later (*see* June 7th).

------◆------

2007: The redevelopment of Manchester United's Old Trafford meant that a new attendance record for the ground was made, with 76,098 spectators watching the game against Blackburn Rovers. At 99.85 per cent attendance, a mere 114 seats remained empty. The home side were victorious 4–1. Subsequent reorganisation reduced the capacity by 255, so this record will stand for the near future.

APRIL 1ST

1403: On this day, the town's baron and priest Thomas la Warre financed King Henry IV's Welsh and Scottish campaigns, to the sum of 500 marks.

———————◆•◆———————

1789: Manchester was host to the world's first ever application of a rotary steam engine for use in a cotton mill. The contract, signed on this day, refers to an eight horse power engine with a 16in cylinder and a 4in stroke piston. This was housed at Peter Drinkwater's mill off London Road, now part of Aytoun Street, whose owner was an early pioneer of improved sanitary conditions, having had a great influence on his manager Robert Owen.

APRIL 2ND

1865: John Cassell, Manchester-born temperance pioneer and founder of the publishing house Cassell & Co. Ltd, died on this day. Born into poverty, he became an apprentice carpenter but soon gave that up to travel the country preaching abstinence from drink as the 'Manchester Carpenter'. He promoted drinking tea and coffee as an alternative to drinking at the alehouse, later concentrating on publishing self-help literature. Lord Brougham later described him as, 'One whose services to the cause of popular education entitled him to a place in the front rank of English philanthropists.' (William E.A. Axon, *Annals of Manchester*, John Heywood, Manchester, 1886)

———•◆•———

1865: Sussex-born Richard Cobden – who would later identify himself as a Manchester manufacturer – died on this day. His services to the cause of Free Trade were unsurpassed, as was his role in the Anti-Corn Law League. At the time of his death he was MP for Rochdale and an alderman of the Manchester Corporation – a role which he had held from its foundation. Prime Minister Lord Palmerston, Benjamin Disraeli and his old comrade John Bright gave tributes in Parliament upon hearing of his death, and moves were soon underway to commemorate him in the town.

———•◆•———

1990: Today saw the beginning of the riot at HM Prison Strangeways where, two days earlier, a note had been passed to a prison officer stating that, 'There's going to be a riot in the Church of England'. However, the warning went unheeded and rioting soon began in the chapel. It lasted twenty-five days; the longest such riot known.

APRIL 3RD

1578: On this day, Manchester's Court Leet condemned its 'wicked watchmen', who had been 'hired, or rather bribed with money of the gamers, and so permitted them to use their unlawful game all the night through at their pleasure; neither regarding the commodity, preservation, or good government of the town, nor yet their oath, which is most lamentable.' They therefore decreed that no man be employed but 'Honest, discreet and sober men, being able to yield account of their living favourites to virtue and enemies to vice. No person of misbehaviour, no suspected person, no persons heretofore with bribes corrupted, or any such like. And in so doing God shall be glorified, the Queen's majesty's watch duly observed, the town in safety preserved, all unlawful games repressed, and good order maintained; which we pray God grant and wish the same unfeignedly.'

———— ◆ ————

1990: The *Manchester Evening News* editor, Mike Unger, braved flying roof slates as he visited HM Prison Strangeways to investigate the ongoing riot (*see* April 2nd). Present alongside solicitors, he witnessed the beginning of negotiations in what would prove to be a very long, drawn-out process lasting twenty-five days. Later that day, a sex offender who had been beaten by other inmates died – he was to prove the sole casualty of the riot.

APRIL 4TH

1569: On this day, the Court Leet recorded that, 'The jury doth request Mr Steward, for and in the name of the lord, to make a pair of stocks and butts for the inhabitants of the town with speed convenient.' The stocks stood in the Old Market Place, at the eastern end of the Old Shambles until 1812, when they were replaced by a more portable means of humiliation as Aston rhymed in his Metrical Records of Manchester: 'In the autumn this year was remov'd a disgrace, which for ages had stared this large town in the face, the stocks and the pillory were found in decay, And without a renewal, were carried away.'

1790: Revered John Wesley, aged eighty-eight, preached for the last time in Manchester today, to a congregation of around 1,600 at Oldham Street Chapel.

1868: On this day, Cross Street shopkeeper John Howarth was found guilty of knowingly accepting stolen stamps from children, and sentenced to five years' labour.

APRIL 5TH

1793: On this day, Manchester's long-serving amateur postmistress Sarah Willatt was pensioned off. She died on Christmas Day 1801, aged seventy.

———•◆•———

1860: Today, the income tax returns report recorded that, 'The wealth of Manchester is enormous. According to the returns of the Property and Income Tax in the year 1860, the yearly value of property and income in Manchester was £5,775,453 [including] £3,715,272 from profits of trade. According to the same return the valuation of property and income in the division of Manchester was £7,212,054.' A further half million may be added for Salford. (Thomas Baines, *Lancashire and Cheshire, Past and Present*, William MacKenzie, Glasgow, 1867)

———•◆•———

2002: The film *24 Hour Party People*, starring Middleton-born Steve Coogan as Tony Wilson, founder of Factory Records and the Haçienda nightclub, premiered on this day. It tells the story of the Manchester music scene, from the Punk days of the Sex Pistols and their historic Lesser Free Trade Hall concert on June 4th 1976, through to the Post-Punk, Electronic and Madchester phases, up until the early 1990s.

APRIL 6TH

1838: Reporters at the *Manchester Times* came across a report today that they dismissed as a 'gross fabrication'. Their rivals at the *Manchester Guardian* looked further into the matter and claimed that the same rumours were, in the main, 'true'. A Yorkshire man by the name of Henry Stoakes, a renowned builder of flues and chimneys employing nine men and a resident on Cumberland Street in Deansgate since 1829, was revealed by his wife to be a woman. He had been living as Henry for over twenty-five years, with nobody being any wiser, except his seventeen-year-old bride he had married twenty-two years before in Sheffield. Henry had even joined the Special Constables in Manchester, on which the *Guardian* states: 'We are assured that, on all occasions when the services of the division were required, as at elections, Orange processions, and meetings of trades' unions, turn-outs, etc., so far from absenting herself from what, as in the case of well-founded apprehension of a riot … she is remembered to have been one of the most punctual in attendance, and the most forward volunteer in actual duty, in that division.' Henry's wife had only revealed her husband's secret because he had refused to give her housekeeping money, and been too handy at following his male colleagues' example of getting aggressively drunk.

April 7th

1446: On this day, Henry VI granted Sir Edmund Trafford of Trafford the right to pursue the semi-heretical art of alchemy, in the hope that he might find the fabled Philosophers' Stone.

—◆—

1861: The census lists that on this day there were 357,604 people living in Manchester, an increase of over 13 per cent since 1851. An extra 105,000 or so may be added for Salford's side of the river too. It also lists that 13.9 per cent were Irish-born, a drop from 1851's high of 16.6 per cent. (Thomas Baines, *Lancashire and Cheshire, Past and Present*, William MacKenzie, Glasgow, 1867)

—◆—

1879: On this day, Dr Andrea Crestadoro, Manchester's Genoa-born Chief Librarian of the Corporation Free Libraries, died. A professor of Natural Philosophy at the University of Turin, he somehow found his way to Salford in 1852. It was here where, like his countryman Leonardo Da Vinci, he dabbled in mechanical invention, including the development of flight. Appointed chief librarian in 1864 and then Cavaliere dell'Ordine de Corona d'Italia by King Vittorio Emanuele, he was the first to compile a catalogue of the Manchester Reference library, in line with his 1856 work *The Art of Making Catalogues*.

APRIL 8TH

1752: On this day, the *Weekly Journal* reported, 'A public infirmary for this place and neighbourhood has long been talked of, and is no doubt as much wished for as it is really wanted.' As a result, money was collected for the first Manchester Infirmary to be built. The public-spiritedness of Joseph Bancroft in particular is worthy of mention, as he offered to defray all expenses for a whole year if nobody else would join him in providing funds.

———◆———

1812: Today, reactionary townsfolk proposed to hold a meeting in order to pen a note of thanks to the Prince Regent for retaining the serving Tory government in power. This was met with violent and outspoken opposition, and as a result the meeting was called off and no message was sent. However, some members of the crowd refused to leave it at that and chose to demonstrate their outrage by smashing up the newsroom at the Exchange. The army were called out to suppress the disorder.

———◆———

1978: Today, aspiring Manchester band Brian & Michael became one-hit wonders. Their L.S. Lowry tribute song 'Matchstalk Men and Matchstalk Cats and Dogs', released on November 25th, reached number one in the charts, where it remained for three weeks.

APRIL 9TH

1821: On this day, Scottish writer Sir Walter Scott visited Manchester. His political notions were to the taste of local radicals, having advocated a tax on manufacturers according to the size of their workforce, with the proceeds going to the wellbeing of the latter.

❖

1846: Today saw thirty cartloads of snow brought to town, in order to be deposited in the ice house under the Shambles. It was sold at 22s per ton; fishmongers had been suffering from a scarcity of ice throughout the season and were glad to purchase the shipment.

❖

2012: Today was the opening day of the first Manchester Fashion Week. It is hoped that it will become a successful annual feature of the Mancunian cultural scene, as well as revitalising some of the town's clothing manufactures. The packed programme included many events, such as the Misguided Festival Grunge Show and Private White Fashion Show. The week ended on Friday 13th with a closing party at the Venus Nightclub hosted by Calum Beat, Bjorn Borg and Caprice, featuring the musical contributions of Boy George and Marc Vedo.

APRIL 10TH

1596: Manchester widow Alice Grene remarried today, to Sir Julius Caesar! Sir Julius was Master of the Rolls and Chancellor of the Exchequer, and owed his rather extravagant name to his father, an Italian doctor who had treated both Queen Mary I and Queen Elizabeth I, Giulio Cesare Adelmare.

———— • ◆ • ————

1848: Today saw thousands of Chartists converge on Manchester. As the Continent was embroiled in revolution, England's Chartists caught the insurrectionary bug. They were dispersed by the local police, warning them of the mobilisation of troops. The Chartists certainly had their share of hotheads, and matters could easily have escalated. Twelve thousand special constables had been sworn in for the emergency, however, and the situation was defused; a great success for the newly formed civilian force faced with its first major public order challenge.

APRIL 11TH

1577: On this day, the Court Leet expressed its grave dissatisfaction that large numbers of people were not grinding their corn at the Lord of the Manor's mills. This was prescribed by law and custom, as well as being the financial support of the grammar school, which derived its income from the tolls extracted. They also ordered James Smith, a capper, and William Savage, the catchpoll (an officer of the court), to monitor the wearing of illegal types of hat in church on Sundays. Royal decrees, intended to promote the domestic wool industry, had ordered that only woollen caps be worn to worship.

———◆———

1789: As the French Revolution unfolded, several Freemasons and ringleaders of local Jacobin sympathisers were arrested on this day. One eyewitness, Anna Walker, stated: 'It seems clubs have been formed here for a long time under the cloak of Freemasonry; the members have been putting the use of Arms in the Manufactories, in order to join the French in case of invasion, corresponding with them & co. Government, informed of their proceedings, have waited an opportunity, and finding enough to justify the proceedings, have seized seven or nine of the ringleaders, who this morning were marched off under a strong guard.' The Manchester authorities were watching the distant bloody events in Paris with horror, as well as grim determination to foil similar aspirations for political change on their watch.

APRIL 12TH

627: According to John Whitaker's *Eighteenth Century Mamecestre*, this Easter Day saw Eadwine 'King of Northumbria and conqueror of Manchester ... baptised by Paulinus, together with his barons, and amongst them the Baron of Manchester ... at York, with great solemnity and ceremony.'

◆

1826: Today, seventy-four men of the 60th Rifle Corps marched on the suspension bridge over the River Irwell, feeling it vibrate beneath their feet. The men thought it highly amusing and carried on marching; making the effect even stronger, until, with a loud crack, one of the metal columns holding the chains broke and forty men fell 17ft into the water. None were killed, but six suffered serious fractures. The British Army has since remained under orders to 'break step' when crossing a bridge.

◆

1818: Oldham Street residents presented their petition to the magistrates today, complaining of the nuisance of 'Profane and debauched ballad singing by men and women', which the neighbourhood then suffered from almost nightly. (William E.A. Axon, *Annals of Manchester*, John Heywood, Manchester, 1886)

APRIL 13TH

1831: 'A Daring Robbery' read the headline of today's *Manchester Guardian*. The article reported that, 'The Badgers of Rose Hill were robbed of their dining silver tonight, the culprits even having the temerity to sneak into the bedroom of Mr Richard Badger to steal his overcoat and shirts. The robbers had broken into the cellar and found their way to the kitchen, where they had enjoyed a slap up meal of veal, ham and milk, though they had commendably avoided the temptation of the open drinks cabinet.' The same edition carried more reassuring news of the break up of a 'Knot of traffickers in horse flesh, who have long infested the town of Unsworth'.

———— •◆• ————

1872: Samuel Bamford of Middleton, aged eighty-four, died at his home in Moston on this day. An old Radical, he had been tried alongside 'Orator' Hunt following the massacre at Peterloo, and was sentenced to twelve months' imprisonment in Lincoln Castle for 'Conspiracy to alter the legal frame of the government and constitution of these realms, and with meeting tumultuously at Manchester.' He had worked as a weaver in Middleton, a warehouseman in Manchester, sailed the North Sea on a coal lugger and, lastly, was a tax clerk in London, all of which he coupled with Reformist journalism, as well as issuing a certain amount of poetry and dialect work.

April 14th

1654: Sir Alexander Radcliffe of Ordsall Hall was buried in the Collegiate Church today. The 'staunch cavalier' had held Salford for the King and attempted to take Manchester with the Earl of Derby in 1642 (for which he was imprisoned in the Tower of London), but did not live to see the Restoration of the monarchy, dying at the age of forty-six. (William E.A. Axon, *Annals of Manchester*, John Heywood, Manchester, 1886)

———•◆•———

1875: Manchester-born 'Prison Philanthropist' Thomas Wright died on this day, aged eighty-six. He spent fifty years as deacon in the Congregationalist Chapel on Grosvenor Street. He began to visit the inmates of the New Bailey Prison in 1838, befriending them and helping them find work when released – one of who later became a clergyman. His efforts came to the notice of the government and this iron foundry worker was offered a £800 annual salary post inspecting prisons which he declined, but did accept a testimonial of £3,248 in 1852 to help him in his endeavours.

———•◆•———

1888: Just five years after his death, Manchester's second bishop, James Fraser, was commemorated in a statue unveiled today on Albert Square. By Thomas Woolner, it shows him on its panels as a Churchman, Charitable Man, and Citizen, in memory of his sympathetic and down-to-earth qualities. (Terry Wyke and Harry Cocks, *Public Sculpture of Greater Manchester*, Liverpool University Press, 2003)

APRIL 15TH

1790: Sprinter John Wild's (*see* November 2nd) racetrack feats as Stump today were later set to rhyme:

> It was in April, the fifteenth day.
> To Kersal Moor Stump came;
> Then side by side these footmen went,
> Which made them shout amain ;
> Saying, Bonny Stump will now be beat
> O how they were mista'en !
> But Stump he was both loyal and true,
> First up to th' chair this hero flew.
> So now to conclude, and make an end;
> For Stump we'll loud huzza!
> Victorious he has always proved,
> And always bore the sway;
> His honour let it always ring:
> God bless bold Stump and George our King!

1842: On this day, campaigning began in Manchester to gather signatures for the Second National Petition for the acceptance of the Charter. 99,680 Mancunian working men signed it, making up a great part of the total national figure of 3,315,752 signatures that were presented to Parliament on May 12th. The Commons voted against it 287 to 49, with Stockport MP Richard Cobden in the minority.

APRIL 16TH

1844: Today, Salford finally received its Charter of Incorporation, catching up with its big brother across the River Irwell. Salford's first mayor was Mr William Locket, and the newly created borough would receive its official grant of heraldic arms on November 5th.

———— • ◆ • ————

1848: Smithfield played host to a huge Chartist gathering today, where upwards of 100,000 met to sign the new petition in favour of the Six Points of the People's Charter. The next day, the National Convention stated that 170,000 signatures had been gathered in all. Fears of an uprising grew and 12,000 special constables were hurriedly sworn in, in preparation.

———— • ◆ • ————

1866: George Murray, the Dumfriesshire-born textile baron, died at Ancoats Hall today. Along with his brother Adam, he had founded the firm A & G Murray in the 1790s, erecting their Old Mill in 1797. Constructed by the millwright Thomas Lowe, who had built Arkwright's first Manchester mill in Shudehill, it is now the oldest such factory in the world; its record-breaking eight-storey height was a thing of wonder at its opening. The Murrays dominated the world cotton industry, employing well over 1,000 people, until overtaken by McConnel and Kennedy in the mid-1800s. The great mill complex was recently converted by Urban Splash into modern office space and flats.

April 17th

1805: On this day, Mancunian romantic painter Charles Gough and his terrier, Foxie, set out for a ramble on Helvellyn in the Lake District – the last he would ever make. His subsequent fate would make him more famous as a subject of art than he had ever been as an artist himself. His remains were not found until July, alongside the healthy (and suspiciously plump) Foxie. According to the *Carlisle Press*, 'The bitch had pupped in a furze near the body of her master, and, shocking to relate, had torn the cloaths from his body and eaten him to a perfect skeleton.' Sir Edwin Landseer later immortalised the scene in oils, stressing the motif of canine loyalty.

◆

1856: Failsworth-born world traveller and author John Armitage died in Manchester on this day. He sailed for Rio de Janeiro as a young man, and wrote *A History of Brazil*. In 1836 he moved onto Ceylon, where he was a merchant and became a member of the Legislative Council. He returned to England in 1855, lauded for his services to the colony but broken by the tropical climate.

◆

1926: Today saw Manchester host its first international football match. England met Scotland at Old Trafford, losing 0-1 in front of a crowd of 49,429.

APRIL 18TH

1560: In a move to promote archery, the Court Leet ordered the making of 'Two pairs of butts; that is to say, the inhabitants upon the south side of the church to make one pair of butts in the Manchester Lane; and the inhabitants on the north side of the church, one other pair of butts, upon Collyhurste, afor the feast of St John Baptist next, sub pena each division *6s 8d*.'

———— • ◆ • ————

1745: On this day, John Kay of Walmersley (the inventor of the flying shuttle) developed the water powered weaving of cloth ribbons with Joseph Stell. Unsuccessful in England, Kay was then forced to go to France, where he spent many years, but his machines spread rapidly throughout England, and there is now a mural of him in Manchester Town Hall, as well as pubs named after him in Bury.

———— • ◆ • ————

1812: Today saw the women of Shudehill start a riot. Market traders accused of selling unwholesome meat and giving short weight finally provided the back-breaking straw, charging an outrageous *2d* for 3lb of potatoes. The local women took matters into their own hands, toppling carts and making off with the goods. The army was called in, but the traders sensibly dropped prices and sold the remainder of their wares at 5¼lb per tuppence. Food riots continued on April 21st and the repercussions were severe (*see* June 16th).

APRIL 19TH

1781: Noted local entrepreneur, author and personality, Elizabeth Raffald (*née* Whittaker) died on this day. Mother of sixteen daughters in eighteen years, she had somehow found time to publish Manchester's first directory, a best-selling cookbook, a midwifery guide, and to encourage the budding leisure sector (*see* March 20th and July 4th).

———◆———

1881: Thomas Seddon of Bradford Colliery was elected secretary of the newly formed Lancashire Miners' Federation. A coal miner from Manchester, Seddon would later serve in the same role for the subsequent Miners Federation of Great Britain from 1889 to 1910.

———◆———

1933: Today saw a 3,000-strong meeting held in the Free Trade Hall to protest the persecution of Jews in Hitler's Germany. With the Lord Mayor presiding and Lord Bishops of Manchester and Salford supporting the platform, it was pointed out that no newspaper had exerted more effort in banishing the ill will left behind from the First World War towards Germany than the *Manchester Guardian*, even though it constituted the one British newspaper that was banned in the Reich. The editor, W.P. Crozier, then stood up to assure those gathered that 'Both my colleagues and I are deeply gratified at this unusual popularity', which was followed by the crowd's laughter.

APRIL 20TH

1584: On this day, the heads of the Catholic Recusants, James Bell, John Finch and James Leybourne, were displayed on top of the Collegiate Church in Manchester following their execution at Lancaster.

———•◆•———

1653: Colonel Charles Worsley of Platt in Rusholme burst into the House of Commons today, under the orders of Cromwell. On Sir Oliver's famous comment, 'Take away that bauble' (referring to the speaker's Mace), Worsley took up the ancient royal symbol and kept it until July 4th. He would subsequently stand as Manchester's first MP in Cromwell's parliament, and was remembered as being of 'Great severity and puritanical rigour.' (Richard Wright Procter, *Memorials of Manchester Streets*, T. Sutcliffe, Manchester, 1874)

———•◆•———

1987: Today saw the completion of Manchester's Chinese Imperial Arch. The first of its kind in Europe, it was assembled by artisans from Beijing, at a cost of £350,000. The local climate hasn't been kind to the structure, and it required major renovation in 2002-05. Apparently, the timbers from northern China, on the edge of the dry Mongolian steppes, aren't particularly suited to Manchester drizzle, nor can the pigs-blood enriched mortar stand up to the damp as well as local alternatives.

APRIL 21ST

1557: The earliest known boroughreeve of Manchester, Robert Becke, died on this day. During his lifetime, Manchester was still a village, despite its already flourishing textile industry and popular annual fairs.

1785: Following a concerted campaign by the town's manufacturers and rumblings of discontent among many thousands of weavers, delegates Walker and Richardson arrived in town today. They reported that Mr Pitt had moved for repeal of the fustian tax, and his opponent Mr Fox had seconded it. Thomas Walker (later the town's boroughreeve) made a short speech in the crowded market place in front of the Bull's Head, before he and his companion were carried through the streets on chairs.

1812: On this day, a riotous mob attacked and plundered the shop of greengrocer John Holland, on the corner of Priestner Street (now Liverpool Road) and Deansgate. The whole region was in turmoil, with the Middleton Fight, mob seizures of foodstuffs and Luddite attacks on industrial machinery, and the army were kept busy rushing between each scene of unrest. Anger at the scale of the repression reached its peak when murder was committed on May 10th, which resulted in eight hangings at Lancaster on June 16th.

APRIL 22ND

1800: Released on this day, G. Bancks's Manchester and Salford Directory lists 6,336 of the principal inhabitants and tradesmen of the conurbation, and 658 streets. These new figures highlighted an appreciable increase from the previous directory of 1797. New features included reference to municipal street lighting and 'scavengers'.

———— ◆ ————

2012: On this day, Manchester Airport welcomes the first visit of the Boeing 787 Dreamliner – 'The best thing in aviation since Concorde' – and one of the largest aeroplanes in the world. Standing 55ft tall and with a 197ft wingspan, it is truly a monster. But perhaps most striking of all was the enthusiasm of the plane-watching hobbyists, many of whom had waited three hours in the cold morning mists to catch a glimpse of the flying behemoth.

APRIL 23RD

1579: Today's Court Leet records state that, 'Whereas there is great abuse in a game used in the town called "Gede Gadye", or the "Catt's Pallett" [Giddy Gaddy] ... no manner of person shall play at the same game, being above the age of seven years, upon pain of every person so playing, to be imprisoned in the dungeon for the space of two hours; and every parent or master of such persons so playing ... for every time so serving them after warning given, 4*d*. This order is made because divers of the inhabitants do find them aggrieved that their children be hurt and in danger of being hurt.' Giddy Gaddy involved a 6in-long tapered piece of wood, first whacked into the air and then again at a target. The same complaint and punishments were reiterated in 1583, the game of Giddy Gaddy proving near in-eradicable.

———— ◆ ————

1601: John Booker was born in Manchester today. He was the official licenser of all books printed in England on mathematics, astronomy and astrology. Credited with having psychic powers, 'He had a curious fancy in judging of thefts, and was quite as successful in resolving love questions.' He wrote *The Bloody Irish Almanac*, among other astrological books. (William E.A. Axon, *Annals of Manchester*, John Heywood, Manchester, 1886)

———— ◆ ————

1661: On this day, the market place's conduit ran with claret instead of water to celebrate the coronation of Charles II, after a decade's interregnum.

April 24th

1855: Radical Bible Christian preacher Revd James Scholefield, aged sixty-five, died on this day. A devout vegetarian for forty-four years, his works in favour of the lifestyle, *Man is not a Predator!* had most impact in Germany – it was translated by Weilshaeuser as *Der Mensch – Kein Raubtier*. In the political sphere he was notable for his support of the Chartists, who he permitted to hold their 1842 conference in his Every Street Chapel. For this, he was tried and acquitted before the Lancaster Assizes in 1843.

———◆———

1875: The last of the auctions to sell off the great art collection of the German Mancunian merchant Sam Mendel, who had been so suddenly bankrupted by the opening of the Suez Canal, was held on this day. The auction took place at his palatial home of Manley Hall in Staffordshire, which Mendel was then forced to sell for £85,000; with the artworks making £101,184, 14s 6d. Mendel was left with only his memories and an orchid named after him, the graceful white *cattleya mendelii*.

———◆———

1932: The mass trespass onto Kinder Scout – a landmark event in the struggle for ramblers' rights – occurred today. Ewan McColl commemorated the event in his popular folk song 'The Manchester Rambler'. His involvement was matched by that of other leading Communists, especially Benny Rothman.

April 25th

1794: On this day, John Dalton was elected as a member of the Literary and Philosophical Society. A Quaker and mathematics professor from Cumberland, he had only been living in the town for a year when his scientific genius was noticed and he was offered the membership. He later became president of the society in 1817, remaining so until his death on July 27th 1844.

1990: The twenty-five day long riot at Strangeways Prison came to an end today. Only six inmates remained, and the staff began the operation to take back full control. One inmate surrendered and the rest climbed up onto the roof. As they continued to throw missiles (much of the roof was already bare of slates at this point) the Prison Officers managed to move the remaining protesters to where they wanted them by spraying the last bit of roof with soapy water to prevent them from moving further. The last man to leave the roof was Paul Taylor, the man who had initiated the riot. A later inmate, Colin Garnett, recorded the event in poetry:

As years passed by in Strangeways jail, tension grew and grew
Inmate's protests got no response, so what else could they do?
The threat of grief was always there, but no one knew the truth
Bad attitudes by all concerned cost Strangeways jail its roof.

APRIL 26TH

1576: On this day, the Court Leet recorded that, 'No man shall turn forth any swine upon the market days, so that they be found in the streets or market places, 12*d*. Those which be appointed for making clean of the market shall … give diligent heed to keep the swine from sacks of corn for and during the market time.' Cattle were also reported as knocking over the archery butts at 'Alporde Lane' (on Deansgate, near Knott Mill).

———◆———

1817: Margaret Marsden, aged seventy-five, and Hannah Parrington, aged twenty, were brutally murdered at Three-Nooked Field in Pendleton, on this day. A bent, bloody poker and cleaver were found, and £160 in gold and notes was missing. Four men were speedily arrested the next day – William Holden, David Ashcroft and two James Ashcrofts, who were father and son. Despite steadfastly pleading their innocence right until the last, they were hanged at Lancaster on September 8th, after singing the hymn 'I'll Praise My Maker Whilst I've Breath' on the scaffold. (Richard Wright Procter, *Memorials of Manchester Streets*, T. Sutcliffe, Manchester, 1874)

———◆———

2006: Today saw the Beetham Tower finally completed. Fireworks marked the 'topping out' ceremony as the 561ft skyscraper (the tallest outside of London) reached its maximum height. Architect Ian Simpson was especially pleased – he now occupies the vast 8,000 sq. ft penthouse suite, another national record breaker for its height.

APRIL 27TH

1713: Edmund Harrold's diary entry for this day reads, 'This day thought to have drunk no ale, but got to Hardy [Ardwick] Green and bowled eleven games; so I drank about three gills in all, and spent 7d of losses ...'

1773: On this day, an early enumeration was made of the town. It was found to be home to some 10,358 males and 11,933 females, totalling 22,291 people in 8,402 houses. Adding to that the populations of Salford and outlying townships, the total populous amounted to 40,842.

1974: Manchester United were unlucky today, in the famous 'Denis Law Game' – a derby match which was all that stood between United and relegation to the Second Division. United were in desperate need of a victory and City were loathe to deliver the final blow. The game seemed set to end in a 0–0 draw until, with only ten minutes to go, Law, who was standing with his back to the goal, back-heeled the ball into the net. He walked off the pitch with his head down, believing he had scored a death blow against his former team. Attempting to force an abandonment of the match, United fans then launched a pitch invasion, but the Football League later determined that the score would still stand. Law subsequently retired from professional football.

APRIL 28TH

1786: The escaped Stretford-born Jacobite John Holker (*see* July 16th) died at Rouen in France today. It was here that he had been made a Chevalier of the Order of St Louis by Louis XV on September 27th 1770. Escaping execution for being a Jacobite rebel, he had joined the French Army and later gone into textile and chemical manufacturing in Rouen. He was the first to introduce leaden chambers in the process of making sulphuric acid. Later in life, he travelled secretly to England to lure away English artisans. He also hosted Benjamin Franklin at his home in Paris, and sent his son to set the fledgling US textile industry on a good footing.

———◆———

1996: On this day, Oasis, the group formed by brothers Noel and Liam Gallagher, perform one of their biggest concert appearances at Maine Road, as part of their '(What's the Story) Morning Glory?' tour. With half a dozen other pieces recorded elsewhere, footage of the bulk of the concert was later released as the 'There and Then' DVD and video.

APRIL 29TH

1679: On this day, Manchester inhabitants swore an oath of loyalty to King William III. The Dutch sovereign was invited over to oust the Stuarts by a conspiracy headed by the City of London and the magnates. Temporarily cowed at the 'Glorious Revolution', the townsmen would later prove to have been largely crossing their fingers, and the exiled Stuarts would later find many supporters in Manchester.

1862: The continuing disastrous trade slump saw up to 3,000 unemployed factory operatives gather in Stevenson Square today, for a meeting. The Cotton Famine due to the civil war in America was already well in evidence, though relief measures were still woefully inadequate to deal with the resultant distress.

2008: On what would have been his seventieth birthday, the larger-than-life bronze statue of steeplejack and industrial enthusiast Fred Dibnah was unveiled in his native Bolton. Two year later, his old back yard (complete with 70ft working coal mineshaft) opened as the Fred Dibnah Heritage Centre.

APRIL 30TH

1667: On this day, while visiting Manchester, Revd Oliver Heywood was awakened late at night by a curious and now forgotten local custom called Bringing in May. After midnight, houses were strewn with flowers and garlands. Heywood considered this 'foolish', and was most irritated by the disturbance.

———◆———

1863: The Cotton Famine stretched on and on, with no immediate sign of an end to hostilities in America. Many saw little other hope than emigration, and so set up the Emigration Aid Society, whose first boatload of 1,000 former operatives sailed out from the Mersey to a new home in New Zealand on this day.

———◆———

1994: This day was an emotional day for Manchester City fans, as they said goodbye to the legendary Kippax stand. Traditionally home to their most vocal fans, City had prided themselves on the fact that their singing stand occupied a full long side of the pitch, not one behind the goalposts like other clubs. A new safer stand was built, decreasing the capacity from 18,300 to around 14,000. Three tiers tall, it was remarkable in its own way as the tallest such structure in the country, and was officially opened by City goalkeeping hero Bert Trautmann.

MAY 1ST

1473: An early rental survey was made of the town on this day, recording around 150 burgages in the still small townlet.

— • ◆ • —

1842: On this day, Manchester was granted its present coat of arms. The shield of the Norman de Grelley Barons was topped with references to trade and industry in the form of a ship and globe covered with bees. Later, a lion and antelope were added, and the motto *Concilio et Labore* was chosen to point to the town's good counsel and hard-working populace.

— • ◆ • —

1912: Salford-born Edwin Alliott Verdon-Roe set a new milestone in the history of flight today, as his Avro Type F made its first flight. The aircraft had a rather ungraceful resemblance to an old-fashioned pram, but was the first ever cabin aircraft to stand up to testing. Being a monoplane, as opposed to the biplanes of the period, it had an advantage in lightness and reached the never before heard of altitude of 1,000ft. The novelty invited a certain amount of over-use, however, for the result of which see September 13th.

— • ◆ • —

1965: Today, Manchester band The Hollies achieved their first number one spot with their single 'I'm Alive'. Their second would come many years later (*see* August 1st).

MAY 2ND

1687: The first mention of the races at Manchester is found in today's *London Gazette*. At the time, Kersall Moor remained quite an open and democratic field, with no walls or turnstyles, where all manner of Manchester folk rubbed shoulders while enjoying the festivities of the day.

———◆———

1844: The first stone of the Presbyterian (Scotch Covenanter) Church in Ormond Street in Chorlton-upon-Medlock, was laid on this day. Seating a congregation of 400 and designed by A. Nicholson, it was the first church of this particular denomination to be built south of the border.

———◆———

1899: On this day, controversy over the Cromwell statue in Victoria Street prompted a counter-reaction at a meeting in Milton Congregational Church near Rochdale. Describing the Lord Protector as a 'God-made man, as much raised up by God to do a special work as were John Bright and Richard Cobden in later days', those gathered averred that 'Manchester ... had done itself honour in erecting a monument to Cromwell, and as for the dastards who proposed the other day to throw it into the Irwell, they themselves were first likely to go there.' (*Manchester Guardian*, May 3rd 1899)

MAY 3RD

1854: On this day, Richard Arkwright's 'Old Factory' was gutted by fire. The town's first purpose-built cotton mill, this hulking structure made of massive brickwork and heavy wooden floors, had amazed townsfolk when it was built in the 1780s. Although built of seemingly primitive but solid edifice, it was unsuited to the scale of the newer machines. Following the fire, parts of the mill's carcass were incorporated into later works, and the remaining structure was finally laid low by the Luftwaffe (*see* October 23rd).

1871: Connecticut-born inventor Joseph Cheesborough Dyer died on this day. He came to Manchester in 1802, and patented the carding engine in 1811 and the roving frame in 1825, before settling in the town for good from 1816. Many of his other projects were less successful; losses from his failed Somme machine works amounted to £120,000, and the failing of the Manchester Bank cost him a cool £96,000. His work in the political sphere bore better fruit, however, especially his promotion of the newly fledged *Manchester Guardian*.

1956: Granada Television made its first television broadcast today. Based then, as now, at their Granada Studios site on Quay Street, its flagship programmes include the record-breaking *Coronation Street* and other stalwarts such as *University Challenge*.

MAY 4TH

1801: Today saw the first Whit Sunday Procession. It included the Anglican Sunday school pupils parading in pomp and show to the Collegiate Church to hear Warden Blackburne give a special sermon. Careful records were kept down the years of the numbers attending, reaching up to 20,000 or so in their Victorian heyday.

———— • ◆ • ————

1904: On this day, Manchester's Midland Hotel held a history-making meeting in the world of motoring between Stewart Rolls and Frederick Henry Royce. The rest, as they say, is history!

———— • ◆ • ————

1991: Ryan Giggs, then a youngster of seventeen years, scored his first ever professional goal at Old Trafford today – the only goal of that day's derby match. (Notching up a further thirty-five appearances, Giggs also happens to be the player with most appearances in Manchester derbys.)

———— • ◆ • ————

2002: Kylie Minogue performed for a sixth night at the Manchester Evening News Arena on this night. This pushed the proceeds from tickets past £2 million, and she outperformed any other single artist at that venue since its opening. Breaking the record for revenues of any female performer, her tickets were selling like hot cakes, well suiting the name of tour – 'The Fever'.

MAY 5TH

1821: The first edition of the *Manchester Guardian* left the presses for the newsstands and paperboys' bags today. Issued weekly on Saturdays, the paper sold at 7*d*, was printed and published by John Edward Taylor and Jeremiah Grant, and would become a major Manchester icon. The paper would come to be known as the *Guardian*, the national paper we have today, in 1959.

1857: Today saw the opening of the largest art exhibition ever held in this country – The Art Treasures of Great Britain, held at the Botanical and Horticultural Society gardens, the present day site of the White City Retail Park in Old Trafford (*see* October 17th).

1956: On this day, Manchester City played Birmingham City in the FA Cup Final, winning 3–1. However, the lasting fame of the match is reserved for City's goalkeeper, Bert Trautmann. A Wehrmacht prisoner of war, he had been named Footballer of the Year only two days before and for seventeen minutes of the match he managed to play with five dislocated vertebrae, one of which was broken in two. The peculiar way they had wedged together was all that had kept Trautmann alive, and he even blocked two attempts on goal. Nobody realised the extent of his injury until several days later, despite being unconsciousness for several minutes after the injury was inflicted. Cheered off the pitch to 'He's a Jolly Good Fellow', he received his winner's medal from Prince Philip who remarked on his crooked neck.

MAY 6TH

1597: Today, the Warden of the Collegiate Church, its clerk and many other townsfolk walked the bounds of the Parish of Manchester. The complete circuit would take six days and was a vestige of an ancient medieval rite, 'Beating the Bounds', practised at only a handful of rural parishes. The warden of the day was eminent scholar of the occult, Dr John Dee, a one time confidante of Queen Elizabeth I and King of Bohemia. To imagine such a man tramping along the muddy field boundaries and ditches of a still rural south-east Lancashire is amusing in the least.

———— • ◆ • ————

1790: Father and son doctors White and White, with Messrs Hull and Hull founded the Manchester Lying-In Hospital today. It would operate from their homes until permanent premises were found at the former Bath Inn on Stanley Street in 1796.

———— • ◆ • ————

1803: On this day, weaver-cum-political writer Robert Walker died at Littlemoss in Audenshaw. He had taken exception to Edmund Burke's reference to the 'Swinish multitude' and put pen to paper in a series of pieces in dialect that were printed in the *Manchester Gazette*, and later in a book called *Plebeian Politics* – such was the golden age of local self-taught craftsmen scholars!

MAY 7TH

1747: John Wesley, founder of the Methodist movement, visited Mancunian laypreacher Nelson on this day. His visit resulted in an impromptu sermon: 'I had not thought of preaching here till I was informed John Nelson had given public notice that I would preach at one. I was now in a great strait. Their house would not contain one-tenth part of the people, and how the unbroken spirits of so large a town would endure preaching in the street I knew not. Beside that, having rode a swift trot for several hours, and on so sultry a day, I was both faint and weary. But, after considering that I was not going a warfare at my own cost, I walked straight to Salford Cross ... I then began, "Seek ye the Lord while He may be found; call upon Him while He is near" None interrupted us at all, or made any disturbance till I was drawing to a conclusion, when a big man thrust in with three or four more, and bade them bring out the engine. Our friends desired me to remove into a yard just by, which I did, and concluded in peace.' (William Arthur Shaw, *Manchester Old and New*, Cassell and Company, London, 1894)

———— • ————

1875: Today saw Manchester's Pomona Gardens host the second annual international show of horses, mules and donkeys.

MAY 8TH

1597: John Knott, of Knott Mylne, was buried today, giving the lie to those amateur linguists that have sought to find a trace of the eleventh-century monarch King Knut (or Canute) in the name of Knott Mills. In fact, it merely commemorates the sixteenth-century owner. The site had earlier been known as Hulme Mills and, far from being so ancient, records exist for the first damming of the river here on November 10th 1509, by miller Elyse Prestwich. It now provides the name for an inner city railway station at the southern end of Deansgate.

———— ◆ • ————

1842: Piccadilly station opened today, under its earlier guise as Store Street station, the terminus of the Manchester and Birmingham Railway. From 1846 to 1960, it was also known as London Road station. It underwent £60,000 worth of modernisation in 2003.

———— ◆ • ————

1860: Today saw the founding of the Greek Orthodox Church on Bury New Road in Higher Broughton. Father B. Moros laid the first stone. Manchester was by this time home to around 150 Greek merchants, mostly in the suburbs of Higher Broughton and Kersal.

———— ◆ • ————

1960: On this day, Terry Christian was born in Old Trafford. He worked as a broadcaster and was best known for working on Channel 4 programme *The Word*, as well as various radio programmes. In both mediums he did a great deal to promote the 'Madchester' scene, and remind the world of the existence of Manchester every time he spoke.

MAY 9TH

1584: On this day, the Court Leet reports made no deference to feminism: 'Whereas great inconvenience is felt in this town that single women, being unmarried, be at their own hands, and do bake and brew and use other trades, to the great hurt of the poor inhabitants having wives and children, as also in abusing themselves with young men and others, having not any man to control them, to the great dishonour of God, and evil example to others; in consideration whereof the jury doth order that no single woman unmarried shall be at their own hands, or keep any house or chamber within this town, after [Christmas] next, 6s 8d and imprisonment at the discretion of the steward, the boroughreeve and constables.'

———◆———

1829: Delegates from Manchester, Liverpool and Glasgow met with the Duke of Wellington and his Cabinet Ministers today, to press for free trade agreements with India and China. These same desires would soon result in the Opium Wars and the full annexation of India to the British Empire!

———◆———

2002: On this day, Manchester City hosted the last ever Manchester Derby played at their old ground, Maine Road. As was fitting for such an occasion, Keegan's side achieved their first victory over United in over thirteen years.

MAY 10TH

1812: Sergeant John Moore of the militia and his female relation were murdered at midnight on this day. Sergeant Moore had been 'Active in the performance of his duty', suppressing the discontent of the working classes at the continuing privations occasioned by the French war. The bodies of the soldier and his luckless companion were flung over Ancoats Bridge into the Rochdale Canal. The bodies were soon discovered, and a group of men were seen hurrying away. The offer of a £200 reward was for nought, as the discontented poor closed ranks against the enforcers of the law.

———◆———

1821: On this day, the Bank of England began changing coins for one and two pound paper notes. As a result the Manchester premises were crowded daily for over a month, and £420,000 worth of notes were handed out for more than four tons of gold.

———◆———

1831: Although Manchester was still a year away from having its own Member of Parliament, Benjamin Heywood was elected to represent the County of Lancashire on this day. He was president of the Manchester Mechanics' Institute, sole proprietor of his father's bank in the town, and was made a baronet for his work with the Reform Bill.

MAY 11TH

1812: Prime Minister Spencer Perceval was assassinated on this day. It came as a blow to unlucky Bolton Spinning Mule inventor Samuel Crompton. He had gone to Parliament with evidence that his Mule was producing 80 per cent of Lancashire cottons, and thus £350,000 of annual tax revenue, while he had not received a penny. It was rumoured that Perceval was willing to pay £20,000. In the event, Crompton received only £5,000.

1881: Manchester-born John Blackwall, the oldest member of both the Linnaean Society and the British Association, died today at the age of ninety-two. A member of the Manchester Literary and Philosophical Society for six decades, his zoological studies were printed in the 1834 and 1873 *Researches in Zoology* journal. An inhabitant of Crumpsall Old Hall, his most important work was the 'Monograph on British Spiders'. His contributions to the Royal Society's Catalogue of Scientific Papers span an entire half century, from 1821 to 1871.

2003: On this day, Manchester City played their last ever match at Maine Road; their home ground for the previous eighty years. Fans rushed to buy tickets, some even paying up to £250 for one, and the final attendance was 34,957 – a mere 100 or so from the maximum. City were unfortunately beaten 0–1 by Southampton. Demolition then began, with many artefacts of the old stadium sold at auction (*see* July 13th). The site now holds 474 new homes.

MAY 12TH

1785: England's first hot air balloonist James Sadler went aloft twice today, much to the delight of the Manchester viewing public. The event is immortalised in the name of Balloon Street, behind the modern printworks off Corporation Street.

— ◆ —

1809: Lieutenant Colonel Joseph Hanson, the 'Weavers' Friend' of Strangeways Hall, was sentenced to six months' imprisonment and a £100 fine at the Court of King's Bench on this day. This was in retaliation for his attempts to mediate between angry protesters and riot troops, in the hope that bloodshed might be avoided in the town. The grateful working classes raised a 'penny subscription' for his relief, collecting the modest offerings of some 39,600 contributors. (William E.A. Axon, *Annals of Manchester*, John Heywood, Manchester, 1886)

— ◆ —

2011: On this day Openshaw's Davy Jones rejoined his fellow Monkees for the first performance of their reunion tour 'An Evening with The Monkees: The 45th Anniversary Tour'. Tonight's show was held at Liverpool's Echo Arena, but Davy would be back in his native Manchester at the O2 Apollo the following night, for the band's second appearance. Eight more British shows would see them then fly over to play in Atlanta on June 3rd, and finally end the tour in Milwaukee on the 23rd July – a total of forty-three performances later.

MAY 13TH

1713: Edmond Harrold's diary entry for this day reads, 'Lent Ellen a book about marriage', offering a glimpse into eighteenth-century Manchester courtship practices. It is doubtful that Ellen got the right message, as tomorrow's entry refers to 'Daniel the rival.' On the 17th he wrote that he 'Dreamed of my dear's actions toward me,' before stating, 'she's sharp, has wit enough, if she be but good humoured ... Fortune's but low, £20 or £30 at most.' However, he ended up falling out with her 'in my drink' two weeks later, and finally getting 'rude usage of her hands' in June. By July 28th, he was engaged to another, Ann Horrocks. Harland's footnote to Harrold's comment about being 'with Ann till six in the morning' is interesting: 'The old Lancashire custom in courting allowed the parties to sit or keep company together all night without any scandal.' (John Harland, *Collectanea Relating to Manchester and its Neighbourhood at Various Periods*, Chetham Society, Manchester, 1866)

1983: Manchester band The Smiths released their first single, 'Hand in Glove', today. With both Morrissey and Johnny Marr's songwriting, and Morrisey's distinctive vocal style, it set the tone for the rest of their work, combining lyricality with a certain bleakness. Though it received good airtime thanks to John Peel, it didn't break into the charts. Their best-selling single, 'What Difference Does it Make?', only ever made it to number twelve in the UK charts.

MAY 14TH

1301: Manchester received its first Burgage Charter on this day. This would determine the form that the local government would take for the next 500 years. The document was signed by Thomas Grelle, and provided for the interrelations of burgesses, a reeve and the institution of a regular Lagh-mote, or 'law meeting' to consider any matters that arose. Members of leading local families witnessed the signing, including the Byrons, Traffords, Hultons, Prestwyches, and Pilkingtons.

———•◆•———

1806: On this day, more than 2,000 Manchester folk signed a petition to be sent to the House of Lords, supporting the abolition of the slave trade. One of the largest documents of its kind, it occupies nine sheets of parchment. An act was passed less than a year afterwards outlawing the transatlantic trade, and the abolition of slavery itself would soon follow throughout the Empire.

———•◆•———

1949: Maine Road takes a break from the norm today, in order to host the Rugby Football League Championships, as it had done from 1939 and would continue to do until 1956. Today's particular match was notable for the jaw dropping attendance figures; 75,194 spectators crammed in to watch Warrington versus Huddersfield. The Yorkshire side were leading 8–0 at half-time, and though Warrington almost managed to equalise, Huddersfield won the match 13–12.

MAY 15TH

1579: The hard up Baron West of Manchester resolved to sell his manor, and received £3,000 for it today from John Lacye, a London mercer. He would sell the rights in 1596 to the Didsbury-based Mosley family, who would remain the town's lords for the next three centuries.

1815: This Whit-Monday, as the parish's Sunday school children were all assembled within the Collegiate Church, a hoax call claiming that the roof was falling in led to a panic. One child was killed and five others injured in the ensuing scramble for the doors. The event was not held again for four years.

1865: Veteran Reformer George Wilson chaired a National Reform Conference in the Free Trade Hall today. By this time, the hard won reforms of 1832 were no longer enough to satisfy the ever more confident industrial towns and their politically aspiring 'labour aristocracy' that had not so far been given the vote. The new movement would bring success as early as 1867 (*see* November 17th).

MAY 16TH

1862: A disturbing and tragic story came to its head today, as William Taylor murdered land agent Evan Mellor at his offices in St James' Square. Accompanied by his wife Martha, Taylor had attempted to shoot Mellor but missed, injuring an uninvolved workman. He had then taken out a 12in cheese knife and stabbed him to death, blaming him for the death of his eldest daughter Mary, aged twelve. After his arrest, the bodies of Taylor's other two children (Hannah, aged eight, and William, aged five) were found at his rented rooms in the Britannia Buildings, Strangeways. A boiler had exploded, killing Mary, and it appears William then lost his mind and killed her siblings with chloroform. Sentenced to death, he was hanged outside Kirkdale Prison on September 13th, insisting that Mellor had 'ruined his family'. (William E.A. Axon, *Annals of Manchester*, John Heywood, Manchester, 1886)

1863: Manchester's last boroughreeve, Alexander Kay, died on this day. Simultaneously Mayor of Manchester, from 1845 to 1846, he spanned the divide between the modern form of municipal governance and the old manorial system, making it possible for all the older mechanisms of local rule to be absorbed into the new political structures.

MAY 17TH

1783: On this day, Methodist founder Revd John Wesley preached the sacrament to a vast crowd of over 1,300 communicants. 'Such a sight as, I believe, was never seen in Manchester before … there is no place but London where we have so many souls so deeply devoted to God.' Clearly, the Theatre Royal was failing to have the desired effect (*see* June 5th). (William E.A. Axon, *Annals of Manchester*, John Heywood, Manchester, 1886)

——— • ◆ • ———

1877: On this day, the first proper tramlines of Salford and Manchester opened. Thirteen cars filed down from the Woolpack Inn in Pendleton to the Grove Inn at Higher Broughton, with the cavalcade being led by two tramcars filled with the committees of the two tramway corporations.

——— • ◆ • ———

1966: Bob Dylan played at the Free Trade Hall today, controversially mixing his traditional acoustic performance with the use of a full backing band and electric amplification – a 'betrayal' for the hard-liner folk purists. A shout of 'Judas!' came from the crowd, and the outburst was claimed by several people, one of whom would later state, 'Any pop group could produce better rubbish than that! It was a bloody disgrace! He's a traitor!' Manchester's own Communist folk singer Ewan McColl would also criticise Dylan for abandoning political folk for more consumerist electric band music.

MAY 18TH

1709: Today saw the foundation stone of St Ann's Church laid by Lady Ann Bland of Hulme Hall. Constructed in a former cornfield, it was agreed the church's square should be 30yd wide, to accommodate the ancient Acres Fair that had taken place there since time immemorial.

1942: Nobby (Norbert) Stiles was born in Collyhurst today. He was one of only two Englishmen to have played and won in the finals of both the European Cup and World Cup. Spotted by Sir Matt Busby, Nobby played for Manchester United from 196 to 1971, scoring seventeen goals. He would eventually earn twenty-eight caps playing for England, and he received an OBE in 2000.

1980: On this day, Joy Division's vocalist and song writer, Ian Curtis, hanged himself in the small hours of the morning. Troubled by frequent depression, worsening epilepsy and marriage problems, he took his own life on the eve of an American tour. His best known song, 'Love Will Tear Us Apart', was, appropriately, chosen for his epitaph. The song reached the UK top twenty the following month. After losing an irreplaceable voice and lyricist, Joy Division reformed as New Order.

MAY 19TH

1767: Today's *Manchester Mercury* carried a most unusual advertisement: 'Any gentleman, or lady, wanting to purchase a Black Boy, 12 years of age, with a good character, has had the smallpox and measles. Whoever this will suit, may, by applying to the Higher Swan and Saracen's Head, in Market Street Lane, Manchester, meet with a Proper Person to deal with them on reasonable terms.'

———— • ◆ • ————

1785: Pioneer balloonist James Sadler made a second assent today, but was discomforted this time by strong winds (*see* May 12th).

———— • ◆ • ————

1839: Major-General Daniel Seddon, born to a local family and educated at Manchester Grammar School, died in Paris on this day. He survived thirteen months in the dark, filthy dungeons of Chiteledroog in India, served in both Russia and Egypt, and successfully defended the town of Antrim from 500 Irish rebels, against whom he led a mere twenty-six dragoons, and of which he was one of only three survivors. He rose to the rank of major-general during the Peninsular Wars, in which he trained Portuguese troops to fight the French.

May 20th

1754: On this day, Mr Miles Bower laid the first stone of the Manchester Infirmary's new home. It was a grand, specially designed, classical building which once stood where Piccadilly Gardens now stand. £4,000 and many more stones later, it opened to patients the following year.

1860: Eccles-born (specifically at Hope Hall) William Butterworth Bayley died today. He had risen to the top of the Imperial apparatus in India, where he had served as acting governor-general in 1828. A fluent Hindi and Parsi speaker, he was also made a director and chairman of the British East India Company throughout the vital years of 1834-58 when Britain was establishing rule over India.

2012: Robin Gibb died on this day at the age of sixty-two. He had enjoyed a massively successful career with the Bee Gees, as well as a long and varied solo career. He has been lauded in his own right by music historian Paul Gambaccini as 'one of the major figures in the history of British music', and 'one of the best white soul voices ever'. Robin had spent an incredible sixty years in showbiz, and his last performance was just three months before his death at the London Palladium, in a benefit concert for wounded servicemen. (BBC News, May 20th 2012; *Daily Telegraph*, May 21st 2012)

MAY 21ST

1894: On this day, Queen Victoria opened the Manchester Ship Canal in her royal yacht, the *Enchantress*. This was merely a formal affair, as the canal had been in commercial use since January 1st, when *The Norseman* had led seventy-one ocean-going cargo ships up to Salford Quays. The Co-operative Wholesale Society's *The Pioneer* was the first to unload its wares.

1982: Nightclub The Haçienda first opened its doors on this day. Founded by Tony Wilson and the group New Order, it took its name from a Situationist Internationalist slogan, 'The Haçienda Must Be Built.' Ben Kelly designed the industrial-style interior, and the three bars were each named after Soviet agents, including 'The Gay Traitor', named after Anthony Blunt, the British art historian who spied for the Soviets. Bernard Manning compèred the first night, joking that, 'I've played some shit-holes during my time, but this is really something.' The crowd were not impressed.

MAY 22ND

1421: On this day, King Henry V licensed Manchester's new Ecclesiastical College, the pet project of the parish priest and the lord of the manor, Thomas la Warre. The latter's pious motives were laid out in the charter itself: 'The church of Manchester having a large and ample parish, and very populous, had been accustomed to be ruled and governed in bygone times by rectors, some of whom never, and some very seldom, cared to personally reside in the same; and that from their long absence followed a diminution of divine worship and a great danger of souls', thereby indicating that a concern for the spiritual wellbeing of the people of Manchester was uppermost in his mind. The news of the royal assent was well received in the town, 'And all and every parishioners gathered together at the sound of the bell, and the community and university of the sayd parish, so farre as this might in any way concerne them, did for themselves, their heires and successors, give their free assent and consent thervnto.' (W.H. Thomson, *History of Manchester to 1852*, John Sherratt & Son Ltd, Altrincham, 1967; Richard Wright Procter, *Memorials of Manchester Streets*, T. Sutcliffe, Manchester, 1874; William E.A. Axon, *Annals of Manchester*, John Heywood, Manchester, 1886)

———— ◆ ————

1554: George Charleton, a Manchester goldsmith, was 'committed to the ffleete' today, for minting counterfeit coin.

———— ◆ ————

1959: Steven Patrick Morrissey was born in Davyhulme on this day. Usually known only by his surname, he became the vocalist of Manchester band The Smiths.

MAY 23RD

1782: On this day, Edward Hobson – a weaver, warehouseman and amateur botanist, mineralogist, geologist and entomologist – was born on Ancoats Lane. His humble background could not restrain his natural talent and intellectual drive, which found their focus in the self-improvement associations of working men, and he wrote several remarkable scientific works; mainly on the mosses of the British Isles, the most notable being his work called the *Musci Britannici*. He died of consumption at Bowdon on September 7th 1830, and was buried at St George's in Hulme. A fellow botanist remarked that, 'I hardly ever saw a man possessed of more enthusiasm than this poor fellow' – a judgement borne from Hobson's penchant for climbing trees and buildings in all weathers, in order to gain a closer look at any interesting mosses that might be found.

———— • ❖ • ————

1866: Damages incurred by a great fire at the London and North Western Railway Company's warehouses, near Ordsall Lane, would reach surprisingly modern figures – £200 to £300,000, though this would be in the multi-million scale today.

———— • ❖ • ————

1877: A cocoa room opened at Shudehill today, heralding the wave of temperance taverns serving non-alcoholic drinks that would sweep the city – none remain, for better or worse.

MAY 24TH

1808: A weaver was fatally shot during a meeting over a dispute in wages on this day. This was the first bloodshed in the town during the era of Radicalism and Reaction. Lieutenant-Colonel Hanson of Strangeways Hall had attempted to cool things down, but to no avail. Polarisation of opinion was evident in this period, and such incidents contributed greatly to the ill-feeling. The town was lucky to avoid any serious insurrectionary outbursts, with the chief blame for violent overreaction going to the reactionary authorities. Unfortunately, this unease spilt over most regretfully at Peterloo eleven years later.

1833: Duc Ferdinand d'Orleans, heir to the French throne, visited Manchester today, with his suite of distinguished officers.

1845: The *Manchester Guardian* reported the last known mention of the Manchester Public Baths. These were located in Piccadilly beside the Infirmary and Lunatic Asylum, having opened in 1781.

1919: On this day, the Alexandra Park Aerodrome was scene to the first UK domestic air service, operating between Manchester and the resorts of Southport and Blackpool.

MAY 25TH

1605: Today's entry in the parish register reads, 'Richard Boile, in ye Sugar Lane. Buried.' Richard stands in here for the no fewer than 1,078 victims killed by the plague in Manchester that year, representing one in five of the then inhabitants. Six acres of wasteland at Collyhurst were donated by Rowland Mosley to be devoted to a makeshift shantytown for plague victims, and many were buried there. Subsequently, several skeletons and a lead coffin were dug up during road improvements in the area 200 years later.

———•◆•———

1871: The last lord of the manor, Sir Oswald Mosley, died on this day. Educated at Rugby and Oxford, he sat in Parliament from 1806 to 1837. A learned man, he had penned *The History of Tutbury*, *Family Memoirs*, *and A Short Account of the British Church*, and made a number of useful contributions to the journal *Zoologist*. In 1845, he sold his ancestral rights to the Manor of Manchester for £200,000, ending an institution that had existed since Anglo-Saxon times.

———•◆•———

1885: This Whit-Monday, 23,082 scholars marched in the annual procession of Sunday schools. The annual holiday also brought record numbers to the Mosley Street Art Gallery – more than 5,000 people in eight hours! (William E.A. Axon, *Annals of Manchester*, John Heywood, Manchester, 1886)

MAY 26TH

1612: Today's document of the lease of a property on Market Stede Lane (now Market Street) by John Hunt to Robert Lever is of interest, in so far as it enumerates the adjoining plots of land, including the Great Meadow, the Brick-Kiln Meadow, the Kiln Field, and the House Field.

———◆———

1733: Bury's John Kay invented the Flying Shuttle for the handloom on this day. One of Ford Maddox Brown's murals in Manchester's Town Hall depicts him being bundled up by his friends and hurried out of his cottage in a blanket, away from the Luddites who saw his innovation as a threat to their livelihoods.

———◆———

1788: On this day, Manchester opened its second bank, following the failure of the first. Benjamin Heywood, Son & Co. set up shop in the Emporium on present-day Exchange Street. Mr Allen's Manchester Bank failed the same year, and the Heywoods, who had recently moved from Liverpool, bought the premises and assumed its name. In 1847, Benjamin's grandson was made a baronet, and the firm later joined with others to form the Manchester and Salford Bank.

MAY 27TH

1826: Riots broke out at Hugh Beever's mill today. This was not uncommon for the time, during depression in trade, and as attacks on factories continued, the Cabinet got involved and the army was brought in. Several local men were later convicted of rioting.

1866: Tommy Lye, born in Spinning Field, died at the age of seventy-one on this day. One of Manchester's most popular jockeys, he was described as a 'quaint, sagacious little fellow', and it was reported that 'for a two-handed crack on old times few men were better'. (*Manchester Guardian* and *Sporting Life*)

1831: Today, the world's first Co-operative Congress meeting was held at Manchester. They had gathered to resolve and establish several trading collectives, as well as to discuss opening a school in the town. The latter was particularly successful, having 170 pupils attending within six months of opening – mostly working men anxious to improve their literacy. The Co-operative Wholesale Society and its associated entities now occupy a whole complex of buildings in the city centre, including the CIS Tower – once Manchester's tallest skyscraper – and the soon-to-be-completed NOMA building.

MAY 28TH

1821: On this day, the population in Manchester tops the 100,000 mark for the first time, reaching 108,016; this was a marked increase from 1811's figure of 79,459.

1866: Today, robbers of the Cross Street Stamp Office made away with around £10,000 worth of stamps … an impressive philately. Brett, Leeson, Douglas and Douglas (the robbers) were subsequently sentenced to over ten years a piece hard labour.

1869: George Bedson laid the foundation of Holt Town Ragged School today. Around £900 had been spent on its construction, providing for the needs of 500 poor scholars.

1994: A copy of Gilbert Baye's 1953 statue of idealist social reformer Robert Owen was unveiled today, on Corporation Street, as part of a nationwide celebration of 150 years of the Co-operative movement. Owen had lived, worked and married in Manchester for much of his youth, before going on to create his experimental model community at New Lanark in Scotland. Hughie Todner, president of the Co-op Congress, unveiled it in the presence of the Lord Mayor, Councillor Sheila Smith and other dignitaries. (Terry Wyke and Harry Cocks, *Public Sculpture of Greater Manchester*, Liverpool University Press, 2003)

MAY 29TH

1814: Today being Whitsunday, the Church Commission ordered the provision of 'a number of cakes to be sold at 1*d*, for the children', so that they might refresh themselves before the Whit Walks began from St Ann's Square. This would be the beginning of the Whit Week tradition of 'buns and milk'. (William E.A. Axon, *Annals of Manchester*, John Heywood, Manchester, 1886)

———— • ◆ • ————

1967: Oasis songwriter and guitarist Noel Gallagher was born in Longsight this day. Elder brother of Liam, Noel was inspired to go into music by The Smiths, and spent some time touring with the Inspiral Carpets, after which he joined his brother's embryonic Oasis in 1991. Years of success followed until the group's break up on August 28th 2009.

———— • ◆ • ————

1968: Manchester United celebrated their first European Cup title today.

———— • ◆ • ————

2008: Forty years on, United celebrated the anniversary of their first European Cup title with the unveiling of a statue of the team's 'Holy Trinity' – George Best, Denis Law and Bobby Charlton. Standing on a plinth across Sir Matt Busby Way, their likenesses face that of Busby himself and Old Trafford's East Stand.

May 30th

1846: Today hosted the last Whit Week Races held on Kersal Moor – a tradition going back to 1730. Unfortunately, one jockey by the name of Byrne was killed in the hurdle race.

———— • ◆ • ————

1906: Newly elected Manchester Labour MP John Robert Clynes made his first major speech in Parliament on this day. Clynes, who would later become Labour leader and Home Secretary, chose to highlight the outrages suffered by working men, whose employers were simultaneously their landlords, citing a recent case of miners in Hemsworth. Evicted from their homes during a dispute, their wives and children had been forced to sleep rough on waterlogged ground. Clynes demanded that the government 'Recognise that property not only had its rights but also its duties. In this case, property had the right to evict men from their homes, and these evictions had taken place despite the offer of rent in the ordinary way. The object of these evictions was not to improve the house or change the tenancy, but to compel the tenants to accept wages and working conditions which otherwise as organised workmen they would not accept.' He added that even in the Boer War better provision had been made for potentially hostile foes, than was the case here involving Englishmen abandoned by English law.

MAY 31ST

1819: This Whit Monday, the less progressive parts of the Anglican establishment were horrified when many Manchester parents sent their sons to the Whit Walks dressed in 'drab coloured hats', then the symbol of Radicalism. Urgent action was clearly required to stamp this out, and the offending headgear was henceforth prohibited. (William E.A. Axon, *Annals of Manchester*, John Heywood, Manchester, 1886)

1837: On this day, Higher Broughton's Zoological Gardens opened. Polar bears and elephants made for an impressive cast, but Manchester's first zoo was forced to close as soon as 1842. Many animals were sold to its Belle Vue competitor, which survived until the 1970s.

1982: Great swathes of Greater Manchester were sealed off today, as His Holiness John Paul II blessed the crowds at Heaton Park. This was the first ever visit to England made by a reigning Pontiff; certainly the first to Manchester. Just over a year before, he had been shot in an assassination attempt and security was well in evidence, but the quarter of a million people crowded in Manchester extended an enthusiastic welcome – one memorable banner reading 'Owdo, John Paul!' A 17-ton granite boulder now stands where he celebrated mass. (*Middleton Guardian*, April 7th 2005)

JUNE IST

1785: On this day, would-be Devonian squire Thomas Newte, visited Manchester. Following his visit, he dispelled certain unpleasant rumours about local woman: 'The women of Manchester, and indeed of all Lancashire, are esteemed handsome, and in this respect the title of witches may be bestowed on them with great impropriety.' (W.H. Thomson, *History of Manchester to 1852*, John Sherratt & Son Ltd, Altrincham, 1967)

———◆———

1890: On this day (Trinity Sunday), the first ever procession of Manchester's Italian community with their Madonna del Rosario, takes place. Padre Pappalardo was the organising force behind the Festa, and the statue of Our Lady of Mount Carmel set out from the Convent of St Vincent in Ancoats's Little Italy. The tradition continues to this day.

———◆———

1935: Norman Foster, now Baron Foster of Thames Bank, was born in Reddish this day. A world-renowned architect, he started out as a clerk in Manchester Town Hall – the perfect surroundings to become inspired with such a career! He was behind such striking structures as Wembley Stadium, the London 'Gherkin', and the HSBC Building in Hong Kong. Recognition includes knighthoods, Orders of Merit, Life Peerages, and the prestigious Pritzker and Principe de Asturias prizes.

JUNE 2ND

1806: Kaiser Franz, the last Holy Roman Emperor, visited Manchester today. He later assumed the more limited title of Emperor of Austria.

———— • ◆ • ————

1817: On this day, Catherine Prescott died at her home in George Leigh Street, at the reputed age of 108. She learnt to read when she was over 100, at the Lancasterian School and St Clement's Sunday school. Revd C.W. Ethelston conducted the burial of this remarkable woman at St Mark's Church on Cheetham Hill.

———— • ◆ • ————

1885: On this day, Manchester, still a major centre of coalmining activity, hosted a national conference of miners' permanent relief societies. They had gathered to discuss a proposal made by the Northumberland Hartley Relief Fund to form a joint national fund, with their own surplus of £20,000 to be the base upon which to build. The societies were broadly in favour and appointed a committee to work out how such a scheme could be realised.

JUNE 3RD

1852: What should have been a pleasant entertainment turned to tragedy at Belle Vue Gardens today. Aeronaut Signor Giuseppe Lunardini fell to his death from his hot air balloon, the result of a fault within the flying device.

———— • ◆ • ————

1863: On this day, Manchester held an anti-slavery conference as a gesture of support to the Union forces in America. At the time, General Lee's forces were marching northward, not yet halted by July's coming Battle of Gettysburg.

———— • ◆ • ————

1885: Today, Salford Council met to discuss a most pressing issue; that of the 'cries of persons vending newspapers or other articles in the streets'. This was clearly detrimental to the public decorum of such an august municipality as Salford, the nuisance referred to even reaching blasphemous levels, given the following clause 'especially on the Lord's Day'. The Council were unanimous and the Watch Committee was instructed to frame the appropriate by-laws at once. (William E.A. Axon, *Annals of Manchester*, John Heywood, Manchester, 1886)

JUNE 4TH

1792: Today was the King's birthday, but was also host to local Tory riots! Attacks were launched on Non-Conformist chapels, and publicans were coerced into displaying signs saying 'No Jacobins admitted here'.

———— ◆ ————

1821: On this day, a young man was crushed to death between the wheel of a carrier's cart and the wall of a building, in the still un-widened part of Market Street. His untimely death stimulated the existing demand for improvement into action, and an Act of Parliament was obtained the following July.

———— ◆ ————

1859: The Manchester and Salford Equitable Co-operative Society open their first store in Ancoats today. The society was originally the initiative of the Roby Brotherhood, a group of young men who had met at the Sunday school of Roby Chapel.

———— ◆ ————

1976: The Sex Pistols performed at the Free Trade Hall today, to a crowd of only forty people. This concert has now become legendary in pop music's annals as a catalyst for the Punk Rock and New Wave movements. They would perform here again on the 20th, this time to a much larger crowd.

JUNE 5TH

1580: On this day, Warden John Woolton of the Collegiate Church was promoted to the See of Lincoln. This would result in transferring the Manchester position to the Bishop of Chester, William Chadderton. Woolton had been born in Wigan around 1535 and was described by a fellow bishop as a 'pious, painful and skilful divine'. Throughout his time at Manchester, Woolton authored several works, including a Christian manual. (William E.A. Axon, *Annals of Manchester*, John Heywood, Manchester, 1886)

———— • ◆ • ————

1775: The Theatre Royal opened in Spring Gardens on this day. Oddly enough, in order for it to open an Act of Parliament was required, and it was by no means unopposed. The Bishop of London had proclaimed in the House of Lords that 'Nothing could be more destructive to the welfare of a manufacturing town', to which the Earl of Derby countered it would do wonders in combating Methodism – 'I know not of any way so effectual to eradicate that dark, odious, and ridiculous enthusiasm as by giving to the people cheerful, rational amusements, which may operate against their methodistical melancholy.' (William E.A. Axon, *Annals of Manchester*, John Heywood, Manchester, 1886)

———— • ◆ • ————

1945: The 'King of Forgers', Herbert Winstanley, was caught handing over forged pound notes whilst placing a bet at the Albion Stadium in Salford. At his home on Lindum Street in Rusholme, police found a complete forger's workshop and thousands of forged pound notes which were stacked in bundles. He received ten years' imprisonment for his crime.

JUNE 6TH

1642: On this day, Charles I replies to Manchester's petition of February 28th. He deemed it was 'evasive and unsatisfactory', and so Manchester declared in favour of the cause of Parliament. Warden Heyrick then formed a Puritan committee to defend the town against the King's supporters (*see* July 15th). (William E.A. Axon, *Annals of Manchester*, John Heywood, Manchester, 1886)

<hr>

1721: Following the act of December 8th 1720, the River Irwell was now navigable to Manchester vessels of 50 tons, all the way to the port of Liverpool – a great stimulus to the town's trade.

<hr>

1841: Today, the first full modern census records the population in Manchester and Salford's as 309,607. (William E.A. Axon, *Annals of Manchester*, John Heywood, Manchester, 1886)

<hr>

1881: On this day, a long-distance bicycle race began in Manchester. This was a truly gruelling event which lasted for several days. At one point, the contestant Battensby had ridden without a rest for forty-six solid hours, having travelled over 625 miles around the track. The race ended on the 11th, with Newcastle's J.W. Lamb winning the £150 prize, having ridden 931 miles. (*Manchester Times* June 14th and *Penny Illustrated* June 18th)

JUNE 7TH

1757: Enraged at potato prices in the market place, two women upended the traders' sacks and a scramble ensued in which the traders lost all their spuds. Riots ensued, with attacks on corn dealerships, and the two women were arrested. They were soon broken free from the Dungeon (on the Old Bridge) by a crowd armed with hammers. Looting continued until order was restored by the cudgel-bearing servants of the principal inhabitants. The Sheriff of Lancaster would arrive the next day with yet more persuasive means.

———— • ◆ • ————

1805: On this day, a tragic accident befell two cousins in Colonel Hanson's Rifle Corps. While practising on the range at Strangeways Hall, one Faulkner shot another right through the body while he was hidden behind a target.

———— • ◆ • ————

1954: Alan Turing OBE, the 'Father of Computing', died at his home in Wilmslow today. His statue in Sackville Gardens holds an apple, referring obliquely to the means by which he took his life, after having fallen foul of the strict anti-homosexual legislation of the day (*see* March 31st). There was some ambiguity surrounding his death though; he had died of cyanide poisoning, and had been working on apparatus in his home that involved a legitimate use of this substance. It is thought that he made his death look doubtful for the sake of his mother.

JUNE 8TH

1571: The Collegiate Church underwent an inspection today, in which many peculiar local traditions were recorded, some to be condemned by the inspecting archbishop as relics of popery. One fellow of the college was found to be keeper of an alehouse, and would go there while still dressed in his surplice at sermon time. Another fellow was found to be a part-time surgeon, despite being 'altogether unlearned'. Many pictures in the church had not been whitewashed over, and the choristers accompanied funeral processions in the town with singing and bell-ringing. Other fellows 'Went about the town with a hand bell, moving the people to works of mercy'.

1902: Painter Rosa S. Hope was born in Manchester on this day. Having been schooled at Manchester High School for Girls, she later found work teaching art in Cape Town, and spent much of the rest of her life in South Africa, becoming one of that country's most memorable landscapists.

1960: On this day, Mick Hucknall, Simply Red's instantly recognisable lead singer, was born in Denton. Like many key figures of the Manchester music scene, he was present at the 1976 Sex Pistols concert in the Free Trade Hall, and went on to form the band Frantic Elevators, before becoming a core member of Simply Red.

JUNE 9TH

1783: Manchester's first Blackpool coach sets out today, taking day-trippers to the Golden Mile. Pickford and Co.'s *Diligence* set out from the Royal Oak in the Market Place at 6 a.m., charging 15s per person; a little above the budget of the later working-class visitors, but a beginning at least.

———— • ◆ • ————

1840: Chief booking clerk to the Manchester and Leeds Railway, Thomas Edmondson, received a patent in London for 'Certain Improvements in Printing Presses'. He died a wealthy man, having been able to charge rail companies (English, Scottish, Irish and American) a royalty of 10s per mile per annum for the privilege of using his tickets; a direct ancestor of those still in use today.

———— • ◆ • ————

1964: Manchester-born John Readitt, Sergeant of the 6th Battalion South Lancashire Regiment, died on this day. He was awarded the Victoria Cross for his selfless actions at Alqayat al Gaharbigah Bend in Iraq, on February 25th 1917 during the First World War.

JUNE 10TH

1715: Prince James – 'Old Pretender' to his foes and 'James III' to his adherents – celebrated his birthday on this day. A Jacobite mob marked the occasion by attacking and looting Cross Street Non-Conformist Chapel, tearing down the majority of the building, for which £1,500 compensation was later awarded by Parliament. Rioting spread to Moston, Blackley, Stand, and Failsworth, but the ringleader, Tom Syddall, a wig maker, was seized and sent to Lancaster Castle. Soon freed by his Scottish comrades, he joined their forces and marched to Preston. Defeated in battle by General Willes, Syddall was condemned to death at the Bloody Assizes. His young son would soon grow to manhood and attempt to avenge his father in the next Jacobite invasion of 1745.

1953: June Osborne was born on this day. As the Dean of Salisbury, she is the first woman to serve in such a position at any of England's medieval cathedrals. Born and educated in Manchester, she was among the earliest women to be ordained by the Church of England. She is tipped to be one of, if not the first female bishop.

JUNE 11TH

1812: On this day, thirty-eight working men were charged with administering the Luddite oath at a public house. Kept incarcerated for three months, until their acquittal at Lancaster on August 28th, all they had done was discuss the writing of an address to the Prince Regent and a petition to the House of Commons.

———— • ◆ • ————

1813: Royal Assent was given to the Manchester Police Bill, in which provisions were made for the long overdue modernisation of the organs of local administration. Though the boroughreeve remained in place, many administrative functions were now entrusted to the new Police Commission. Unelected and unanswerable to the populace, this would soon be replaced by a proper town corporation.

———— • ◆ • ————

1868: This day was an unlucky day for John Rhodes of Stevenson Square. He was robbed of £1,500 in bank notes and bills at a pub in Hilton Street, just one block away from the police station on Faraday Street.

JUNE 12TH

1656: Roundhead Colonel Charles Worsley of Platt in Rusholme died at the young age of thirty-five today. He was Manchester's first MP in Cromwell's parliament, as well as his direct representative in the Midlands. Buried with much pomp in Henry VII's chapel in Westminster Abbey, he was remembered as being of 'great severity and puritanical rigour'. Unlike those of his comrades, his remains were not later dug up for public humiliation. It has been said that in his death, Cromwell lost his only hope of a worthy successor.

———•◆•———

1785: On this day, hypochondriac Jane Diggle of Kersal Moor died. She was buried in garments and a coffin she had ordered thirty years before.

———•◆•———

1792: 'To be sold, by order of the churchwardens and overseers of the poor of Manchester, the fee-simple and inheritance of and in all that large and substantial pile of building, with the workshops and appurtenances thereunto belonging, situated, standing, and being in Cumberland Street, in Manchester aforesaid, now used as the Manchester poorhouse; the site or ground-plot contains upwards of one thousand eight hundred and twenty-seven superficial square yards.' The previous June had seen the foundation of the new more modern Strangeways workhouse. (Richard Wright Procter, *Memorials of Manchester Streets*, T. Sutcliffe, Manchester, 1874)

JUNE 13TH

1729: The first Manchester Races took place on Kersal Moor on this day. Manchester man of letters John Byrom opposes the innovation in a very strong-worded pamphlet, and Bishop Peploe of Chester (also Warden of Manchester) forbids the clergy from attending.

1792: On this day, Manchester Constitutional Society members Thomas Cooper and James Watt (son of the steam pioneer) were invited to speak at the Societe des Amis de la Constitution in Revolutionary Paris. The latter would later achieve permanent infamy under the more familiar name of the Jacobin Club, orchestrating a great deal of deaths by Guillotine in the coming darker days of the French Revolution. Prominent Tory Edmund Burke 'poured forth a volume of invective' in Parliament upon hearing of this near treasonous act, as it was considered by many at the time. (W.H. Thomson, *History of Manchester to 1852*, John Sherratt & Son Ltd, Altrincham, 1967)

1799: St Andrew's Presbyterian Chapel on Lloyd Street opened on this day. Manchester had been no stranger to such sects, but Scottish migrants were reinforcing numbers as the town grew into a city.

JUNE 14TH

1421: On this day, consent was given for an Ecclesiastical College to be founded in the town. Historian Richard Procter waxed lyrical on the event, saying 'What a glorious "parish vestry" must this have been! Here, unanimously congregated at the sound of the bell, were the great magnates of the district – Lawrence Hulme and Henry Bulkely, the churchwardens at that time; Sir John le Byron of Clayton and Sir John de Radcliffe of Ordsall, two worthy knights of the neighbourhood, with a profusion of esquires and gentlemen of rank … with stout yeomen, whose veneration for the Church was only equalled by their determined zeal in giving it their defence. It requires but little stretch of the imagination to realise the gathering within the walls of the old church, to note the look of approval as the pious De la Warr, in the benevolence of his own good heart, unfolds his plans for the collegiation of their parish church, offering to give up his ancestral home, and at his own expense erect a suitable residence for the clergy on its site … we may almost fancy we hear the clank of sword and spur upon the pavement as the knightly throng retires from the scene, talking over the disinterested zeal and Christian benevolence of the worthy old priest-lord.'

───◆───

1928: Moss Side-born suffragette leader Emmeline Pankhurst died in London on this day.

JUNE 15TH

1919: On this day, former Manchester Central High School students J.W. Alcock and A.W. Brown complete the first ever non-stop transatlantic flight. Landing in a rocky Galway field, they thereby won themselves the £10,000 prize that had been offered by the *Daily Mail*, upon the completion of the flight. Jack Alcock was a native of Seymour Grove in Old Trafford, and Arthur Whitten 'Teddie' Brown, though born in Glasgow, had also grown up in Manchester. Both had served as fighter pilots in the First World War and been taken captive as prisoners of war. They were both knighted by George V. (*Flight* magazine)

———— • ◆ • ————

1996: At 11.17 a.m. on this day, the IRA detonated a huge bomb on Corporation, wrecking the city centre. Despite it being the largest device they have ever used on the British Isles, the terrorists failed to cause a single death – a miracle given the time and place. A particularly prominent survivor was a red pillar box which stood close by; it withstood the blast and still stands there today, with only a few dents and a commemorative plaque to show for it. The city seized the opportunity to redevelop the retail district and actually move two of the town's oldest buildings (the pre-industrial Shambles formed by the Wellington Inn and Sinclair's Oyster bar) into a more photogenic site by the cathedral.

JUNE 16TH

1812: On this day in Lancaster, eight Mancunian rioters were hanged. Several others were acquitted, with many machine-breaking Luddites being transported or imprisoned, but eight were selected to be made an example of, including Abraham Charlson, aged sixteen, who cried for his mother on the gallows, and Hannah Smith, aged fifty-four, for rioting and seizing sacks of potatoes.

———◆———

1933: Crowds looked on helplessly as two men drowned while trying to save a kitten today, in the River Irwell. Former boxer William Burke had noticed the animal trapped under Victoria Bridge, and slid down a rope to rescue it. The rope snapped and he plunged into the filthy polluted river. Police Constable Thomas Jewes, who had recently been awarded the Watch Committee Medal for his bravery in restraining a runaway horse, then dived in to rescue Burke, but both men sank beneath the surface only 3ft from the bank. A third hero, John Tudor, then jumped in to help, but was too late and firemen recovered the bodies hours later; they also saved the kitten. Twenty thousand people came out to witness Jewes' funeral procession. (*The Times*)

JUNE 17TH

1838: On this day, Joseph Corbett Peel, a cashier at the Bank of Manchester, absconded with a large sum of money. He was pursued and arrested at Rotterdam by Officer Sawley of the Manchester police, and transported for seven years. Four years later, the entire bank would collapse, with losses of £300,000 and liabilities of £713,082. Manager Burdekin, perhaps remembering how Peel hadn't ran far enough, absconded a little further, to America.

1839: Manchester's first semi-modern police force, organised by the new borough corporation, commenced its duties on this day. Richard Beswick was Head Constable and received a £400 salary.

1857: Today saw the inaugural meeting of the Manchester Entomological Society at Mr Rickett's Temperance Hotel in Great Bridgewater Street.

JUNE 18TH

1760: On this day, an evening of genteel Georgian musical entertainment was given in the gardens of the Infirmary (now Piccadilly Gardens), the proceeds of which were added to the Infirmary's funds.

———•◆•———

1816: Surgeon and chemistry pioneer Thomas Henry died in Manchester today, aged eighty-two. Born in Wrexham, he moved to Manchester and was soon nicknamed 'Magnesia Henry' for his invention of a new process for producing magnesium oxide. He helped found, and served as president of, the Manchester Literary and Philosophical Society, and was made a Fellow of the Royal Society.

———•◆•———

1835: William Cobbett, veteran of local political activism, died while serving as MP for Oldham, at the age of seventy-three. It was reported that 'Few men had greater influence with the working men of this district'. (William E.A. Axon, *Annals of Manchester*, John Heywood, Manchester, 1886)

———•◆•———

1885: An underground explosion at the Clifton Hall Colliery in Pendleton killed 176 miners on this day.

JUNE 19TH

1215: On this day, King John signed the Magna Carta at Runnymede, under the watchful eye (and ever so slight duress) of the Lord of Manchester, Robert Grelley.

———— • ◆ • ————

1782: Lord of the Manor Sir John Parker Mosley won a victory in court against Messers Chadwick and Holland on this day. Chadwick and Holland had set up a meat market at Pool Fold (an old open space, now the site of the top end of Brown Street) in July 1781. The dispute had been taken to Lancaster Assizes, been debated in Westminster twice, and reached the Court of King's Bench. Mosley's manorial rights received confirmation, to the unfortunate injury of local commerce.

———— • ◆ • ————

1991: Mancunian television writer Tony Williamson died today. Some of his more memorable scriptwriting can be seen in classic series such as *The Avengers* and *Randall and Hopkirk (Deceased)*.

JUNE 20TH

1596: On this day, Sir Alexander Radcliffe, younger son of the squire of Ordsall Hall by the Ship Canal, was knighted at Cadiz in Spain, for his valour in taking that town during battle.

1815: Today, Manchester-born Daniel Bayley was knighted for his services as Consul-General in Russia, during the Napoleonic Wars. He was also a member of the Manchester Agricultural Society.

1839: A grand procession marked the opening of Victoria Bridge, for which the hundred of Salford had paid £20,800. They also managed to obtain the reigning monarch's permission to christen the bridge after her – the first stones were laid in Queen Victoria's first regnal year. The first vehicle to make use of the replacement for the medieval Old Salford Bridge was the dray cart of Lupton and Adamthwaite Brewery.

1874: On this day, 15,000 Manchester trade unionists marched through the main city streets. With bands and banners, according to Axon, they managed to be both 'gay and imposing'. The marchers gathered at Pomona Gardens, where a further 45,000 crowded around six sets of hustings to hear speeches on solidarity with the 'locked-out' agricultural labourers of Southeast England.

JUNE 21ST

1819: On this day, distressed cotton workers of Manchester attended a meeting to discuss their emigration to the United States. The tone turned radical, and delegates were then appointed for a general reform union. But, the boroughreeve, Edward Clayton, tried to check this by announcing an official meeting for July 9th to discuss the preservation of peace.

———— • ◆ • ————

1831: Manchester's long forgotten but extensive (sixteen acres in total) Botanical and Horticultural Gardens were opened today at Old Trafford.

———— • ◆ • ————

1884: Today, 50,000 Mancunians gathered at Pomona Gardens to demonstrate their approval of the Manchester Ship Canal Bill.

———— • ◆ • ————

1948: Today witnessed a world first in computing – the Manchester Mark I ran the first stored computer program. The brainchild of Stockport-born Mancunian engineer Sir Frederic Calland Williams and his Yorkshire-born colleague Tom Kilburn, this was a triumph for the University of Manchester and a major step on the way to producing the modern computer. The Mark 1 had received much input from Alan Turing too, who had recently began working at the university, having used many of the theoretical concepts he had developed before the war. The great mathematician improved some of its programs. The machine weighed over a ton but used only 128 bytes of memory.

JUNE 22ND

1679: Manchester-born three-year-old Charles Bennett was 'displayed' at the Bear Inn at Smithfield in London, as a child prodigy. According to a pamphlet published at the time, Charles' first words had been to correct his father who was stumbling over a certain Biblical passage, and it was later discovered that he could converse with ease in Latin, Greek and Hebrew, as well as his native English. Nothing more was ever recorded of Charles.

———•◆•———

1835: On this day, an unlucky steeplejack plunged 225ft to his death while working on the smokestack of the Salford gasworks.

———•◆•———

1881: The Manchester Statistical Society held its annual meeting on this day, with the, at the time, shocking decision to admit female members!

JUNE 23RD

1821: Street crime at this period was rather different to that known today. Methodist Samuel Waller appeared in court today at the New Bailey Sessions, charged with preaching in the highway at Ashton-under-Lyne. He received three months in prison.

◆

1896: On this day, entrepreneur Ernest Terah Hooley purchased Trafford Park from Sir Humphrey de Trafford for £360,000. Initially intended for development as a prestigious residential suburb, it became the first purpose-built industrial estate in the world, and one that remains the largest in Europe. Its fallow deer had roamed freely since feudal times, but Sir Humphrey, who had recently opposed the digging of the adjacent Ship Canal, had had it with the industrial views that marred his enjoyment of his ancestral deer park. Hooley would subsequently be bankrupted four times and imprisoned twice for contempt of court and fraud.

◆

2001: A memorial to Alan Turing was unveiled today in Sackville Park, inscribed 'Father of Computer Science, Mathematician, Logician, Wartime Codebreaker, Victim of Prejudice.' The work was executed by Glyn Hughes, upon the initiative of Stockport barrister Richard Humphrey, after £16,000 had been raised by the public – just enough to pay for casting in China. He is sitting on a park bench, an ambiguous apple in his hand (*see* June 7th).

JUNE 24TH

1340: On this day, John la Warre, Baron of Manchester, fought the French at the great naval engagement off the coast of Sluys. It was one of the most important battles in the Hundred Years War – it destroyed the French fleet and thus their capability of bringing the warfare onto English soil.

— ◆ —

1694: Cross Street Chapel opened on this day. It was the first Non-Conformist chapel in the town, upon the passing of William III's Act of Toleration. 'Prince of Preachers' and 'Father of Manchester Non-Conformity' Henry Newcome led praise there, having been previously forced to retire from his position in the Collegiate Church on the Restoration of the monarchy. Close by was Plungeon Field, where Manchester's old 'plungeon' was installed – a ducking stool for nagging housewives. Subsequently, the town's Anglicans referred to the Dissenters' place of worship by the derisive 'Saint Plungem's'.

— ◆ —

1751: On this day, Berry published the first detailed plan of the town, 20in to a mile. Advertised as, 'A Complete Map of the Towns of Manchester and Salford, with all the inclosures and gardens bordering on the same ... Price bound, two shillings.' Some interesting street names are printed, now lost or altered: Catnest (Cateaton St?), Toad Lane (now Todd), Back o'th'Church, Coffee House Entry, Cockpit Hill, Daube Holes, Seven Foot Lane, Fox Entry, Cupid's Alley, Wring Spiget Hall, Sandy Well Lane, the list goes on.

JUNE 25TH

1519: Manchester-born and bred Bishop Hugh Oldham of Exeter, founder of the town's grammar school, died on this day. He was officially anathema at the time, due to Papal disapproval of his altercations with the Abbot of Tavistock, but was nevertheless buried in a chapel built by himself expressly for the purpose, at Exeter Cathedral, where a handsome monument was erected to his memory. However, this was not in the cathedral, but on the brink of it, to get round the Pope's judgement.

—◆—

1886: Two prestigious visitors came to Manchester today. Mr Gladstone, who was cheered in the streets and later gave a speech on the Irish Question in the Free Trade Hall, and the other rather more exotic: Ambassador Tseng of the Imperial Court of China. Marquis Tseng was cordially received by the Chamber of Commerce and then dined with Mayor Goldschmidt in the Town Hall.

—◆—

1938: Ringway, later Manchester, Airport officially opened today. Eventually swallowing up the village of Ringway itself (of which only a few houses and chapel remain), Manchester Airport is now the largest outside London, and sees double the amount of passengers of the nearest competitor, Edinburgh. Third busiest in the UK and twenty-third in Europe, it is the only British airport with two 3,000-plus metre runways.

JUNE 26TH

1825: On this day, Ben Brierley, Failsworth's renowned dialect writer and poet, was born. His birthplace still stands in the row of venerable houses known as The Rocks, where Oldham Road passes over the Rochdale Canal, and he was honoured recently by a statue at Failsworth Pole. Old Ben's bones lie in Harpurhey Cemetery.

◆

1827: Spinning Mule inventor Samuel Crompton died aged seventy-four on King Street in Bolton. Born and living at Th'Hall i'th'Wood – a timber-framed old hall still open to visitors – he combined weaving with fiddle playing, and employed his mechanical aptitude in perfecting the mechanisation of the textile industry. Like many in this field, he received little recompense for his labours – the paltry grant of £5,000 awarded to him by Parliament being quite typical, despite the rapid growth of fortunes of those employing his Mule (by way of context, cotton exports (mostly spun on his Mule), amounted to £36,824,270 the following year).

◆

1869: The Hindu reformer Baboo Keshub Chudner Sen preached in the Unitarian Chapel at Strangeways on this day.

JUNE 27TH

1810: Reverend Thomas Barnes died at Little Lever on this day. He was the one time pastor at Manchester's Cross Street Chapel, where he was buried, and a founder of the Manchester Literary and Philosophical Society. Axon rated him 'A leader in the intellectual and philanthropic movements of the time'.

* ◆ *

1873: Nassr-ed-Din, King of Kings and Shah of Persia, visited the town on this day. After an address was accorded to him by the Town Hall, he went on to visit, with his large entourage of ministers, the Salford works of Mr Haworth.

* ◆ *

1882: Daniel Adamson of Didsbury hosted a meeting of the Mayors of Manchester and Liverpool, to discuss the feasibility of a canal fit for seagoing vessels being built between the two cities. Adamson was an engineer who had made his fortune through his invention of Manchester Boilers, as well as various other innovations, and being based in Stockport and Dukinfield would clearly profit from such a canal. He was elected chairman of its provisional committee, and fought a long battle on the project's behalf against the opposition of the Liverpudlian port interests and railways. In 1885, he became the first chairman of the board of directors for the Manchester Ship Canal Company.

JUNE 28TH

1838: Manchester celebrated the coronation of Queen Victoria on this day. In the words of Thomson, 'Flags floated from churches and public buildings, while the day was ushered in by the booming of cannon, the rattle of musketry and the merry peal of bells ... Vast crowds gathered in St Ann's Square and the Market Street at 7 a.m. to witness the assembly of the schoolchildren, estimated at 41,500, who marched to Ardwick Green.' These were followed by the 3rd Dragoon Guards, Artillery and the 98th Regiment of Foot, as well as the various trades bodies, and £200 was lavished on the fireworks at Ardwick Green.

1997: On this day, the iconic nightclub the Haçienda opened its doors for the last time. A converted textile factory on Whitworth Street, it first opened on May 21st 1982, and since then had helped to put the declining city firmly back on the cultural map. It never made money and was kept afloat by its founders' music sales, and the growth of the 'rave' culture did little to help bar takings. After just over fifteen years of business, amid growing drug and violence problems, it finally shut its doors. Several years later it was demolished by construction company Crosby Homes, who erected a modern apartment building on the site, which retains the name of the club. (Peter Hook, *How Not to Run a Club*)

JUNE 29TH

1824: On this day, Hugh Prichard sold his twenty-six-year-old wife for the princely sum of 3s.

———◆———

1857: Queen Victoria, Prince Albert, several of her children and Prince Friedrich Wilhelm of Prussia arrived at Patricroft on this day. They were driven to Worsley Hall to stay with the Earl of Ellesmere, in order to visit the Exhibition of the Art Treasures of the United Kingdom at Old Trafford (*see* May 5th).

———◆———

1870: On this day, W.T. Blacklock died at Hope Field in Eccles. He had been a great supporter of the Ragged Schools and the Clinical Hospital, as well as the numerous religious missions in the city. To the undoubted distress of his daughter he died suddenly, on the morning of her wedding.

JUNE 30TH

1555: Manchester-born John Bradford was made a martyr on this day. Born in Blackley in 1510, he studied at Bishop Oldham's Grammar School. Quick with a pen, he was appointed secretary to Sir John Harrington, treasurer of the English forces in France. In 1547, he studied law in London but converted to Protestantism and entered Cambridge a year later. He became chaplain to Edward VI, and toured his home region preaching the reformed faith. When Mary came to the throne, Bradford carried on preaching his faith, only to then be tried and found guilty of sedition and heresy on January 22nd 1554 – he was burnt at the stake in Smithfield, attended by his brother-in-law Roger Bexwicke of the family of Manchester benefactors. In the words of Fuller, 'It is a demonstration to me that he was of a sweet temper, because Persons, who will hardly afford a good word to a Protestant, saith, "that he seemed to be of a more soft and milde nature than many of his fellowes".' (Thomas Fuller, *The History of the Worthies of England*, London, 1662)

1909: On this day, Mancunian militant suffragette Mary Brown is arrested for the first time, for stoning 10 Downing Street. This was the first of very many arrests! (*see* September 22nd and July 18th)

JULY 1ST

1830: On this day, Manchester engineer Richard Roberts – the owner of a very well-reputed machine-making workshop – patented his new improvement for the self-acting Spinning Mule.

●◆●

1880: The Manchester Central station, once the 'GMEX' Exhibition Centre and now the Manchester Central Convention Complex, opened on this day. It is famous for its Paxton roof which, at 210ft across, is the widest unsupported span in the country, after London's St Pancras. Designed by Sir John Fowler, it was built by Andrew Handyside and achieved Grade I listed status in 1963. At the height of its time as a station, 400 members of staff were employed there, with as many arrivals and departures a day, but it saw its last trains on May 5th 1969. It is now a major conference venue.

●◆●

1898: On this day, the Great Northern Railway Company's Goods Warehouse opened. Still proudly bearing its long name across its 217ft front, it was notable in its day for being one of the earliest multi-storey steel-framed buildings in the world. It is now one of only three warehouses remaining in existence which provide transport links to road, rail, and canal. A Grade II listed building, it is built from riveted steel box girders supporting steel beams bearing brick arches, served by four hydraulic lifts, and was executed by engineer W.T. Foxlee.

JULY 2ND

1849: Bury-born Prime Minister Sir Robert Peel died on this day, after falling from his horse. He is remembered with great respect in the town for repealing the hated Corn Laws.

———◆———

1860: On this day, Queen Victoria opened the first meeting of the British Rifle Association in Wimbledon. She fired a shot at target using the Whitworth Rifle, which was designed and produced by Manchester engineer Joseph Whitworth at his workshop on Chorlton Street (*see* December 21st). Rejected by the British Army but adopted by France, a number of the rifles also ended up in the Confederate States of America, where they were known as the Whitworth Sharpshooter.

———◆———

1863: Parliament passed the Public Works Manufacturing Districts Act today. This Act enabled the unemployed to be better equipped to survive the ongoing Cotton Famine. At the time, 65,000 women were attending sewing school while receiving Poor Law Aid, and 20,000 men and boys were learning literacy in the schools that were opened or extended to deal with the crisis. However, there were still around 25,000 men not catered for, so the Act removed the legal obstructions for borrowing money, and numerous projects were started, including updating the sewage system, public park creation, road improvements, river cleaning and street paving. (www.cottontown.org)

JULY 3RD

1845: Thomas Briggs of the Richmond Hill Ropery, made a rope 4,374yd in length – almost 2½ miles – for the purposes of the machinery of the new Theatre Royal. Perhaps a record!

———◆———

1839: Today's *Manchester Guardian* reported how Ashton-under-Lyne cotton spinner, Timothy Higgins (aged thirty-three) had recently received a nasty awakening at the hands of Deputy Constable Newton and his men. Newton had burst into his house at 1.30 a.m. to find him in bed with his wife, as well as two crates of 'seventeen muskets, with bayonets, and a spare bayonet; four double barred guns, a rifle, one large horse pistol, four common-sized pistols, besides a quantity of bullets and cases.' The gun laws were somewhat slacker at the time, but Higgins's, being an avowed republican and secretary of the local Chartist society, lent suspicion to his hoarding of firearms, despite his protestations that he had intended to sell them on. He was convicted of conspiracy at the Autumn Assizes and locked up in Chester Castle for eighteen months. In 1841, a government inspector noted that this 'man of considerable intelligence' had spent his term reading Walter Scott novels and improving his arithmetic, but feared for the wellbeing of his wife and four children, then supported by the Chartists' 'victim fund'. Armed rebellion had been averted this time, but just nine years later another Ashton policeman, Constable James Bright, would be shot dead by Chartists. Subsequent reform defused the situation, though it is curious to reflect on how many in the region had looked to the Revolutions on the Continent with more than idle interest.

JULY 4TH

1780: A more genteel side to the occasionally controversial and rowdy race meetings on Kersal Moor was revealed in a notice issued on this day: 'The ladies' stand on Kersal moor will be opened on Wednesday next for the accommodation of ladies and gentlemen of the town and neighbourhood of Manchester, where coffee, tea, chocolate, strawberries, cream, etc. will be provided every Wednesday and Friday during the strawberry season. By the public's most obliged and humble servant, Elizabeth Raffald.' (William E.A. Axon, *Annals of Manchester*, John Heywood, Manchester, 1886)

1838: On this day, the first steam-powered boat sailed up the River Irwell. Carrying 11 tons of goods, the *Novelty* had a 4-horse power motor and was the property of the Mersey and Irwell Navigation Company.

1857: William Bradley (aged fifty-six) died in poverty at his Mancunian birthplace on this day. At the age of sixteen he began painting portraits for a shilling a piece in Manchester, before he was taken on by Mather Brown (famous painter of Jefferson and other prominent American Founding Fathers) who was resident of Manchester. Bradley then went to London and became much in demand, painting familiar portraits of prominent men, particularly that of Gladstone. In 1847, he returned to Manchester in poor health, dying in obscurity a decade later.

July 5th

1796: Though Manchester was never in real danger of becoming a spa town, it was not always totally lacking in such amenities. Today's *Mercury* made an announcement concerning the long-forgotten spa on the Salford side of the Irwell: 'Public Cold Bath, at the Lying-in Hospital, Stanley Street, New Bailey Street, Salford. The ancient cold bath called the Spaw, known for its coldness, and the plentiful supply of spring water, which is constantly running through it, is now fitted up for the use of the public. Terms of bathing, sixpence per time, or ten shillings and sixpence per quarter; towels included.' (Richard Wright Procter, *Memorials of Manchester Streets*, T. Sutcliffe, Manchester, 1874)

———— ◆ ————

2002: On this day, the Imperial War Museum North opened at Salford Quays. Clad in stainless steel, it takes the form of the shards of a shattered globe, and was designed by Daniel Libeskind. It is a major contribution to the striking new twenty-first-century architecture going up in the city.

JULY 6TH

1886: The treasurer of the Manchester Chamber of Commerce, John Copeland Zigomala JP, died on this day. Born on the island of Chios in 1816, he was one of very few to survive the 1821 massacre of the islanders by the Turks. Rescued by an American merchant, Zigomala added his surname to his own in gratitude. From the USA he made his way to Glasgow, and finally, in 1837, to Manchester where he struck a partnership with William Stavert manufacturing and shipping printed fabrics. The company continued in business up until 1959, when the Cuban Revolution removed its last big market.

———— • ◆ • ————

1996: On this day, the long-lost submarine *Resurgam II* was officially listed under the Protection of Wrecks Act (1973). Rediscovered by Liverpool Bay diver Keith Hurley, it had been invented by Moss Side clergyman George Garrett, and had sunk in 1880, after a series of unfortunate accidents. Had Garret been slightly luckier, he might have gone down in history as the father of sub-aquatics, but instead he died penniless in New York. A full-size replica may be seen by the Birkenhead docks, where she was built.

———— • ◆ • ————

2012: The National Football Museum opened in the Urbis building in New Cathedral Square today. Something of a coup for Manchester, the town was selected over Wembley for the honour.

JULY 7TH

1712: An eventful day in the life of Mancunian *perruquier* (wigmaker) Edmond Harrold: 'This morning I had my old melancholy pain seized on me, with a longing desire for drink; so I went and paid my rent, then I sold J.G. a lock of hair pro loss five shillings, sixpence; then I spent then I spent twopence with Hall and co., then fourpence with Mr Allen, 'tourney; then fought with S.B. at Jane Win's about chat; then went a rambl – Key, Dragon, and Castle, and Lyon, till near twelve o'clock, till I was ill drunken; cost me four-and-a-half-pence from six till twelve. I made myself a great foole …'

———•◆•———

1856: Seventy-nine-year-old William Lockett, first Mayor of Salford (1844-45), died on this day. The last Boroughreeve of Salford (1844), Lockett's election to the two posts oversaw the transition to modern municipal government in much the same way that Kay had on this side of the River Irwell (*see* May 16th).

JULY 8TH

1712: Manchester diarist, Edmund Harrold, regretted his previous day of gallivanting. The entry in his diary for this day reads: 'This day I lay in bed till almost eleven o'clock; I've drunk no ale today, yet on six at night I'm vext about my ramble last night. I've mist public and private prayer two times. It's a very great trouble to me that I thus expose myself, hurt my body, offend against God, set a bad example, torment my mind and break my rules, make myself a laughing-stock to men, grieve the Holy Spirit, disorder my family, fret my wife (now quick), which is all against my own mind when sober, besides loss of my credit and reputation in the world. What must I do? What can I do? Use the creatures, and I abuse them, be sure before I've done. Use them not, and I'm like nobody else. I'm resolved what to do – not to drink any in a morning in the alehouse (a very good rule if followed) upon no occasion whatever for the time to come. I'll go to prayers now.'

1875: The Sultan of Zanzibar, Seyyid Barghash, arrived in Manchester on this day. His two-day stay was filled with visits to the Egerton Cotton Mills, Peel Park, the Assize Courts, the Royal Exchange, Hoyle's Printworks, the new Town Hall and Manley Hall.

JULY 9TH

1645: On this day, Parliament voted to grant £1,000 in relief to Manchester, which had been suffering under a severe pestilence. The town had been under quarantine for months, and it was reported that, 'Tradesmen were not only ruined in their estates, but many families are like to perish for want who cannot be sufficiently relieved by that miserably wasted country.' A further collection took place in the churches of London, whose congregations were grateful to Manchester for supporting the Parliamentarian cause in the north. (William E.A. Axon, *Annals of Manchester*, John Heywood, Manchester, 1886)

———•◆•———

1842: Giles Bedford of Pendlebury, one of the last survivors of the Manchester Volunteers, died on this day, aged ninety. He had been a part of the team who had been at the Great Siege of Gibraltar (1779-1783), the blockade which lasted for three years and ten months.

———•◆•———

1992: On this day, Kerry Morrison's oak sculpture of a huge bottle draped with raspberries and currants is unveiled on Granby Row. It was commissioned in honour of the 1908 invention of the area, by Noel Nichols – the iconic soft drink Vimto. The drink has recently celebrated its centenary and enjoys world-wide popularity, often more abroad than at home; for example, in parts of Polynesia or the Arabic world it outsells its rivals, especially during Ramadan! (Terry Wyke and Harry Cocks, *Public Sculpture of Greater Manchester*, Liverpool University Press, 2003)

July 10th

1580: Humphrey Chetham, the founder of Chethem's Hospital and Chethem's Library, was born in Crumpsall Hall on this day. He attended Manchester Grammar School, before going into business with his brother George, becoming a great benefactor of the town (*see* December 16th).

◆

1596: On this day, renowned cartographer Christopher Saxton 'described and measured' Manchester on a visit to the town. However, his visit is something of a mystery as no map is ever shown. Suspicions were raised by his visit happening shortly after esoteric scholar John Dee became Warden – it has even been supposed that he was engaged in geomantic work with the aged alchemist. Others point to Dee's role in the English Secret Service – he used '007' as his signature, and had been an agent on the Continent for Queen Elizabeth I. Saxton's mapmaking was a sensitive matter in the early days of empire, of which Dee was an early proponent. Saxton left Manchester on July 14th.

◆

1840: The last installation of a Warden in Manchester's Ecclesiastical College occurred on this day. The appointee was William Herbert, son of the Earl of Carnarvon, and quite a polymath, publishing works on botany, Attila the Hun, and Icelandic poetry. On the reformation of the Collegiate Church as a Cathedral, Herbert became its first Dean.

JULY 11TH

1834: On this day, Dr Grindrod held several temperance meetings in Miles Platting, founding a teetotal society. This was, perhaps, the first general public and exclusively teetotal society in England according to the movement's historian, Winskill. (William E.A. Axon, *Annals of Manchester*, John Heywood, Manchester, 1886)

——◆——

1837: Early Victorian Manchester was no stranger to the thrill-seeking of modern-day 'extreme' sports. Today saw 'the Jumper' – local man Samuel D. Scott – make two daredevil leaps into the Irwell from the roof of Shanklin, Manley and Co.'s premises by the New Bailey Bridge. The drop measured some 65-70ft, and having tried it once feet first, the Jumper made the second plummet headfirst.

——◆——

1845: The Manchester and Leeds Railway Company began the process of inserting a channel to culvert the River Irk from below the College, for 120yd of its length, in order to expand their general offices. Once renowned for its eels, much of the river's lower course is now deeply hidden underground, many residents not even aware of its presence.

JULY 12TH

1762: A riot broke out over food prices on this day. The mob smashed up dealers' premises and a corn mill, carting away flour, beans and oatmeal, and flinging that which they could not carry off into the river or otherwise 'rendering it unserviceable'. The damage amounted to a remarkable £1,000. (W.H. Thomson, *History of Manchester to 1852*, John Sherratt & Son Ltd, Altrincham, 1967)

1847: Cloth-dresser William Hardcastle of Back Piccadilly died on this day, aged sixty-seven. A notorious sleepwalker, he had leapt through his bedroom window whilst fast asleep.

1924: Mrs Bingle – an Ancoats woman who had lost three sons in the First World War – joined with the Earl of Derby in today's unveiling of the Manchester Cenotaph in St Peter's Square. Dean McCormick then blessed the memorial, which had been designed by Sir Edwin Lutyens. (Terry Wyke and Harry Cocks, *Public Sculpture of Greater Manchester*, Liverpool University Press, 2003)

1961: On this day, the first man to leave the atmosphere, Kosmonavt Yuriy Gagarin, flew into Manchester Airport to visit the town. He came upon the invitation of Mancunians anxious to get a look at him, he said, 'If all those people are getting wet to welcome me, surely the least I can do is get wet too!' He visited Metrovicks at Trafford Park (then still the biggest factory in the world) and the Town Hall, where he was greeted by a brass band playing the Soviet anthem. (The *Guardian*, July 13th)

JULY 13TH

1846: On this day, a peculiar election in St Ann's Square took place. No other candidate having even bothered to turn up, MP Thomas Milner Gibson was elected by a simple show of hands from the crowd. Only three were in opposition.

1872: A terrible flood – 'the most disastrous which ever visited Manchester' – submerged Peel Park and the racecourse by Throstle Nest on this day. The Medlock rose by 12ft at the calico printworks at Clayton Bridge, wrecking the machinery. The worst of the flooding occurred at Philips Park Cemetery, where many coffins were washed away, their bodies flowing down into Manchester. Two fully laden coal barges were lifted up onto the Castlefield Wharves. Some residential areas were flooded by up to 15ft of water, with many people having to be rescued from their upper storeys – by some miracle only one life was lost in the catastrophe.

2003: Over £400,000 was raised for charity today at the auction of the relics of Maine Road, Manchester City's home ground for over eighty years. In the very first hour, more than £10,000 was raised before an audience of 1,000 fans who had come to see and perhaps acquire a piece of memorabilia. Everything was in demand, including turnstiles, doors and floodlights. The front doors went for £600, the doors to the manager's office for £70, and the office table for £460. Many smaller and more portable mementoes had already been sold off, including seats at £12 each, and pieces of turf were auctioned off for £10.

July 14th

1832: Today's *Manchester Guardian* reported on a brawl in the town. The people who live in the area in which this occurred, Green Erin, are described thus: 'As tending to illustrate the peculiarly pugnacious disposition of the natives of Green Erin, particularly as illustrated in that district which, from being inhabited chiefly, if not wholly, by them, possesses the appellation of "Little Ireland".'

1840: Today, in a peculiar reversal of roles, the district coroner W.S. Rutter appeared in front of the borough court. He was charged with the assault of his colleague, the borough coroner. He was held on bail and the case was referred to the following sessions.

1880: After the Royal Charter was granted on April 20th, the first Court of Governors met at the Owens College on this day, to oversee its transformation into the Victoria University of Manchester. Mayor Patteson later entertained the Governors at the Town Hall, in the presence of the Archbishop of York, Duke of Devonshire, and Professor Huxley.

1989: Clare Leighton, aged sixteen, died after taking an ecstasy tablet at Manchester's Haçienda nightclub. This was the first death caused by the drug in the United Kingdom, and resulted in a crackdown on the clubbing subculture by the local police. Partly as a result of this, the club closed for a period in 1991. It reopened after improvements to security provisions, but soon closed its doors for good on June 28th 1997. (BBC News Online)

JULY 15TH

1642: On this day, Manchester witnessed perhaps the first bloodshed of the Civil War. Royalist troops swarmed into Manchester while reading the King's proclamation against the forces gathering for Parliament. They paraded through the streets, declaring 'The town's our own' but then Richard Percival, a linen weaver of Kirkmanshulme, was slain in a skirmish as Parliamentary forces under Captains Holcroft and Birch marched into town. (W.H. Thomson, *History of Manchester to 1852*, John Sherratt & Son Ltd, Altrincham, 1967)

1847: Manchester was the scene of an outrageous child labour case on this day. 'Climbing boy' Thomas Price, aged seven years and seven months, died of suffocation and burning while up a flue at Tennant, Clow and Co.'s premises in Chorlton-upon-Medlock. It was clear that 'ill-usage' from his master was involved, and the man was subsequently put on trial for manslaughter. (William E.A. Axon, *Annals of Manchester*, John Heywood, Manchester, 1886)

1858: On this day, Emmeline Goulden was born in Moss Side. Twenty years later, marriage to a local barrister saw her become Emmeline Pankhurst. Widowed at forty, Emmeline formed the Women's Social and Political Union, which introduced militant struggle into the heretofore legal and respectful movement for female suffrage. Assaults, vandalism and destruction of public property saw her and her followers repeatedly arrested, with many being force-fed while on hunger strike in jail. In later life, concerns at the excesses of Bolshevism caused her to join the Conservatives.

JULY 16TH

1746: Today saw officers of the Manchester Regiment brought to trial in London for treason. The surrendered or captured officers had fought for the Young Pretender in the Rebellion of 1745. Two men, however, managed to escape a grisly fate by escaping from Newgate Prison – Moss and Holker (*see* April 28th).

1844: The King of Saxony visited Manchester on this day to inspect its factories and public institutions. The Saxony town of Chemnitz would later, as 'Karl-Marx-Stadt', be twinned with Manchester.

1884: Wealthy book dealer Thomas Hayes was found dead in the Bridgewater Canal today, sparking a rather unpleasant fight over his £16,000 fortune. Though his will could not be found, it was thought that he had left £10,000 to an adopted son, William Tatham, who he had educated as his heir. After he had provided for his wife, the remainder was to go towards scholarships for the Owens College. A next of kin appeared in the midst of the confusion to contest this, taking the case to court on April 16th 1885. In the end, enough evidence was found in favour of Tatham. The relative dropped his suit and was given the expenses out of the estate.

JULY 17TH

1761: Today saw the first barge-full of coal make its way up the Bridgewater Canal from the Duke of Bridgewater's mines at Worsley beyond Eccles. As a result of this the coal prices were cut by half, and a celebration was held on waste ground between the canal and what is now Jackson Street. This would take place annually as three days of festivities known as Knott Mill Fair, which, in 1806, was moved to fields on Liverpool Road.

1712: On this day, St Ann's Church was consecrated. Manchester diarist and wigmaker Edmond Harrold, wrote his entry for the day: 'Bishop Dawes performed the consecration, Mr Bagaly endowed it, the clergy responded at entrance, Mr Ainscough read prayers, Beatman 'sponsed, the Bishop read the gift in both Latin and English, Mr Bond preached on "Holiness becometh thine house, O Lord". Then the Bishop and the Clergy, and who would, stayed sacrament. Thus they was about four hours in this great work.'

1821: Mancunian soldier Colonel Thomas Ilderton Ferriar died on this day. He had received wounds at the Battle of Carabobo in Valencia, Columbia, on June 24th. At the time he had been captaining the volunteers of the British Legion against the forces loyal to Spain; an action that was vital in winning South America its independence from Madrid.

July 18th

1578: On this day, the Manchester College Charter is reissued by Queen Elizabeth I.

------◆------

1654: On this day, the High Sheriff of Lancaster, Peter Bould, signed the return by which Colonel Charles Worsley of Platt in the parish of Manchester was confirmed as the town's elected representative. As the town's first MP, Worsley was summoned to the Commons on September 3rd to sit in the so called 'Barebones Parliament'. Cromwell's frustration with the pedantry and inaction of the House caused it to dissolve a few months later, on January 22nd 1655. A trusted and able lieutenant, Worsley was kept on by the Lord Protector as his vice-regent in the north-west Midlands.

------◆------

1912: Manchester suffragette Mary Leigh (*née* Brown) carried out one of her most audacious acts of militancy for the cause today. At the Theatre Royal in Dublin, just visited by PM Herbert Asquith, she managed to set fire to the curtains, throw a burning chair into the orchestra pit, and let off some small bombs. She was sentenced to five years for this, but was released after a debilitating hunger strike. Her criminal record later disqualified her from war service, but she found a position as an ambulance driver by using her maiden name.

JULY 19TH

1821: At the coronation celebrations held today for George IV in the town, 40,000 tradesmen marched in the processions. The later festivities involved 25 oxen, 60 sheep, 29,000lb of bread, and 400 kegs of strong beer. Many in town had been thoroughly disgusted with the monarch's expression of thanks made while Regent to the butchers of Peterloo, and found more to grumble over on this occasion, whose wasteful carnage has been described as 'rudely Hogarthian'. (W.H. Thomson, *History of Manchester to 1852*, John Sherratt & Son Ltd, Altrincham, 1967; Richard Wright Procter, *Memorials of Manchester Streets*, T. Sutcliffe, Manchester, 1874; William E.A. Axon, *Annals of Manchester*, John Heywood, Manchester, 1886)

———— ◆ ————

1939: Irish-born artist John Cassidy died in Manchester on this day. He lived in the town for the last fifty or so years, and some of his better known works are the sculptures he made for the John Rylands Library, including those of the founder and his Cuban wife Henrietta, that stand at either end of the main reading room.

———— ◆ ————

1986: The Festival of the Tenth Summer drew to an end today, after a week 'celebrating Manchester'. Put on by Factory Records, the festival combined fashion, merchandise, film, art, photography, literature and of course music, including the celebration of the Sex Pistols debut album release (*see* June 4th). The programme ended in an all day event at the GMEX venue, in which The Smiths, New Order, Happy Mondays and many others of the Manchester music scene took part.

JULY 20TH

1640: On this day, Charles I made Royalist Lord of the Manor Sir Edward Mosley a baronet. Two years later, his home at Alport Park (modern-day Castlefield) would be burnt down by Parliamentarian townsmen in the Siege of Manchester (*see* September 25th).

1646: Lancastrian Jesuit priest Richard Bradley died on this day, in the Gaol on Hunts Bank while awaiting trial. He had contracted 'gaol disease', which no doubt refers to the less than sanitary conditions in which he was confined. (William E.A. Axon, *Annals of Manchester*, John Heywood, Manchester, 1886)

1840: On this day, twenty-three delegates representing the Chartists of the Midlands and North gathered in Manchester. Following the disappointment of their hopeful beginning in the 1830s, they met to determine how best to organise and focus their strength to achieve their ends. The delegate of the Manchester working men was William Tillman, who was appointed secretary. By the 24th, many plans had been considered and it was resolved to incorporate themselves into a National Charter Association – a risky move unsanctioned by the laws of the day.

July 21st

1603: On this day, the plague reached its height, claiming more than 200 victims to date, in a town with little more than 5,000 people.

———◆———

1806: Mr George Phillips lays the first stone of the new Exchange today. The impressive new civic edifice would open, room by room, throughout 1809.

———◆———

1876: A meeting was called at the Town Hall on this day, in response to a bill proposed by Lord Carnarvon on May 22nd. The bill was concerned with animal cruelty, specifically with regard to the provisions against vivisection (also supported by the Queen, who had been shocked to hear of the details of the practices involved). The Bishop of Manchester was the chief speaker in support of the humane position.

JULY 22ND

1736: On this day, prominent Manchester Tory John Byrom was given a Jacobite snuffbox with a portrait of King Charles the 'Pretender' inside the lid – a dangerously incriminating artefact in those days of dynastic struggle!

1852: Manchester hosted a vegetarian banquet in the Town Hall today, under the presidency of Mr James Simpson. This reaffirmed Salford's credentials as the birthplace of vegetarianism, having already produced the Father of the movement in Revd Cowherd (*see* March 24th).

1868: On this day, Hannah Beswick was buried in an unmarked grave in Harpurhey Cemetery. Better known as the 'Manchester Mummy', she had already been dead for over 110 years (*see* February 20th). Since 1828, Hannah's embalmed corpse had stood in the entrance hall of the Manchester Natural History Museum, between a far older Egyptian mummy and one from Peru, being 'one of the most remarkable objects in the museum', according to a visitor of 1844. When Manchester University inherited the collection in 1867, it was decided that Hannah – now 'irrevocably and unmistakably dead' and well out of any danger of the burial alive that she had so dreaded – should finally be buried. Bureaucratic innovation since 1758 demanded a death certificate, and the matter went to the Secretary of State. Bishop Fraser than gave his permission for a Christian burial, and Miss Beswick was finally interred.

JULY 23RD

1777: Cheetham Hill-born linen draper, James Heywood, died on this day. He is most remembered for being the author of *Poems and Letters on Various Subjects* (1726), which contained an admirable section called 'A compendious character of the celebrated Beauties in Manchester'. In it he defended the honour of the ladies of the town, who had too often been subject to metropolitan sniping and 'scurrilous lampoons' as 'Lancashire Witches'.

———•◆•———

1789: St Michael's Church on Angel Street was consecrated on this day. Its smoke-blackened tower was a recurring feature in Lowry's works, and its curates had the pastoral care of one of the most infamous slums of the city. The neighbouring burial ground was used for mass graves in epidemics and for unmarked graves of paupers in other times. One of its vicars, Jowitt Wilson, died 'worn out' a year after retiring. It was demolished in 1935, and Angel Meadow was made into a park.

———•◆•———

1948: On this day, historian and broadcaster Michael Wood was born in Moston. A Fellow of the Royal Historical Society, he made a career of popularising history via the medium of televised documentaries. Covering the exploits of Alexander the Great, as well as the Spanish Conquistadores, he has also taken viewers into the foundations of English history, discussing the world in which the Domesday Book was written, and the very foundation of Manchester's ethnos in his *In Search of the Dark Ages*.

JULY 24TH

1790: On this day, Magistrate Leaf laid the first stone of the Manchester Workhouse at Strangeways. It opened on February 14th 1793, and was witness to many a grim Dickensian scene in the lives of generations of impoverished Mancunians with nowhere else to turn.

———•◆•———

1854: The Manchester and Salford Temperance Society met today at the Friends' Meeting House on Mount Street and resolved in favour of closing public houses on the Sabbath day. This was a direct result of Manchester's teetotallers turning militant in their desire to enforce prohibition in the country, as their comrades in the USA would later succeed in doing.

JULY 25TH

1851: On this day, Cardinal Wiseman consecrated two bishops at St John's in Salford: Fr Errington of the said church, and Fr Turner of St Augustine's, who became the first Bishop of Salford.

———— •◆• ————

2002: Manchester hosted the 17th Commonwealth Games, and on this night the Queen presided over the opening ceremony, in which the 3,683 athletes of the seventy-two states paraded around the City of Manchester Stadium. Seventeen different sports would be played at more than a dozen venues, many of which were specially built for the purpose. Unique to the Games was the Queen's Jubilee Baton Relay – electronically picking up the pulse of the runner holding it, the baton shone a beam of blue light in time with the heartbeat of the holder. It had been carried round 23 countries and 500 towns across the UK by 5,000 athletes and local heroes, culminating in David Beckham and the six-year-old Kirsty Howard, a Manchester girl who had been born with her heart back to front. The remainder of the £12 million spectacle involved a 'Madchester'-themed mixture of pomp and pop, and featured performances by Salford's Russell Watson, S Club, the Grenadier Guards and a flypast by the Red Arrows – more than 4,000 people ultimately took part, all cheered on by a crowd of 40,000 spectators.

JULY 26TH

1712: Edmund Harrold's diary entry for this day: 'About a quarter past ten my wife was neding and she had teem'd ye berm of o'th two buled [handled] pot, a new one, which she set down in the tub quickly. It gave a crack. What's that? Said she; is that the pot?Says Sarah Sharples, Ay; it's a sign of death, says she. So as they was talking it gave 2 cracks more. At last my wife took up the pot and rung it and it is as sound as can be. I have told several people. Some are of one opinion and some another. Some says it's ominous, others not; but I have noted it down in order to observe the event concerning theirs or our families to come.'

———◆———

1837: Today, Salford's first MP, Joseph Brotherton, held onto his seat yet again in a by-election, but this time by a majority of only one vote; 889 to William Garnett's 888.

———◆———

1859: Moss Side witnessed a terrible tragedy on this day. Two boys were swimming in a great pit that existed at the locality, due to generations of peat extraction, when they sank in the mud. A man heroically dived in to try to save them and was also drowned.

JULY 27TH

1398: The eleventh Baron of Manchester, John la Warre, died on this day. He was fifty-four when he passed, and a veteran of the wars in Gascony. He was childless, so the manor passed to his brother Thomas, a priest, and now thus Baron and Rector of Manchester (*see* May 22nd).

1844: On this day, John Dalton, one of the leading lights of Manchester science, died at the age of seventy-eight. He was president of the Manchester Literary and Philosophical Society for a full half century, and had moved to Manchester from his native Cumberland in 1793, to take the professorship of mathematics and natural Philosophy in the new College on Mosley Street. His greatest work was the beginning of modern atomic theory. He received his Doctorate from Oxford when already over the age of seventy.

1871: The Emperor of Brazil, Dom Pedro II, visited Manchester on this day, to see the wonders of the city's industrialisation.

1956: On this day, England bowler Jim Laker took 19 Australian wickets for 90 runs in Australia's first test at Old Trafford, a feat since unmatched with no other having taken more than 17.

JULY 28TH

1578: On this day, Elizabeth 1 renames the Ecclesiastical College of Manchester, as the College of Christ. Following the reformation of the institute, she halved the number of Fellows to four, and removed two of the six choristers, and the warden would henceforth be an appointee of the Crown. John Woolton was given the position and a salary of 4s a day; the four fellows would receive 16d each, and the choristers 4½ d.

———— ◆ ————

1846: John Owens, Manchester-born hat maker and a man of Radical politics, died today at the age of fifty-six, due to a ruptured blood vessel. Owens left his immense £100,000-plus fortune to the foundation of an educational institution, which would be named Owens College in his honour – this would late become Manchester University.

———— ◆ ————

2002: On this day, Jonathan Edwards CBE managed to win the Manchester Commonwealth Games gold medal, while breaking the Commonwealth record for the triple jump. The record-breaking series of leaps was his third attempt, almost as though to increase the dramatic tension – his winning jump was 17.86m! Commenting on the Manchester crowd of 38,000, the European, Olympic and World Record holder Edwards later remarked 'It was just like a party. Amazing. There were 112,000 in Sydney for the Olympics and I don't think they made any more noise than this.'

July 29th

1676: On this day, Mr William Barrow was appointed High Master of the Grammar School. Barrow's headship is noted for a schoolboys' mini-rebellion, in which they took control of the school for over a fortnight, all with the connivance of the townsfolk. Actual firearms were passed to the rebels, though it is assured that the boys aimed only for the legs of their foes! (Alfred A. Mumford, *Manchester Grammar School*, Longmans, Green and Co., London, 1919)

———•◆•———

1814: Disaster struck at Hunt's Bank on this day, as several houses and part of a soapery tumbled down the steep and cluttered bank of the River Irwell. Three people lost their lives in the river that day.

———•◆•———

1850: The medieval parish of Manchester (possibly more than a millennium old) was finally divided up into the separate parishes of today, by act of Parliament.

———•◆•———

1874: On this day, the Bishop, Dean and the Chapter of Manchester Cathedral met privately to discuss the rather shocking topic of the Owd Church – the town's medieval parish and collegiate churches – being inadequate for the needs of the new Diocese. Thankfully, there was sufficient objection to the idea of overly altering the old edifice, but the general mood was one in favour of erecting a new cathedral on a different site.

July 30th

1746: Thomas Syddall, Jacobite wig maker of Manchester, was executed today. He followed in his father's footsteps, who had been executed for the same charges of treason in 1715. He was beheaded after hanging in London, his heart and bowels consumed by fire. His head was then sent to Manchester to be placed upon a spike over the Exchange there on September 18th. With him died the other Mancunian Jacobites listed for 24th December. They have been commemorated in song:

> 'My name is Tom Syddall, a barber
> In Manchester I am well known
> And now I am going to suffer, for fighting for King Charlie's
> own.' (Harland 235)

> 'The Deel has set your heads to view
> And stickt them upon poles;
> Poor Deel! 'twas all that he could do, since God has ta'en their
> souls.' (Procter)

———•◆•———

1765: Today it was announced that all those drowning cats and dogs, as well as washing dirty linen at Shude Hill pits without consent, would, in future, be 'prosecuted to the utmost rigour of the law.' (Procter)

———•◆•———

2002: On this day, Australian swimmer Ian Thorpe broke the world record for the 400m freestyle at the Manchester Aquatics Centre. His record-breaking time of 3 minutes and 40.08 seconds earned him the Commonwealth Games gold medal – one of the five gold medals and one silver medal he won at the games.

JULY 31ST

1845: On this day, the first stone of Manchester's Bank of England branch in King Street was laid by its agent John Reid and the architect Charles Cockerill.

———— • ◆ • ————

1868: The Trafford Arms was host to a disaster on this day. A false fire alarm caused a terrible crush in which twenty-three people perished on the stairs, with many more seriously injured. Now cleared away to widen Victoria Street, this tavern was once home to a singing gallery, which was quite an institution in its day; Proctor describes it thus: 'Who has not heard of Ben Lang's, or Th' Trafford, or Th' Vic? Within those walls appeared, during many years, a succession of surprises for the people. Matchless singers, inimitable dancers, champion pedestrians, belted bruisers, and so forth, to the utter exclusion of the golden mean – the happy medium.'

———— • ◆ • ————

2002: Derbyshire's Zoe Baker won gold in the Manchester Commonwealth Games today, competing in the 50m breaststroke event. At 30.6 seconds, she completed the race a full second before the next swimmer and only 0.03 seconds slower than the world record she had set the previous day in semi-finals.

AUGUST 1ST

1573: The first entry in Manchester's first parish register was made today, for the burial of one Robert Fisher.

——— • ◆ • ———

1713: Edmond Harrold's diary entry for this day reads, 'I'm in a midered condition.'

——— • ◆ • ———

1883: Bibliophile James Crossley died on this day. Though born in Halifax, he had lived in Manchester for sixty-seven years, where he had practised law (working alongside the novelist Ainsworth) in a firm of which he later became proprietor – Crossley and Sudlow. In 1843, he was the first to suggest the foundation of the Chetham Society to print historical documents of pertinence to the history of the region. In 1847, Crossley became the Society's second president, editing several documents himself. His library was immense – 90,000 volumes! – and he was elected honorary librarian of Chetham's Library in 1867.

——— • ◆ • ———

1988: On this day, the enduring Manchester group The Hollies made it to the number one slot for the second time, with a gap of over twenty-three years since the first! 'He Ain't Heavy, He's My Brother' was the chart-topping song, and it is still a firm jukebox favourite. Yet another generation on and the band are still touring and releasing records (*see* March 15th).

AUGUST 2ND

1659: Five hundred armed Manchester men of the 'trained bands' march to Warrington to join other regional forces today, who were gathering to counter the Royalist 'Cheshire Rising' headed by Dunham Massey's Sir George Booth. He had switched sides due to Richard Cromwell's refusal to allow him to take up his old seat in the reconstituted Rump Parliament that Oliver had dissolved, and aimed to make the North West a bridgehead for a Stuart Restoration (*see* August 5th).

1662: On this day, the Act of Uniformity is passed, in order to push dissident churchmen from their positions. Warden Heyrick refused to be moved from the Collegiate Church, and Charles II later overlooked this, thanks to the request of the Earl of Manchester, a friend of Heyrick. Two Fellows of the College, Henry Newcome and Christopher Richardson, resigned but continued to preach privately in the town, which became something of a hotbed of defrocked Non-Conformists. The ministers of Salford, Blackley, Eccles, Gorton and Newton Heath were likewise dismissed.

1996: The Ishinki Touchstone sculpture by Kan Yasuda was installed in the town on this day. As its backdrop, the new Bridgewater Hall was fast approaching completion. The 18 tonnes of Italian marble cost £200,000 to be made, which was paid for jointly by the City Council, Airport, Arts Council and the National Lottery.

AUGUST 3RD

1573: The first baptism in Manchester's was recorded in the first ever parish register today – that of Ellen Darby, daughter of William. The first marriage to be recorded is entered on this date also – Nicholas Cleaton wed Ellen Pendleton.

1746: The heads of executed Jacobites Syddall, Chadwick, and Deacon were brought from London on this day, to be mounted on spikes on the roof of the town's Old Exchange. Dr Deacon was the first to see the head of his son, Captain Thomas, and overcame his emotions enough to salute it, reportedly 'rejoicing that he had possessed a son who could firmly suffer martyrdom in the Stuart cause.' Others mocked the heads as 'the gods spiked upon the Exchange'. (William E.A. Axon, *Annals of Manchester*, John Heywood, Manchester, 1886)

1848: The magistrates' fears of Chartist insurrection finally prompted them into action. On this night, 300 police constables under Captain Willis and Mr Beswick launched a simultaneous surprise raid on the Chartist clubs in the city. Fifteen leaders were arrested, including Leach and Donovan who had recently attended the National Convention in London.

1876: The Knott Mill Fair (*see* July 17th) should have taken place on this day. But, thanks to the Council's decision that 'All fairs now holden in the city be discontinued', the fair was cancelled. Other ancient gatherings to be cancelled were the Whit Monday Fair, Dirt Fair, and Acres Fair.

AUGUST 4TH

1847: St Chad's Roman Catholic Chapel in Cheetham Hill opened on this day. Over sixty clergymen took part in the ceremony, creating quite a spectacle.

———— • ◆ • ————

2002: Torrential rain aside, the Manchester Commonwealth Games certainly went out with a bang. The Queen, Prime Minister and 40,000 spectators gathered to watch the closing ceremony on this day. In just a minute and a half, 1,600 local schoolchildren painted probably the biggest ever (and fastest), portrait of Elizabeth II on 1,000sq m of fabric. There were giant doves made of lanterns, and stars such as the Eurythmics, M People, the cast of *Coronation Street* and both Manchester football teams played their part. The David Dixon Award was then presented to the 100m and 50m disabled swimmer Natalie Du Toit, who was recognised as the outstanding athlete of the Games. Fireworks finished the event off, accompanied by 'Land of Hope and Glory', but the legacy of the Games is still with us, in the superb sports facilities remaining in the city. The 2008 Olympic triumph of British Cycling owed much to the velodrome at Sport City, and the main stadium has seen the improvement of Manchester City's fortunes.

AUGUST 5TH

642: On this day, King Oswald was killed by Penda of Mercia in a battle at Makerfield. Manchester may have been annexed to that kingdom for a period, perhaps reflected in the local dialect's commonalities with Midland speech.

1495: Henry VII passed through Manchester on this day, after visiting his mother at Latham House. The first Tudor monarch stayed no more than a day in the as yet undistinguished market town.

1839: Manchester's first cab stand, in Picadilly, is established today. William White of Spear Street was the entrepreneur and the cab itself was the property of W.H. Beeston of Tib Street.

1839: On this day, famous philanthropist Robert Owen laid the foundation stone for the Hall of Science before delivering an oration to the supportive crowd. The stone bears the motto 'Sacred to the Investigation of Truth'. This was the largest lecture hall in Manchester, holding up to 3,000 people, and was situated on Byrom Street in Campfield, and cost £7,000 to erect. In 1842, Engels visited the hall and made a note of the 'Most ordinary workers speaking with a clear understanding on political, religious, and social affairs.' It was sold to the Corporation to be used as a Free Library in 1850, for £1,200 on the initiative of Alderman Potter.

AUGUST 6TH

1667: Richard Heyrick died on this day, while still Warden of Manchester Collegiate Church; a post he held onto despite attempts to unseat him by both Cromwellian and Restoration regimes. Appointed in 1636 as a result of a debt owed to his father by Charles I, he supported the legitimist cause despite his Presbyterian leanings.

———◆———

1831: On this day, William Fairbairn and James Lillie's foundry on High Street burned down. The damages amounted to £8,000, but the firm's reputation kept it afloat and they continued to get contracts for work. Lillie left the business in 1839 and it was reformed as William Fairbairn and Sons. Fairbairn moved to Manchester from the Scottish Borders and set his engineering genius to the challenges offered by the cotton industry of the town. He later collaborated with the leading minds of the day to produce many of the flagship engineering super-projects of the Victorian period. Fairbairn was made the first Baronet of Ardwick in 1869.

———◆———

1979: Labour peer Baron Harold Lever of Manchester died on this day. Manchester-born and educated at the town's grammar school and university, he worked as a lawyer until he was elected MP by the Manchester Exchange constituency in 1945 (his brother Leslie representing Ardwick). He joined the House of Lords in 1979, campaigning for Third World debt relief in his old age.

AUGUST 7TH

1861: Though the omnibuses were still pulled by horse, Salford Council met today to approve the laying down of iron tramlines from Cross Lane up to Albert Bridge. The new metal lines were to a design of Messrs Greenwood and Haworth, and were based on 'Haworth's Patent Perambulating Principle'. (William E.A. Axon, *Annals of Manchester*, John Heywood, Manchester, 1886)

1888: John Jackson was hanged at Strangeways on this day, for the murder of prison officer Ralph Webb. The execution was carried out by James Berry, a good friend of Webb. Jackson had been serving time for a burglary until, as he was a plumber, he was asked to fix a problem in the prison matron's quarters. Taken there by Webb, he set to work. The matron then heard a cry and, along with three wardens, burst into the room to find Webb beaten to death with a hammer; Jackson had escaped through a hole in the ceiling. He was apprehended weeks later in Bradford and brought back to Strangeways to meet his end.

1912: Wilfrid Parke completed the first flight in a fully enclosed cabin biplane aircraft today. In the test flights before August's Military Aeroplane Competition, he flew the Avro Type G over Salisbury Plain. Overturning on landing, it was hurriedly shipped back to the Brownsfield Mill basement in Ancoats, where it had been designed and built. Parke would soon be making more aviation firsts (*see* August 25th), resulting in the construction of the Avro 504 biplane, of which 20,000 were made for the First World War.

AUGUST 8TH

1829: Today's *Manchester Guardian* railed against 'the great evils of immigration'. In a manner that would be most distressing to the readers of its present-day successor, it stated that 'The Irish were the most serious evil with which our labouring classes have to contend'.

———◆———

1765: On this day, Revd John Whitaker surveyed the 'Romano-British fort of Mancunium' to illustrate his rich but fanciful history of the town. 'The garrison appears to have consisted of a single cohort ... the First Cohort of Frisians raised among the natives of Friesland ... If this cohort had its entire complement of men, the garrison of Mancunium must have ordinarily consisted of 762 foot soldiers. In sports they introduced the fighting of trained cocks.' A millennium would pass before the civic authorities would succeed in banning this bloody entertainment, though Cock Pit Lane only gave way to the Arndale Shopping Centre in living memory.

———◆———

1844: A public meeting was held in Manchester's Town Hall today, to discuss the need for some green space within the town. After a few weeks, more than £8,000 had been raised, all from private donors, of whom the greatest contributors were Mark Philips, Sir Benjamin Heywood and Lord Francis Egerton, each donating £1,000.

AUGUST 9TH

1832: On this day, Manchester celebrated the passing of the Great Reform Act. Manchester finally received two MPs and an MP for Salford. A magnificent procession was followed by Charles Green's ascent in a balloon.

***

1886: Ashton-under-Lyne's Mary Ann Britland was hanged at Strangeways on this day. Intent on clearing the way for her and her lover Tom Dixon, she poisoned her own daughter and husband, along with the wife of her intended. The third death raised suspicions, and the corpses of Elizabeth (aged nineteen), Thomas and Mary were exhumed, incriminating Mary Ann. Dixon had known nothing of the murders and was left the sole survivor of the fatal love triangle.

***

2011: On this day, as a result of the London riots, Manchester was witness to its own riots. The rioters broke into shops, attacked cars, and targeted police. Fire engines drove past arsonists, looters flaunted their stolen goods in front of lines of policemen, and for twelve hours, one of the country's biggest and most important cities was lawless and out of control. Eight hundred riot police attempted to manage the situation but the mob revelled in its impunity: 'It was better than anything. You just cun't describe it, cuz you was in the atmosphere, and it might not 'appen again.' Greater Manchester Police described it as the worst violence the city had seen in a generation, emphasising the purely criminal motivation: 'We want to make it absolutely clear – they have nothing to protest against … there has been no spark.' (BBC *Newsnight*)

AUGUST 10TH

1596: Warden John Dee was paid a visit by his cousin Thomas Jones of Tregaron, alias Twm Sion Cati – the 'Welsh Robin Hood' – on this day. Twm was as well known for magic as his cousin John, but the chief purpose of his visit seems to have been to drive up a herd of cattle from Wales.

———— •◆• ————

1823: On this day, the first stone was laid for the first Town Hall on King Street, by Boroughreeve James Brierley. Inspired by the Athenian Erechthenion, it cost £40,000 to build but would be outgrown by municipal needs in 1877.

———— •◆• ————

2003: Having inherited the brand new Commonwealth Games stadium, Manchester City played their first match there, beating Barcelona 2–1. Serious remodelling had added an extra 10,000 seats at a cost of £40 million and brought the capacity up to 47,805.

———— •◆• ————

2007: Tony Wilson, Granada TV journalist cum music mogul, died today. He had helped to give Manchester a new meaning in a world fast forgetting the Cottonopolis. Forming Factory Records in 1978, he founded the Haçienda nightclub in May 1982, helping to shape the 'Madchester' phenomenon. He has been portrayed twice in film: by Steve Coogan in *24 Hour Party People* and Craig Parkinson in *Control*. At his death, the Union flag flew at half-mast on Manchester Town Hall, and he was buried under an epitaph from Isabella Banks' *The Manchester Man*. (*Manchester Evening News*)

AUGUST 11TH

1829: Today's *Manchester Guardian* translated the striking impressions Manchester had upon Prussian envoy, Herr Schinkel: 'Mr Connell, Mr Kennedy, and Mr Murray have buildings seven and eight storeys high. They are constructed completely fireproof, and a canal runs along one side and another within ... above street level they are linked by connecting passageways. There are buildings of this sort all over Manchester; they are the spinning mills for the finest kind of cotton ... Since the French War, 400 new factories have been set up in Lancashire; one sees buildings where three years before there were still fields, but these buildings soon look so black that one might take them as having already been a century in use. The immense edifices all built as they are by one contractor, without any attempt at architectural beauty and carried out only to meet the barest necessities, in red brick alone, make on one a very weird impression.' (W.H. Thomson, *History of Manchester to 1852*, John Sherratt & Son Ltd, Altrincham, 1967)

——— ◆ ———

1839: William Benbow, political agitator and Manchester coffee house proprietor, appeared today before the magistrates. For his writings, publishing and campaigning activities he was sentenced to sixteen months; he took some revenge, though, by making a ten-hour speech, comparing himself to Jesus, the Whigs to the Jews, and the judge to Pontius Pilate. Born in Manchester in 1784, he had come up with the notion of a 'grand national holiday' as a means of social revolution – a tactic later christened 'the general strike'. Much of his thinking was influential in the Plug Plot strikes of 1842. (Max Beer, *A History of British Socialism*, G. Allen and Unwin, London, 1940)

AUGUST 12TH

1656: On this day, Manchester elected its second ever MP, Richard Ratcliffe Esq. of the Lodge in Pool Fold – an old moated house once found between Market and King Street. The restored Charles II resolved that large Puritan sympathising towns were a liability to his rule, and Manchester lost its parliamentary representation until 1832.

1839: The local Chartist working men began their 'Chartist Holiday' or 'Sacred Month' – as a general strike was referred to in those times – on this day. Riots broke out all over the region.

1844: The funeral of John Dalton, world-famous developer of atomic theory, occurred on this day. He had been lying in state in the Town Hall since August 10th, as up to 40,000 people filed by to get a last glimpse of the great man. On the day of his burial, he was carried in a procession of 500 members of local societies, 300 gentlemen, and 100 members of various institutions, including the mayor, Alexander Kay. The hearse was drawn by six horses, and six mourning coaches carried his relatives and friends, as well as members of the Manchester Literary and Philosophical Society. At the cemetery, his fellow Quakers gathered to pay their last respects. Most businesses in Manchester were closed, along with all the shops. Dalton was buried in a vault in Ardwick Cemetery, which was kept open until 5 p.m., in order for many more to view his coffin. There has been nothing quite like it before or since in the town.

AUGUST 13TH

1861: Manchester-based architect turned explorer Thomas Witlam Atkinson, died on this day. He was the writer of *Oriental and Western Siberia; Explorations* (1858), and *Travels in the Region of the Upper and Lower Amazon* (1860).

———◆———

1930: On this day, Manchester's larger-than-life comic Bernard Manning was born. He started out by entertaining his fellow troops in post-war Berlin, before he turned professional and moved into stand-up and opening the World Famous Embassy Club in Harpurhey. Appearing on the 1970s show *The Comedians*, he went on to compère at The Wheeltappers and Shunters Social Club, recreating the atmosphere of the Working Men's Clubs. He passed away in 2007.

———◆———

1964: Strangeways Prison in Manchester saw (simultaneously with Liverpool's Walton Prison) one of the last executions by hanging in the United Kingdom at exactly 8 a.m. on this day. Gwynne Owen Evans was the condemned, for the murder of John Alan West.

AUGUST 14TH

1579: In the words of a sensational writer of the day, 'A most dreadfull and meruclous Monster born in Manchester upon Tusdaye, being the fourteenth of August'. The unfortunate Siamese twins were buried on the 19th of the same month, being referred to in the parish register as 'a mayde child and a monstrous man childe wantinge boeth neck, head, and armes.' (William E.A. Axon, *Annals of Manchester*, John Heywood, Manchester, 1886)

———— • ◆ • ————

1660: Manchester's last Presbyterian Classis was held on this day. The death of Lord Protector Cromwell and the Restoration of the Stuarts with Charles II brought a return to the old Episcopalian form of church organisation. Manchester returned to the authority of the Bishop of Chester, but lost its representation in Parliament for the next 172 years, thanks to its part in the downfall of the first Charles.

———— • ◆ • ————

1878: Alderman Walmsley opened the Langworthy wing of the Peel Park Museum on this day. It contained a reading room and picture gallery, and was 178ft in length. It was named in honour of Alderman Langworthy, who had left a bequest for the purpose in his will.

August 15th

1599: Sir Alexander Radcliffe, of the ill-omened Ordsall Hall family, was slain at Curlew Pass in Roscommon today. Ambushed by Red Hugh O'Donnell, the English forces were almost annihilated, but for a brave uphill cavalry charge in which the Manchester warrior played his part, allowing many of the infantry to get away – one of the two heaviest blows ever received by the English in Ireland, according to contemporary Sir Robert Cecil. Meanwhile, his brothers Edmund and Thomas simultaneously perished while fighting in Flanders.

1785: Thomas de Quincey, writer of *Confessions of an English Opium-Eater*, was born on this day on Princess Street. His parents moved to then rural Greenhay, and he was baptised at St Ann's church. The *Mercury* had announced the wedding of his parents five years previously; 'Wednesday last was married, at St George's, Queen Square, Mr Thomas Quincey, linen merchant in this town, to Miss Penson of North Street, London.' (William E.A. Axon, *Annals of Manchester*, John Heywood, Manchester, 1886)

1878: Mancunian plant collector James Mudie Spence died at the age of forty-two today. A Fellow of the Royal Geographical Society, he wrote *The Land of Bolivar* (1878) about his travels in Venezuela. A member of the Alpine Club, he had climbed the 9,430ft Pico de Naiguata there, gathering rare and unknown plants, one of which – *chusquea spencei* – now bears his name. He enjoyed similar exploits in Norway and California.

AUGUST 16TH

1819: It is hard to sum up the importance of the massacre of peaceful protesters that took place at Peterloo on this day, in either the history of Manchester or that of the whole country. A crowd of 60,000 men, women and children had gathered on St Peter's Field with banners calling for political and social reform, to hear the speeches of Henry Hunt and others. This was no violent mob, but a mass articulation of a generation's frustrations and hopes. And into it all rode forty of the Manchester Yeomanry, 'more or less intoxicated', slashing at the people with no thought for sex or age. A body of the 15th Hussars then rode in to extricate the Yeomen, while the people trying to get away from hooves and sabres ended up piled high. Officially, eleven were thus killed, and many hundreds grievously maimed. This cowardly mockery of chivalry was soon christened 'Peterloo', contrasting it with the real business of soldiers in actual battles, like Waterloo. (William E.A. Axon, *Annals of Manchester*, John Heywood, Manchester, 1886)

———— • ◆ • ————

1821: On this day, radical Reformers met to mark the second anniversary of Peterloo. They walked to the site of the outrage and then to Christchurch in Hulme, where several had their children baptised as 'Henry Hunt' in honour of the politician, still languishing in gaol after the events of 1819.

AUGUST 17TH

1890: On this day, miners protested on Kersal Moor. They eloquently expressed their sentiments in the following announcement: 'Was you to go down to the bottom of the pit, and there to see the dangers that the colliers are exposed to, you would never think their wages too much, was they to get a pound per day, that to work in those doleful and dangerous places – was we to lay down all the dangers we are in, with the carrying on of our work, it would be more than this paper would hold – we are in danger of our lives every moment, and all this we endure for the good of the country at large. Gentlemen, without us, no kind of business can go on; and we think it very hard that we must be confined to the bowels of the Earth from 9 to 12 hours or more to the day, and from that to 14s per week.' (pittdixon.go-plus.net)

———— • ◆ • ————

1933: On this day, having been placed in the city centre for the precious six years, the decision was finally made to remove the Cromwell statue from opposite the cathedral tower. It was reasoned that, 'The crossing is one of the most dangerous in the city and few will question the wisdom of transferring the familiar statue to the quieter neighbourhood of the parsonage.' Presented to the city in 1875 by Alderman Abel Heywood on behalf of Mrs Heywood and her late husband, Alderman Goadsby, the statue was the work of Matthew Noble, the sculptor of the town's Albert Memorial. (*Manchester Guardian*)

AUGUST 18TH

1858: On this day, the first transatlantic telegraph message was sent by Queen Victoria to President Buchanan. The message, 'Glory to God in the highest; on earth, peace and goodwill toward men', was sent via wires manufactured in Bradford, Manchester.

1874: Kelso-born Manchester engineer Sir William Fairbairn died today, at the age of eighty-five. The usual rags to riches tale, the skilful apprentice turned entrepreneur story saw him and his works at Ancoats rise to fame and honours. Amongst his awards the French Legion d'Honneur, awarded by Napoleon III, a knighthood (refused) and a baronetcy (un-refusable!) in 1869. At home in Ardwick, he entertained many a great name in his last years, from Chevalier Bunsen to Mrs Gaskell. Fifty thousand people attended his public funeral at Prestwich.

1933: Today's *Manchester Guardian* reported on how Salford and Manchester were leaders in pedestrian safety, stating that 'A new device is to be installed at the bottom of Portland Street. A strip of black and white stones arranged in chequer pattern ... These 'chekons' are made of a hard natural stone which has such a conspicuous colouring that a strip is seen by motorists two or three hundred yards away ... A crossing of this stone has been laid in Salford – one of the first in the country. The effect of the device in the two cities will be watched with care.'

AUGUST 19TH

1227: On this day, Henry III granted Manchester its annual fair, in the second town charter. Improving upon previous grants, the fair was extended to a three-day event, starting on the Eve of St Matthew the Apostle: the 20th, 21st and 22nd of September.

———— • ◆ • ————

1821: Today, the foundation of St Jude's Church in Ancoats, was laid. It was built in just two months and twenty-three days, the result of an outburst of religious zeal, by the 'Tent Methodists'. A Manchester-born Marlborough banker had sent a tent in which the Gospel was to be preached in urban areas of towns. The tent was pitched in Mather Street on August 19th 1821, and on October 1st in the same year. After a 'stirring sermon', the foundations of a permanent chapel were dug in just six hours by 140 people. (William Arthur Shaw, *Manchester Old and New*, Cassell and Company, London, 1894)

———— • ◆ • ————

1819: Only three days after the Peterloo massacre, the Manchester Magistrates met today to try to cover their errors. They published resolutions which they claimed had been made at a public meeting prior to the gathering, and that authorised force to be used in breaking the peaceful protest up. Public opinion would have none of it, however, and a petition appeared in a matter of days with 4,800 signatures protesting the falsity of these claims.

AUGUST 20TH

1515: On this day, Hugh Oldham, native of the town and now Bishop of Exeter, founded the Free Grammar School on Long Millgate. Hugh is commemorated for 'The good mynde which he hadd and bare to the countrey of Lancashire, consydering the brynging upp in lernyng, vertue, and good maners childeryn in the same countrey should be the key and grounde to have good people ther, whiche both lacked and wanted in the same, as well for grete povertie of the common people ther so that the childeryn in the same countrey, having pregnant wytte, have ben most parte brought upp rudely and idilly, and not in vertue, cunnyng, litterature, and good maners.' Born in a humble family in Crumpsall, he owed his career to the patronage of Henry VII's mother, the Countess of Richmond. Brought up in the household of the Earl of Derby, he was appointed Bishop of Exeter in 1504. (Richard Wright Procter, *Memorials of Manchester Streets*, T. Sutcliffe, Manchester, 1874)

———— •◆• ————

1834: Agustín Cosme Damián de Iturbide y Aramburu, liberator, first President, and briefly Emperor of Mexico, visited Manchester today, in the company of General O'Leary. He stayed at stayed Strangeways Hall.

———— •◆• ————

1864: On the request of the Armenian clergyman Revd Shahnazarian, the Patriarch of Jerusalem sent to Manchester a fragment of the True Cross, which arrived today to form the chief relic of his church.

AUGUST 21ST

1826: Manchester linen and tea dealers Alexander and Michael M'Keand were hanged today at Lancaster, for the murder of twenty-eight-year-old Elizabeth Bate. Michael's remains were handed over to the surgeons of Lancaster, but Alexander's body was sent as a gift to the Manchester Infirmary, where it was exhibited to the public before being passed to the students for disection.

1846: On this day, novelist Charlotte Brontë visited Manchester with her father, Revd Patrick, who was to undergo a cataracts operation in the town. During her stay, she received a rejection letter from a London publisher for *The Professor*.

1893: The world's first and only swing aqueduct saw its first barge crossing today. That the new Ship Canal should accommodate tall ocean-going vessels without disturbing the more traditional traffic of its eighteenth-century Bridgewater Canal forebear clearly demanded the best of Victorian ingenuity. This was supplied by Sir Edward Leader Williams and executed by Andrew Handyside of Derby. Williams had built the Anderton Boat Lift in Cheshire, and his solution for the Manchester ship canal involved a 330ft long metal structure weighing 1,450 tons, mounted on a central pivot. Grade II listed, it is in regular use among pleasure boaters, despite its age.

AUGUST 22ND

1840: Chartist leaders John Collins and Dr Peter Murray MacDonall entered Manchester in proud procession today. Released from Chester Castle Prison, they were entertained in the Carpenters' Hall with an honorary banquet, chaired by Revd James Scholefield.

———— • ◆ • ————

1848: The South Lancashire Assizes indicted forty-six regional Chartist leaders for conspiracy, including the fifteen arrested recently in Manchester. Sentences were not passed until December, but involved various terms of imprisonment, including two years for the prominent Dr P.M. M'Douall.

———— • ◆ • ————

1890: The Mayor, Aldermen and Councillors of Manchester enjoyed an outing to the Lake District today, to lay the first stone of the dam at Thirlmere Reservoir. This outing is attested by a fancy plaque on site, which is crowned with the arms of the city. The first water would reach the town on October 13th 1894.

AUGUST 23RD

1908: On this day, Manchester's suffragette leaders Emmeline and Christabel Pankhurst waited for the release of their fellow townswoman and comrade Mary Leigh from Holloway Prison. On her release, the brass band of the Women's Social and Political Union welcomed her and her twenty-six companions with great pomp. All had been imprisoned for throwing stones at 10 Downing Street. Mary herself then became drum-major of the band, marching in an extravagant uniform at their demonstrations, but still kept her hand in at militant protest (*see* July 18th and September 22nd).

1962: Shaun Ryder is born in Little Hulton in Salford on this day. The lead vocalist for the Happy Mondays, his lyrics were once famously compared to works of Keats (or was it Yeats?) by Tony Wilson. Ryder provided an irreplaceable part of the soundtrack to the Madchester phenomenon all through the 1980s, and still makes appearances in popular culture, collaborating with all manner of performers wishing to inject a little bit of Manchester into their product; most amusingly, in Russell Watson's cover of 'Barcelona'.

AUGUST 24TH

1831: On this day, Manchester coin forgers Jonathan Dade and his associates had their death sentences commuted to transportation to Australia.

———•◆•———

1949: Today saw the first game played at Old Trafford, the 'Theatre of Dreams', since March 11th 1941. Bolton Wanderers were treated to a 3–0 defeat by the home side, and United settled back into their old familiar stadium following several years of playing at their rival's Maine Road facility. United fans would have to wait until 1951 for the return of a roof to the Main Stand, but a subsequent investment of more than £40,000 would see the installation of floodlights, as well as the roofing of all stands, including the Stretford End, by 1959.

———•◆•———

2000: Greater Manchester remained at the forefront of precision engineering, as Chadderton's BAE Systems delivered its first high-tech Nimrod MRA4 wing to the Woodford assembly plant today. At 87ft long and weighing 8 tons, the new reconnaissance plane's wing was escorted by the police along the M60, and motorists stopped to watch the hunk of hardware make its first journey on the way to active service with the RAF.

AUGUST 25TH

1912: On this day, pilot Wilfrid Parke flew the Manchester-built Avro Type G biplane once more, becoming the second pilot in history to survive a spin while diving. His detailed account of how he regained control led to this 'Parke's Drive' went down in the history of aviation. The owner's brother, Humphrey V. Roe, was flown back to Manchester on the same day, becoming the first man ever to type a letter while mid-flight.

1923: Manchester City played their first match at Maine Road today, the stadium which would become the team's home ground for the next eighty years. The opponent was Sheffield United, who they defeated 2–1. With a maximum capacity of between 80,000 and 100,000, it was the second largest ground in the country after Wembley Stadium. The architect, Charles Swain, had even intended a greater capacity of a shocking 120,000. The 16¼-acre site was bought for £5,550, and total construction costs were £100,000. Behind the move were City Chairman, Lawrence Furniss, and the team manager, Ernest Mangnall – the ground was almost named after the former. Curiously, Maine Road narrowly escaped being called Dog Kennel Road; the site was previously the dog kennels of the lords of the manor. The road was renamed in the 1870s after the US state of Maine, renowned among Victorian social activists for its 'Maine Law' which forbade the selling of alcohol.

AUGUST 26TH

1346: On this day, after helping destroy the French fleet at Sluys (*see* June 24th), Baron John of Manchester served with distinction against the land forces of the French at the Battle of Crécy. Fighting under the command of Edward III, the English force of 9,000 to 15,000 men was heavily outnumbered by the 35,000-plus forces of Philippe VI.

———◆———

1846: Today saw great celebration surrounding the opening of three new Manchester Parks: Queens, Peel and Philips Park. The previous year, the public parks committee had purchased the 32-acre Lark Hill Estate from William Garnett for £5,000 (minus the £500 he himself had subscribed to the fund) to form the riverside Peel Park. In May, Jonathan Andrew's 30-acre Hendham Hall Estate in Harpurhey, now Queen's Park, was purchased for £7,250, followed by the purchase of Lady Houghton's 31 acre estate, now Philips Park, for £6,200.

AUGUST 27TH

1451: Sir Reginald West, Baron of Manchester, died on this day. Succeeded by his son Sir Richard, Reginald had been a devout Catholic aristocrat, with two pilgrimages to the Holy Land and one to Rome under his belt. He had succeeded to the manor on the death of the priest-baron Thomas la Warre, his maternal uncle, in 1427.

———— ◆ ————

1819: Cabinet Minister, the Earl of Sidmouth, forwarded the congratulations of the Prince Regent to Manchester's magistrates for their firm and speedy actions for the 'preservation of the public peace'. The future King George IV was referring to the cutting down of innocent men, women and children at Peterloo (*see* August 16th). The firebrand Henry 'Orater' Hunt and his fellows appeared before judges at the New Bailey Courthouse and were sent for trial at Lancaster, except Elizabeth Gaunt, who was discharged in view of the wounds she had received in the stampede caused by the cavalry charges. Public opinion swung in favour of the reformers, and meetings took place all around Britain to condemn the bloodshed employed against peaceful protesters. Politics moved slowly in those days and Parliament refused to come out and condemn or demand inquiry into the disaster, but by 1832 real progress had been made toward the realisation of the Radicals' demands.

AUGUST 28TH

1771: James Butterworth, dialect poet (under the alias 'Paul Bobbin') and author of *The Antiquities of the Town* and *A Complete History of the Trade of Manchester* (1822), was born at Pitses in Alt on this day. The youngest of eleven children, he showed great aptitude and, after a spell at weaving, ran a Sunday school in Mumps in Oldham. His first poetical works were published in 1800, and he rose to the position of postmaster, bookseller and stationer in the town. Upon his return to teaching, he wrote the bulk of his local historical works, despite the lack of interest shown by publishing agents, to whom he once stated, 'If, like the generality of your tribe, you are not willing to encourage a poor author, I'll commit the work to the flames, and forever renounce the business.'

———— • ◆ • ————

1933: Longsight-born twenty-two-year-old swimmer Ethel 'Sunny' Lowry became the first ever British woman to successfully swim the Channel on this day. Only four have repeated the feat, and Sunny was awarded an MBE in 2005 – seventy-two years seems quite a wait, but better late than never! Sunny died on February 21st 2008.

———— • ◆ • ————

2009: Backstage at one of their gigs, Noel and Liam Gallagher had a violent dispute, which proved to be the straw that broke the back of their Oasis collaboration. Noel refused to put up any longer with Liam's antics, and to date the pair have not met since. It took a major event even to bring them into written contact.

AUGUST 29TH

1835: With the Temperance Movement proving all the rage, John Youil, landlord of the Hen and Chickens, felt called upon today, to speak out against the queer new fad. His lecture was later printed as a pro-alcohol pamphlet.

———◆◆———

1885: On this day, Salford's teetotallers celebrated the jubilee of the Independent Order of Rechabites, which was founded in 1835. Their 1885 membership numbers amounted to 100,000 pledged abstainers.

———◆◆———

1970: The *Manchester Guardian* moved from its offices in Cross Street to new premises on Deansgate on this day. Cross Street had been the home of the paper since 1886 – a period of eighty-four years. Only six more years would pass, however, before the paper moved to London, to become the metropolitan paper it is known as today.

———◆◆———

1999: On this day, Moss Side's Darren Campbell helped to break the British record (37.73 seconds) for the 4x100m relay race at the World Championships in Sevilla, Spain. In 2004, his team won a gold medal in the same event at the Athens Olympics, gaining the first UK Olympic victory in this event since 1912. He is now retired from professional athletics, but helps to coach football and rugby teams, including Manchester United and the Sale Sharks.

August 30th

1783: The victorious 72nd Manchester Regiment returned from Gibraltar on this day. Loaded with pay and arrears, they were presented with an honorary 5s a piece – doubtless, the taverns did well that evening.

——— •◆• ———

1832: Twenty-two-year-old beauty Elizabeth Cleghorn Stevenson married preacher William Gaskell in Knutsford on this day, after which the couple moved to Manchester's Plymouth Grove. Mrs Gaskell became an accomplished novelist, still popular for her witty take on provincial Cheshire life in Cranford, and the socially conscious depiction of the hardships of the industrial poor in *Mary Barton* and *North and South*. She entertained many of the greatest figures in literature at her house in Plymouth Grove, including personal friend Charlotte Brontë, as well as Charles Dickens and Harriet Beecher Stowe.

——— •◆• ———

1887: Today saw the inaugural meeting of the newly named Ardwick Athletic Football Club at the Hyde Road Hotel, beside their newly obtained ground of Hyde Road. Formerly named Gorton, the team decided that a new name would better fit their new base. A further, and final, name change would bring the Manchester City of today.

AUGUST 31ST

1852: On this day, the Athenaeum played host to great novelists Sir Edward Bulwer Lytton and Charles Dickens. Among others attending were publisher Charles Knight and Mancunian bibliophile and scholar James Crossley, who were all speakers at a grand dinner held for the Guild of Literature and Art.

1877: In a rather odd turn of events, Dr Vaughan, the Bishop of Salford, held a meeting at the Manchester Aquarium today, in order to determine what exactly to do with this new acquisition. It was resolved that a caretaker management board be set up to run the place for several months and discover whether or not the place was truly in demand with the citizens. By 1877, Bishop Vaughan would bless the site in preparation for its transformation into St Bede's Roman Catholic College.

1883: On this day, Lord Carlingford opened the Manchester City Art Gallery, the new guise of the former Royal Institution in Mosley Street.

SEPTEMBER 1ST

1816: Attorney and diarist, Henry Crabb Robinson, wrote the following for his entry of this day: 'Strolling into the Old Church at Manchester, I heard a strange noise, which I should elsewhere have mistaken for the bleating of lamb. I found two rows of women standing in files, each with a babe in her arms. The minister went down the line, sprinkling each infant as he went. I suppose the efficiency of the sprinkling – I mean the fact that water did touch – was evidenced by a distinct squeal from each child. Words were muttered by the priest in his course, but one prayer served for all. This I thought to be a christening by wholesale, and I could not repress the irreverent thought that, being in the metropolis of manufactures, the aid of steam or machinery might be called in. I was told that on Sunday evenings the ceremony is repeated. Necessity is the only apology for so irreverent a performance of a religious rite.'

———— • ◆ • ————

1946: Gary Gibb, the eldest of the Gibb brothers of Bee Gee fame, was born on the Isle of Man on this day. He moved to Chorlton-cum-Hardy in 1953 (their mother Barbara being from Worsley). Barry was responsible for the signature falsetto voice that marked the Bee Gees out during their successful disco phase, and stands only behind Paul McCartney in the Guinness Book of Records as the most successful songwriter in history.

SEPTEMBER 2ND

1768: King Christian VII of Denmark paid Manchester a visit on this day. The Nordic monarch stayed at the Bull's Head Inn in the Market Place, it being the only place in town to stock wine and a good quantity of spirits.

———◆———

1774: On this day, Manchester woman Rebecca Mee was convicted of embezzling and purloining three points weight of combed wool from Mr Ottwell Kershaw. She was 'committed to the house of correction, to be kept to hard labour for fourteen days, and to be once publicly whipped at the Market Place in Manchester.' (*Mercury*)

———◆———

1852: The Manchester Free Library at Campfield opened on this day, through which the former Owenite Hall of Science carried on its role in enlightening the labouring classes. The building had been built solely on the contributions of the workers for £5,000, but further alterations and the purchase of the freehold by the Corporation added up to an outlay of a further £6,963 6s. Edward Edwards of the British Museum was the first librarian, and the total number of books it housed was 21,300, with 5,300 in the lending department.

September 3rd

1832: Following a cholera outbreak in which around 900 people died, angry workers attacked Swan Street Hospital after its doctors had, in the course of a post-mortem, severed the head of a dead boy, which his infuriated family then put on show.

1892: Ardwick Athletic FC played their first Football League match at their Hyde Road ground, only two years before their reformation as Manchester City. The match was played against Bootle, and the Mancunian side beat the Merseysiders 7-0.

1908: The 250th anniversary of Oliver Cromwell's death was commemorated today, with members of the town placing wreaths on the Cromwell monument sited on the main road by the tower of Manchester Cathedral. Many were placed there by private persons, but there were also wreaths from local campaigners for female suffrage, headed by Miss Mary Gawthorpe, 'To the honour of a statesman who, when the welfare of the commonweal was at stake, in the interests of human justice, did not hesitate to break the fetters of Parliamentary convention.' Also represented was the town's Jewish community, whose wreath was inscribed, 'As a token of thankful remembrance of the Great Protector' – it was Cromwell who had sanctioned their return to England since their expulsion by Edward I.

SEPTEMBER 4TH

1815: Joseph Budworth Palmer died on this day. Born to a Manchester publican, Joseph Budworth of the Palace Inn, he was educated at the grammar school. He joined the Manchester Volunteers, taking part in the Siege of Gibraltar, and published the romanticist *Fortnight's Rambles to the Lakes*, in which he was the first to describe the 'Beauty of Buttermere'. He married very well, to an Irish heiress whose surname he adopted, and his daughter, Emma (granddaughter of a pub landlord), became mother to a duchess.

1838: On this day, the Corn Law Association was established. The organisation that would later become the great Anti-Corn Law League was founded in a small chamber above the stables of the York Hotel on King Street, in the presence of seven parsons. Others had failed to bring a stop to the import duties that kept the price of bread unrealistically high, but this group hit on the notion of keeping the subscription fee at a low 5s, in order to keep membership open to all classes. A week from this date they had already acquired fifty members with no sign of applications slowing down. Four months later and 500 delegates would meet at its meeting in the Corn Exchange. Eventually it included some great names of Manchester industry in its rolls, before it emerged victorious in 1846.

September 5th

1739: A London paper acknowledged that the Manchester trade was, at the time, worth £30,000 a year. (*Daily Gazetteer*)

———◆◆———

1825: On this day, William Wilkinson Westhead, the 'Manchester Gigantic Boy', appeared in a freak show at Bartholomew Fair in London. At the age of fifteen, he was 5ft 2in tall, 5ft around the body, 27in across the shoulders, and weighed 22 stone. (William E.A. Axon, *Annals of Manchester*, John Heywood, Manchester, 1886)

———◆◆———

1877: The Manchester Corporation received a very fine service of plate today, to help it wow the most prestigious domestic and foreign potentates. The chronicler Axon has lovingly described the seventy-four-piece service, with his good eye for weights and diameters! The lot weighed more than 10,000oz, so Axon may be forgiven some of his hyperbole about the 15ft-long plateau and the two 3ft 4in candelabras of thirteen candles apiece. The chief interest is in the design, which combines Early English Gothic with Byzantine ornament – a fitting complement to the Romanesque and Gothic derived Town Hall itself. The service was paid for by public subscription, at the instigation of former mayor Alderman Curtis, who presented it to the Council.

SEPTEMBER 6TH

1849: On this day, blacksmith Lee killed John Richardson of Ardwick by stabbing him with two pieces of red-hot iron. A rather anachronistic death for the generally progressive tenor of the period.

------ • ◆ • ------

1876: John Ivon Mosley, compiler of the English-Manx Dictionary, died at the age of forty-six today, following several strokes. Fluent in many languages, each of which he mastered in a mere twelve months while working as a wood turner, he wandered among Armenians, Jews, Gypsies, and whoever else he could find in Manchester, and conversed with them in their native tongues. He was compiling a Romany dictionary when he died. Sadly, his efforts left no tangible memorial. (Charles Roeder, *Yn Lioar Manninagh*, Vol. 3)

------ • ◆ • ------

1968: On this day, Bradford Colliery was officially closed. Its final year had seen the production of 538,808 tons of coal, at an overall productivity rate of 31.8 cwt per manshift. One thousand five hundred employees were laid off, with half of those being offered jobs in other pits nearby. The mine had been under the control of the National Coal Board since 1947, and had had around £8 million spent on it, sinking some shafts as deep as 900yd below ground level, increasing mechanisation from 17 per cent to 98 per cent, but in the end the geology of the site proved too dangerous to carry on.

SEPTEMBER 7TH

1811: The funeral of Lieutenant-Colonel Joseph Hanson of Strangeways Hall was held today. Known as the 'Weaver's Friend', he died in prison at the age of thirty-seven. He was serving time for taking the side of the textile operatives in a dispute with their employers, and for attempting to mediate between them and the troops called out to disperse them. He had only recently appeared before Parliament to inform the MPs about the state of the textile workers, telling them that 9,000 Mancunian spinners' average wage was a mere 7s a week, with the 12,000 weavers earning 11s. (William E.A. Axon, *Annals of Manchester*, John Heywood, Manchester, 1886)

❖

1830: Ancoats weaver and amateur botanist, mineralogist, geologist and entomologist Edward Hobson died on this day. His 'humble' background could not restrain his natural talent and intellectual drive, and he wrote several remarkable scientific works, notably on the mosses of the British Isles. He died of consumption at Bowdon, and was buried at St George's Church in Hulme.

❖

1862: On this day, the Lancashire Relief Fund received £30,000 from Australia. They had sent the money in order to help relieve the suffering of the Lancashire cotton workers during the Cotton Famine (*see* July 19th).

September 8th

1664: On this day, Sir William Dugdale, Norroy King at Arms (i.e. chief herald of the North of England), held court at the King's Head in Salford, reviewing the genealogies and coats of arms claimed by the local gentry.

———◆———

1831: On this day, the coronation of William IV was celebrated. The various trades and Sunday schools marched in procession, despite the unfavourable weather, to the number of some 36,000. The day was rounded off with the customary fireworks.

———◆———

1919: The Metropolitan Vickers Electrical Company formed today, being the major heavy industry concern on Trafford Park Industrial Estate. Ship turbines, Argentine railway carriages, electrical locomotive engines and heavy duty power-station fittings kept the firm busy for many decades, so that it became the largest factory in the world, employing over 6,000 people. Further work came along with the Second World War, as Metrovicks provided ammunition and AVRO military aircraft, including the famous Lancaster Bombers.

SEPTEMBER 9TH

1779: The 72nd Regiment, composed largely of Manchester volunteers, is disbanded today. The regiment of 1,082 men were the product of Mancunian 'Loyal zeal in a foolish and unavailing attempt to coerce the American colonies' during the crisis of 1777. They were sent to defend Gibraltar instead, and John Whitaker commemorated the town's martial spirit:

> But Britain in this race of fame,
> Which of thy daughter-towns may claim,
> The greatest share of glory for the whole?
> 'Tis Manchester that claims the share,
> 'Tis Manchester re-urged the war,
> 'Tis Manchester re-awaked the British soul.

(William E.A. Axon, *Annals of Manchester*, John Heywood, Manchester, 1886)

———— • ◆ • ————

1856: On this day, the Mechanical Industrial and Fine Art Exhibition was held. It raised £4,000 to put towards the cost of a new building for the flourishing Mechanics' Institute. This would later become the Technical School, and then the Municipal College of Technology.

———— • ◆ • ————

1881: A meeting was held in the Town Hall on this day, between cotton spinners and their employers. They had come together to discuss how best to defeat the Liverpool speculators, who had been manipulating prices. All parties voted in favour of a temporary stoppage in work, in order to force the outsiders to sell their accumulated stocks.

September 10th

1641: Mancunian Roman Catholic priest, Edward Barlow, was executed at Lancaster Castle. Born in Manchester in 1585, he studied at the English seminaries of Douay in France and Valladolid in Spain. He returned to England as an undercover priest in 1617, hiding from the Protestant authorities for twenty-four years in his native Lancashire.

1887: On this day, Ardwick Athletic Football Club, now named Manchester City, were scheduled to play the inaugural match at their new Hyde Road ground. However, this was not to be, as Salford Athletic simply failed to turn up! The team would have to wait another week for the stadium to be first used. There was little in the way of facilities, it even lacked changing rooms, and players had to change over the road in the Hyde Road Hotel public house. The venue was demolished in the 1920s, after the club moved to the Maine Road ground. However, part of the old roofing structure was bought by a Yorkshire club, and is still in use at the Shay Stadium in Halifax.

September 11th

1790: Today saw the public hanging of James Macnamara on Kersal Moor. He had burgled the Dog and Partridge public house in Stretford that January.

———— • ◆ • ————

1867: On this day, Manchester Police arrested two men in Oak Street. These men were later revealed to be two Irish-Americans who had been planning a violent uprising in Ireland. They had evaded capture and travelled to England to carry on their struggle. One of the men caught was named Thomas J. Kelly, the 'Chief Executive of the Irish Republic' that the rebels would have installed in Ireland – this was quite a lucky catch for the police officers who thought they were apprehending run of the mill robbers! The rebels would later spring the two men from custody on September 18th, in an incident remembered as the 'Manchester Outrages'.

———— • ◆ • ————

1996: Bridgewater Hall opened on this day. It was to be the new home of the Hallé Orchestra. The Hallé had moved from the now outdated Free Trade Hall, and the new building more than made up for the limitations of the old. Designed by Renton Howard Wood Levin Architects, it lacks the usual steel or concrete frame of most modern buildings, instead being several connected masses of sculpted concrete. Its 22,500 ton mass sits on a bed of around 300 special earthquake-proof springs, with almost no rigid connection as such with the surroundings – improving the acoustics (*see* December 4th).

September 12th

1836: On this day, the Banksian Society (a working men's botanical association) was dissolved. Established seven years previously, it had grown out of earlier informal groups of self-taught artisans that met in public houses. It would, from this day on, be reinvented as the Natural History Class, under the aegis of the Mechanics' Institute.

1842: On this day, the River Irwell hosted the first Manchester and Salford Regatta. It was later revived on the 3rd August 1874, and, perhaps, a revival might be on the cards for the future?

1868: At this point, Manchester was still a major military town. It was reported that, 'At a review and sham fight at Heaton Park seven thousand volunteers and regulars were reviewed by Major-General Sir John Garvock.' (William E.A. Axon, *Annals of Manchester*, John Heywood, Manchester, 1886)

September 13th

1577: On this day, Manchester's Court Leet issued some stern instructions: 'No man's children or servants shall go abroad in the street nor come into any alehouse, having no lawful business, after eight o'clock in the winter and after nine o'clock in the summer time. And if any innkeeper shall hereafter sell any meat or ale to any servants or children after, he or they, the forfeiture to be leived by distraint, or else by action in the court.'

1877: In what may well have been the high point of Manchester's civic pride, this day saw the official grand opening of the new Town Hall. Mayor Abel Heywood did the honours, leading a grand procession from the old Town Hall on King Street to the new hall, flanked by locally stationed infantry and cavalry, the fire brigade and the police force, all in their finery. In Albert Square Heywood received a golden key from the Town Clerk and opened the great oak doors to a regal fanfare and rendition of 'God Save the Queen'. Naturally, a grand banquet crowned the day's work, with 400 guests in the Great Hall, including the Lord Chief Justice, Bishop of Manchester, local MPs, and many more dignitaries. From the local artisans, Mayor Heywood received a great ornamental glass goblet, carved with a likeness of the new building.

SEPTEMBER 14TH

1777: On this day, Manchester was the epicentre of a considerable earthquake, with a 70-mile radius. Thomas Henry, Fellow of the Royal Society, recorded the following; 'About five minutes before eleven o'clock, I was alarmed by a noise which seemed as if it might have proceeded from a large bale of goods thrown down on a boarded floor ... the house shook ... I cried out that a part of the house was fallen; immediately confirmed by a third and more violent crash, resembling the tumbling down of a large and lofty wall. Each of these noises was succeeded by a separate concussion. I ran to a window to my great surprise found [the building] standing. My wife informed me, that at the instant of the second explosion she had received a very smart stroke on the top of her head, and, imagining that something had fallen off a shelf, looked down on the floor and perceived it heaving under her, but could see nothing that could have given the blow. Several other persons likewise received strokes similar to electrical strokes in different parts of their bodies. Many people complained, for several days after, of nervous pain and hysteric affections, and of sensations similar to those of persons who have been strongly electrified ... a boy at Rochdale, who had been long deaf, had recovered his hearing at the instant of the earthquake.'

SEPTEMBER 15TH

1830: The Duke of Wellington opened the Manchester-Liverpool railway on this day. Tragedy struck, however, and William Huskisson, president of the Board of Trade, lost a leg under a carriage and died that night in the home of Revd Thomas Blackburne at Eccles. The first fatality in locomotive history should not eclipse an engineering achievement, however. The route's 4-mile crossing over Chat Moss presented a major dilemma; Stephenson's eventual solution was to 'float' the tracks on a firm 'raft' that spread the weight over a wide area of spongy peat. During the work rumours were spread around – 'Chat Moss was blown up!' 'Hundred of men and horses had sunk and the works were completely abandoned!' and 'Railways were at an end for ever!' (Samuel Smiles, *Life of George Stephenson*, John Murray, London, 1857; W.H. Thomson, *History of Manchester to 1852*, John Sherratt & Son Ltd, Altrincham, 1967)

———◆———

1983: On this day, the Museum of Science and Industry took up occupancy of the Liverpool Road station, on the 153rd anniversary of its opening (*see* above). The station had closed in 1975, before the Greater Manchester Council purchased it for the purpose of housing the North Western Museum of Science and Industry, which had moved from its previous temporary home of Grosvenor Street in Chorlton-on-Medlock. At the opening, the dignitaries, including the mayor, filed into the Power Hall (one of the first built exhibits at the museum) to see the great wheels spinning away.

SEPTEMBER 16TH

1623: The 1301 Town Charter, granted to the burgesses by Thomas de Gresley, Baron of Manchester, was enrolled in the records of the Chancery of Lancaster today, at the request of the then burgesses.

1753: The body of Grindrod, or Grindret, was brought from the gallows of Lancaster on this day, to be hung on the gibbet of Cross Lane in Pendleton. He had been hanged for murdering his wife and children by poisoning them. Local poet Ainsworth made this the subject of a ballad about a lost bet:

> 'Ho! Grindrod, old fellow!' thus loudly did bellow,
> The Traveller mellow, – 'How are ye, my blade?'
> 'I'm cold and I'm dreary; I'm wet and I'm weary
> But soon I'll be near ye!' the Skeleton said.
> The grisly bones rattled, and with the chains battled,
> The gibbet appallingly shook;
> On the ground something stirr'd, but no more the man heard,
> To his heels, on the instant, he took. (*Old Grindrod's Ghost*, 1855)

He was still up there at the dawn of the nineteenth century.

1797: Margaret Redmay, aged sixty-five, died on this day. She had been her husband Thomas's assistant for more than four decades – she fell to her death from the belfry of St Mary's Church's lofty steeple, in the town centre.

SEPTEMBER 17TH

1616: On this day: 'An extraordinary flood, called from the day Lambard's Flood, in which the water suddenly rose many yards plumme above the ordinary course, that men stood upon Salford Bridge, and laded up water with a little piggin. It is a easy matter with God to drowne a towne; yea, a world.' (Richard Hollinworth, *Mancuniensis, or an History of the Towne of Manchester*, 1839 (unfinished at his death in 1656))

1845: Ex-mariner John Bracewell, of Young Street, aged eighty-eight, died on this day. He was the last survivor of Admiral Rodney's men who destroyed the French fleet in the West Indies on April 12th 1782.

1884: The 'Merchant Prince' Sam Mendel died on this day. His 'reign' was abruptly cut short by bankruptcy due to the opening of the Suez Canal. An enormously wealthy importer and exporter, he lavished much of his fortune on his palatial Manley Hall at Whalley Range, which he filled with many a work of art, and cultivated fine orchids. He was eventually forced to sell off almost everything he owned when his trading empire collapsed.

2010: With the ending of its only rival, the US soap *As the World Turns*, Manchester-made *Coronation Street* broke the official Guinness World Record and became the world's longest-running soap opera. William Roache ('Ken Barlow') simultaneously became the actor to have played the longest ever role in a soap. (*The Stage*, September 24th 2010)

SEPTEMBER 18TH

1565: Today witnessed the humble beginnings of worldwide export, Manchester Cottons. The company is listed among the inventory of a merchant's ship in the Port of Bristol.

1836: The Manchester Musical Festival and Fancy Dress Ball held on this day raised £4,320 for good causes. The performance was to prove fatal for one specially invited virtuoso, however (*see* September 23rd).

1867: On this day, Police Sergeant Brett was killed at the 'Manchester Outrages. Members of the Irish Republican Brotherhood attempted to jailbreak their comrades from a police van under a railway arch on Hyde Road, in between the courthouse and Belle Vue Prison. Brett was the first Manchester police officer to have been killed while on duty, and is remembered in a memorial inside St Ann's Church in the city centre. Two American Civil War veterans and IRB conspirators were being transported to Belle Vue, along with four other prisoners (a twelve-year-old boy and three female felons) as well as the ill-fated Brett who had the keys. A thirty-to-forty strong gang with firearms fell upon the unarmed police escort, who fled for help. Crowbars proved of little avail, and Brett steadfastly refused to open the door. As a result, one individual fired a pistol into the lock, just as Brett was peering through the keyhole – he was killed instantly. Kelly and Deasy escaped to America via Liverpool, but twenty-six men would soon stand trial (*see* October 29th).

September 19th

1356: The tenth Baron of Manchester, Roger la Warre, fought and won honour at the Battle of Poitiers on this day. Grandson of the la Warre who had borne the crest of Manchester at Sluys and Crécy, Roger was himself a great medieval warrior, and along with several other English knights he accepted the surrender of Jean II, the King of France. Roger died in 1370, leaving two sons and a daughter. The la Warre line ended with his sons, and so Manchester passed to his heirs in the female line, the Wests.

1818: Former gunner for the 72nd Regiment of Manchester Volunteers, Henry Jones, died on this day. He had so distinguished himself by his daring at the Siege of Gibraltar that he was afterwards styled 'Harry the Devil'. (William E.A. Axon, *Annals of Manchester*, John Heywood, Manchester, 1886)

1841: On this day, Governor General of Canada, Lord Sydenham, died. He had previously been known as Charles Poulett Thomson, twice elected MP for Manchester.

September 20th

1573: On this day, the manorial Court Leet ordered that 'Neither butcher, nor any other person, shall not from henceforth cast any cow-bag, or belly of any kind of beast, upon any dunghill or other place within the town, to be noisome to any person; [fine] 3s 4d.' The jury presented eight 'notorious' women who were 'forbidden in the town', one of whom was Margaret Warren, otherwise called 'Mag o' Dents'.

———— ◆ ————

1869: John Jennison died at the age of eighty on this day. Many generations of Mancunians have him to thank for the city's premier pleasure ground – Belle Vue Gardens. He had opened the gardens in 1836, overcoming many difficulties to see it expand and improve to the extent that many visited it, some from several counties away. An aunt informs me that a rashly entered into 'mystery trip' from Blackpool, took her all the way back home to Manchester for one day of her seaside holiday, with Belle Vue as the destination!

———— ◆ ————

2009: Today was witness to an astounding Manchester derby match, which United won 4–3. Even the notoriously laconic Ferguson didn't hold back, saying 'Probably the best derby of all time.' Five minutes of extra time saw the two teams still neck and neck at 3–3, only for Michael Owen to tip the balance in favour of the Reds.

September 21st

1584: Today was the start of Acres or 'Ackers' Fair, one of the town's older annual festive occasions, and somebody seems to have taken the opportunity for a settling of scores. As the Court Leet stated, 'It is presented to the jury that upon St Matthew's day being the fair day, there was an assault made and weapon drawn within the church-yard ... there was a brawl made, and blood drawn, upon the watchmen.' The court saved its greater wrath for its own constables, who were deemed 'negligent in doing their duty' by not bringing the concerned parties to the jury.

———◆———

1787: On this day, the Bishop of Chester consecrated a new burial ground in Ashley Lane. The interred came to be laid in anonymity under easily removed stone flags. After its closing in 1816, these became known as St Michael's Flags, and their nature was forgotten about by the following generations.

———◆———

1972: Liam Gallagher, Oasis vocalist, was born in Burnage on this day. A City supporter and no stranger to controversy, he has stated opinions such as 'All Spanish girls have moustaches', and the odd little quip about Bono or Robbie Williams have made him a tabloid favourite.

SEPTEMBER 22ND

1808: A servant woman who had poisoned herself was buried at New Cross this day. At this time, suicides were still buried in such un-consecrated places as this. Later, road works at the crossroads rediscovered her body and those of others similarly interred there.

———◆———

1874: The great Manchester poet Charles Swain died today. According to Hawthorne, Swain's works were even well known in the USA. Southey's famous appreciation of him was that 'if Manchester is not yet proud of him, she will be'. He was buried at Prestwich. (William E.A. Axon, *Annals of Manchester*, John Heywood, Manchester, 1886)

———◆———

1909: Alongside three comrades, militant Manchester suffragette Mary Leigh was in Birmingham on this day. It was here that the women were prevented from attending a meeting at which Herbert Asquith was speaking. As a result, the women scaled the building and set about smashing up the roof with an axe, and flinging the broken slates at the helpless policemen below. It took three policemen to bring Mary down. Imprisoned, she began a hunger strike, ending up undergoing the painful and humiliating treatment of being force-fed through a nasal tube.

SEPTEMBER 23RD

1836: World-famous vocalist, Madame Maria Felicita Garcia Malibran de Beriot died in Manchester today. It is reported that she died from over exertion singing at the Theatre Royal during the recent Musical Festival. Born in Paris to a Spanish tenor, Manuel Garcia, she had lived an exciting life, marrying the elderly Monsieur Malibran in America, and then the Belgian violinist de Beriot. Her remains were laid to rest in the Collegiate Church on October 1st, before being transferred for re-burial in Brussels on January 4th.

———◆———

1870: The Duke of Devonshire laid the foundation stone of the Owens College on this day. The building is still in use by the present university and was designed by Alfred Waterhouse, who also built the Town Hall. The impressive complex cost some £90,000, and the enlarged college would now be able to admit 600 day students.

———◆———

1993: The International Olympic Committee met at Monte Carlo to determine the winning bid for the 2000 Summer Olympics on this day. Beijing and Sydney were the favourites, but also competing were Berlin, Istanbul, and Manchester. The spotlight was on IOC President Juan Antonio Saramanch as he selected Sydney. Although the town lost out to Sydney, Manchester got on with holding the 2002 Commonwealth Games, and the regeneration project of Sport City went ahead regardless.

September 24th

1831: The Manchester Socialists met on this day, for what would be a week-long conference. The 500 delegates adopted Owen's plans for labour exchanges and Co-operative societies.

◆

1838: A great Chartist meeting was held today on Kersal Moor. Leaders Fergus O'Connor MP and Revd James Rayner Stephens spoke to a crowd of more than 300,000 people. The purpose was to demand the acceptance by the government of their Charter of Six Points: universal male suffrage, no property qualification for MPs, paid MPs, equal constituencies, secret ballots and annual parliaments. The assembly elected Bronterre O'Brien as its delegate for the forthcoming London Convention of the following year. Meanwhile, politically active middle-class Mancunians met at the York Hotel to discuss the formation of the Anti-Corn Law League. The differing fortunes of the two movements would be an enlightening experience, despite the crushing disappointment that it brought to the working classes.

◆

1873: The Athenaeum on Bond Street suffered a disastrous fire, which caused £12,000 worth of damage on this day. As a result, the prominent club for lovers of high culture required a complete refurbishment, and its patrons soon saw it restored to its rightful condition as a symbol of Manchester's aspirations to be seen as much more than merely a mill town (*see* January 22nd 1875).

September 25th

923: 'After Harvest' King Eadweard of the West Saxons expelled the Danes from Mameçestre, refortifying the burh and bringing it under the authority of Mercia. Manchester is thus found in the Mercian Diocese of Lichfield until the 1530s, and thenceforth that of Chester until the Victorian period.

———— • ————

1642: The Siege of Manchester began on this day. The Mosleys of Aldport Lodge invited Lord Strange (scion of the Earls of Derby) to set up his headquarters for the Royalist cause in Castlefield. Puritan Warden Heyrick engaged the services of the German military engineer Colonel Roswurm, with a contract of £30 for six months. Roswurm erected barricades and earthworks at the several entrances to the town, and placed chains and posts across Salford Bridge and Deansgate, which served their purpose well. However, he had a hard time obtaining his fee, later terming his miserly employers as 'despicable earthworms'. Lord Strange's forces of 4,000 infantry and 200 horses meanwhile, took up their positions in Salford and Aldport, resulting in Roswurm's musketeers repulsing an evening assault across the Salford Bridge.

———— • ————

1838: Today saw the last races to take place at Heaton Park. The Earl of Wilton won the Manchester Cup, and the race for the Heaton Park Stakes was remarkable for the falls of Harkaway and Cruikseen.

SEPTEMBER 26TH

1763: Doctor John Byrom, aged seventy-two, died on this day. He was the inventor of the predecessor to Pitman's shorthand, Jacobite, man of letters and Manchester's greatest wit. A Fellow of Trinity College Cambridge, he refused a clergyman's career and returned home to marry his cousin Elizabeth, against the consent of both families. He left for London to teach shorthand (then a top secret code) for which he was made a Fellow of the Royal Society. He returned home to inherit his brother's a comfortable fortune. The best impression of the man may be taken from his satirical but good-humoured verses:

> God bless the king! – I mean our faith's defender.
> God bless – no harm in blessing – the Pretender!
> But who Pretender is, or who is king,
> God bless us all! That's quite another thing.

———— • ◆ • ————

1788: The Manchester Literary and Philosophical Society member, George Walker, investigated the town's first foray into artificial power today. Erected by Arkwright several years previously, this 'fire engine' or 'steam engine' was used to raise water at Shudehill to power a cotton mill's waterwheel. Its attendant, Mr Barton, proudly informed the learned gentleman that it raised 64 gallons of water 7ft 9in, eleven times a minute, powered by five tons of coal a day. (*Manchester Guardian*)

September 27th

1642: On this day, the Royalist forces of Lord Strange continued their siege of the town. He ordered his cannons to be placed in Deansgate, but seemed reluctant to use full force, perhaps hoping merely to frighten the townsfolk into surrendering. According to England's Parliamentary Chronicle, the Puritan defenders had 'but one small peece' of artillery, but nevertheless managed to burn Aldport Lodge to the ground. Manchester was held by 'the honest-hearted and most courageous Manchesterians; the principal men in the kingdom, next to the most famous and renowned citie of London, that fight most prosperously for God and true religion, Had not this town stood firmly to the king and Parliament, the whole country would have been brought into subjection to the oppression and violence of the cavaliers.' (W.H. Thomson, *History of Manchester to 1852*, John Sherratt & Son Ltd, Altrincham, 1967)

———◆———

1861: On this day, it was noted that 43,500 people were receiving poor relief throughout the parish. The following week would see the cotton mills running 'short time'.

———◆———

1976: Children's animated series *Chorlton and the Wheelies*, was aired for the first time on this day. It was produced at the Cosgrove Hall studios at Chorlton-cum-Hardy and captured the hearts of a generation. This was the first series produced by the company, and the renowned *Wind in the Willows*, *Dangermouse* and *Count Duckula* would soon follow to earn a worldwide following.

SEPTEMBER 28TH

1784: On this day, Sir John Parker Mosley presided over the Committee for Sunday Schools at its first meeting at the Bull's Head Tavern in the Market Place. Though Anglicans, Catholics, and Dissenters were all represented, there were no sectarian disputes for sixteen years. This ecumenical model was soon copied in many other towns.

1838: On this day, at a meeting of the Chartists on Kersal Moor, Revd James Raynor Stephens summed up what the Charter meant to him: 'I want to see the working man as free in the mill as when he goes into the wilderness – as free spoken when he goes for his wages as he is when he spends a part of it with his companion. I want to see every man so free as to speak his mind, act according to his conscience and do no one any injury … I shall support [the resolution] with heart and soul, so far as I can, and as far as you can with me if you acted the same way, and we shall ultimately carry the Charter.' (*Northern Star*)

1894: Simon Marks and Tom Spencer opened their first joint enterprise today – the Penny Bazaar on Deansgate.

SEPTEMBER 29TH

1642: On this day, Lord Strange was informed of his father's death and inherited his title, becoming the Earl of Derby. Also fighting for the King, Captain Standish of Duxbury was killed by a sniper bullet in Serjeant (now Chapel) Street in Salford at the house of Robert Widdow, whereupon his soldiers fled.

———— • ———— • ————

1645: A plague victim was buried on this day at Mayfield, Moss Side, under the epitaph, 'Here lyeth the body of Margery Beswicke, wife of Hugh Beswicke of Hulme, who departed this life the 29th of September 1645.' The parish register mentioned other victims buried out of town, some in Collyhurst and others at George Street in Hulme, where 'Human remains were there dug up in the summer of last year (1872)'. (Richard Wright Procter, *Memorials of Manchester Streets*, T. Sutcliffe, Manchester, 1874)

———— • ———— • ————

1942: Ian McShane, most well known for his portrayal of the character 'Lovejoy', was born on this day. He also played 'Blackbeard' in the 2010 instalment of the *Pirates of the Caribbean* saga, and voiced the baddie in *Kung Fu Panda*. In 2012 he was set to play the king in a new adaptation of the ancient English folktale *Jack the Giant Killer* folktale. Born in Blackburn, he grew up in Urmston and attended Stretford Grammar.

September 30th

1642: On this day, as the bombardment of Manchester continued, the Royalist forces besieging the town finally raised the siege to regroup with the King's army at Shrewsbury. Defending losses amount to one man killed in action, another in an accident with his gun, and a small boy who had sat on a nearby style to watch the struggle. It had been a short siege, with a hesitant attacker 'Resembling a needle between two magnets'. (Procter) A Cromwellite chronicler made wry fun of the affair: 'There was little harvest weather that week, it was not reaping work, but threshing work.' No further attempts were made on the town throughout the remainder of the war. (W.H. Thomson, *History of Manchester to 1852*, John Sherratt & Son Ltd, Altrincham, 1967)

* ◆ *

1712: Edmund Harrold, wigmaker cum book dealer and diarist, wrote for today's entry on the difficulties of being a Manchester alcoholic, during a period when taverns were plenty, and yet keep his religion:

> O God that I may remember
> That I've both displeased and pleased thee this September
> And give grace this October
> To me to keep sober.

* ◆ *

1809: Today saw the release of the first issue of the Manchester *Exchange Herald*, which was printed and published by Joseph Aston. It marked the opening of the Second Exchange.

OCTOBER 1ST

Year? On this day, until the October 3rd, the Ackers Fair was held. Among the curious medieval traditions of this annual event, the fair was opened each day with the whipping of a pig.

———— • ◆ • ————

1823: The Royal Manchester Institution was founded on this day. This body promoting literature, science and the arts was the brainchild of auctioneer Thomas Dodd, and would later occupy a £30,000 building on Mosley Street, which now houses the City Art Gallery. This day in history is clearly one auspicious to the foundation of new institutions, with the School of Anatomy opening in 1815 and the School of Design opening in 1838, on the same date.

———— • ◆ • ————

1893: On this day, Manchester's 'Sherlock Holmes', Detective Superintendent Jerome Caminada, tackled the Anarchists who had been making a nuisance by holding meetings on Ardwick Green (instead of at Stevenson Square, where the police had requested they relocate themselves). Caminada's hat was knocked off by the young rebel Barton, whereupon he laid about him with his umbrella, which was later commemorated in the song 'The Scamp Who Broke his Gamp at Ardwick Green':

> Caminada showed his valour by knocking people down,
> And using his gamp well, Good citizens to fell.
> He collared all the Anarchists, and marched them through the town,
> And put them in the Fairfield station cell.

(radicalmanchester.wordpress.com)

OCTOBER 2ND

1555: On this day, Skevengers were appointed to sweep and keep clean parts of the town. These included: 'Market Stede Lane, Deansgate, St Mary's Gate, the Old Market Stede from the Booths to the Smithy Door, from Hunt's Bank to the house now or late in the holding of John Curtenhall, the Hanging Ditch and the Meale-gate, the Mylnegate, and the Market Place.'

———•◆•———

1566: The Court Leet decreed on this day, that 'Every person shall keep their swine in the night time in some lawful swine-cote, so that in no wise the same swine do not go abroad in the night, or lie in the Church-yard at any time hereafter, 4*d*.'

———•◆•———

1820: Today saw the last Ackers or Acres Fair at St Ann's Place before its removal to the new marketplace at Shudehill in 1821. (William E.A. Axon, *Annals of Manchester*, John Heywood, Manchester, 1886)

———•◆•———

1871: On this day, the new Royal Exchange opened for the first time. The third such building of its purpose in Manchester, it was 4,405 sq yd. The previous Exchange covered only 1,634 sq yd, while the first Exchange's main hall had measured a mere 452. The Cross Street façade of the new edifice had originally been graced with a highly elaborate eight-columned Corinthian portico.

OCTOBER 3RD

1818: Salford bank's New Bailey Prison received a visit today from prison reformer Mrs Fry, who is lately celebrated on the £5 note.

* * *

1843: George William Wood, MP for Kendal and vice-president of the Manchester Literary and Philosophical Society, died on this day. He had rendered many services to the town, most particularly drawing up the bill almost single-handedly which provided the town with two MPs in 1832, as well as being the initiator behind the establishment of the Savings Bank, Royal Institution, and the modernisation of the town's main thoroughfare, Market Street.

* * *

1885: On this day, Gorton FC, progenitor of the modern Manchester City, played their first game at the Reddish Lane Bull's Head ground. Playing Earlestown, they drew 1–1. The equaliser was scored by Lawrence Furniss, the man who would later become the manager/secretary, then chairman of the club in the 1920s. He would ultimately initiate the club's move to Maine Road.

* * *

1885: To mark the passing of the Ship Canal Act, Manchester's Trades and Friendly Societies held a great parade on this day. Jubilant demonstrations were held at Belle Vue Gardens and Alexandra Park, which were deemed 'large and enthusiastic' in spite of the rain.

OCTOBER 4TH

1552: The oldest preserved Court Leet proceedings originate from today: 'The jury order that Thomas Jonson shall make a pale or wall of stone for a defence, that his dunghill not stop the course of water in the ditch between the said Thomas and Richard Hunte and Francis Pendilton ... sub pena, 6s 8d.' It also went on to state that, 'No persons hereafter shall suffer their geese or ducks to be put in the Market Stede upon pain of every one so offending, for every goose or duck 1d.'

———— • ◆ • ————

1890: Today witnessed the last ever service in the dilapidated St Mary's Church in Deansgate. Dating from 1753, the church was now so neglected that, in the middle of his reading, the minister discovered that the Bible was missing a page and had to pause while another was found. As the town's tallest church (180ft in height), it had been a curious sight, topped by a lantern of eight Ionic columns, a spire, and finally a globe and cross. After a particularly strong gale, the last two were bent almost perpendicular, and were left in that state for several years.

———— • ◆ • ————

1993: Mike Pickering's house music ensemble M People released their second album on this day. It would spend a phenomenal eighty-seven weeks in the album charts, later re-entering it three times in 1996-7. The album, titled Elegant Slumming, won the Mercury Prize, with four tracks making the Top Ten in their own right.

OCTOBER 5TH

1592: The people of Manchester were being too lax observing days of Fast, so, on this day, the Court Leet set a fine of 10*s* for every householder caught eating meat, or even dressing it, within the township on a Fast day.

⬧

1852: On this day, the Corn Exchange hosted a meeting of the Friends of the Irish Church Missions to the Roman Catholics. They discussed attempts to wean the troublesome Gaels off their inexplicable attachment to Popery.

⬧

1905: John Edward Taylor, proprietor of the *Manchester Guardian* and son of its founder and first editor, died on this day. His ownership saw the twice-weekly paper become a daily publication, halving its price to 1*d*. He had also played a part in the 1868 establishment of the present-day *Manchester Evening News*. A supporter of the Owens Institute, the Manchester Education Aid Society, and the Temperance Movement, he declined a baronetcy offered by Lord Roseberry, insisting upon the full independence of the press. The way was now clear for Charles Prestwich Scott to buy the paper, and thus become both editor and owner. Having been editor since 1872, Scott's ethos permeated the paper: 'Comment is free, but facts are sacred. The voice of opponents no less than that of friends has a right to be heard.'

OCTOBER 6TH

1578: On this day, the Court Leet ordered that, 'Every person shall from henceforth wear caps upon the Sabbath Day, according to the statute in that cause provided, upon pain of such forfeiture as [is] in the same statute contained; and we make officers for to see the same executed, John Shawe and James Smithe.'

* * *

1899: After almost a decade of work on its cathedral-like building, John Rylands Library on Deansgate was formally dedicated to the public on this day. The brainchild of John's Cuban-born widow Enriqueta, the library is her monument to her husband, Manchester's first multi-millionaire. It contained 70,000 books and less than a hundred manuscripts at this date (a small fraction of its present globally significant collections). The library was the first in Manchester to have been specifically designed with electric lighting in mind, but its lights have a very peculiarly shaped bulb specific to the building. Thankfully, their longevity has ensured that the batch manufactured in 1900 are still in working order!

* * *

1966: Dove Stone Dam was completed on this day. The last British dam to be built with a traditional clay core inside the concrete and stone facings, it is 38m high and 550m across, with a volume of 34,000 cubic metres.

OCTOBER 7TH

1661: On this day, 582 citizens of Manchester were recorded, by name, as swearing an Oath of Allegiance to the newly restored Crown.

———◆———

1828: The first ever Manchester Musical Festival was held on this day. A rather more elite affair than those of more recent times, the season of 'general and delightful relaxation' collected the princely sum of £5,000 for charity, £2,500 of which was presented to the Infirmary. The week-long event was hosted in the Theatre Royal on Fountain Street, with the main performance being held in the wide nave of the Collegiate Church. (W.H. Thomson, *History of Manchester to 1852*, John Sherratt & Son Ltd, Altrincham, 1967)

———◆———

1840: On this day, the young Queen Victoria was presented with a full cartload of petitions from Manchester, begging her not to prorogue Parliament without considering first the distress of the people.

OCTOBER 8TH

1856: Today saw the grand opening of the Free Trade Hall. Free Trade – the abolition of all state-sponsored obstructions to the free movement of goods across all borders – had long been synonymous with the town's 'Manchester School' of thought. The hall stands as a permanent reminder of the great successes achieved, especially the repeal of the Corn Laws that had robbed many of a cheap crust in times of hardship. Costing £40,000, it replaced a wooden structure, which had been erected in 1843. Designed by Edward Walters, architectural historians have praised the Cinquecento architecture as a 'Classic which belongs in the canon of historic English architecture.' Declared a Grade II listed building in 1963, it is now a 263-bedroom hotel. (John J. Parkinson-Bailey, *Manchester: An Architectural History*, Manchester University Press, 2000)

1921: On this day, King George V inaugurated the extension of the Royal Exchange, which had been opened by his grandmother seventy years before. The directors of this great centre of Manchester trade read out a list of statistics to impress upon His Majesty the might of the Exchange in their official address, stressing its great size – the Great Hall being the largest then existing at 8,000 square yards – and the numbers of firms active – 12,000 members and 2,000 firms; some £300 million of invested capital in all. The King expressed his hopes that the opening might prove a stimulus to trade in that time of high post-war unemployment. (*London Gazette*)

OCTOBER 9TH

1770: Today's *Manchester Magazine* reported that, 'The inhabitants of this town are desired to take notice, that the old engines for extinguishing fires are at the Lodge in the Old Churchyard, and in the Engine House, Tib Lane, as heretofore.' It also reported that, 'Others at St John's, St Mary's, the Market Place, High Street and Milngate are kept in constant readiness; and the constables beg this opportunity of requesting all manner of persons to be most careful in preventing the necessity of using them.'

———◆———

1779: Serious riots broke out in Manchester on this day. The traditional cotton spinners' anger at increasing mechanisation erupted into a violent Luddite frenzy. It was all in vain, however, for Samuel Crompton of Bolton was then perfecting the Mule, to render hand-spinning fully obsolete.

———◆———

1818: Matthew Laycock, the Manchester to Skipton carrier, died of rabies on this day. Blackwood's *Edinburgh Magazine* reported that, on his journey, 'He was bit by a dog supposed to be mad, on which he took the medicine, but when returning, strong symptoms of the hydrophobia appeared. On the Friday following, he expressed a fear of the returning malady, and wished to see his children; they were brought to him, he gave each of them a kiss, and very soon after, the malady returned, and he died the same day in the greatest agony, barking like a dog.' (*Edinburgh Magazine*)

OCTOBER 10TH

1851: On this day, Queen Victoria and Albert, accompanied by the Duke of Wellington, visited Manchester. Eighty-two thousand Sunday school children and the patients of the Infirmary greeted them. The weather held out remarkably, and Queen Victoria sailed up the Irwell in a Royal Barge, arriving to church bells, military bands and children's choirs. At the reception in the Exchange, the mayor was knighted Sir John Potter. The Queen noted that 'The order and good behaviour of the people, were the most complete we have seen in our many progresses through capitals and cities ... everyone says that in no other town could one depend so entirely upon the quiet and orderly behaviour of the people.' (W.H. Thomson, *History of Manchester to 1852*, John Sherratt & Son Ltd, Altrincham, 1967; Richard Wright Procter, *Memorials of Manchester Streets*, T. Sutcliffe, Manchester, 1874)

—— • ◆ • ——

1901: Edward Onslow Ford's monument to Queen Victoria was unveiled on this day, five months after her death and two before that of the sculptor. The ceremony was presided over by Lord Roberts, commander-in-chief of the army, but the positioning of the stands was such that a disorderly crush resulted, and many 'privileged citizens' were obliged to climb the railings of the Infirmary. The *Manchester Evening News* reassured readers that, 'The people packed behind the barrier were men of a distinctly rough type, who could well withstand the many rude buffetings they were necessarily subject to.' (Terry Wyke and Harry Cocks, *Public Sculpture of Greater Manchester*, Liverpool University Press, 2003)

OCTOBER 11TH

1852: Queen Victoria, Albert, Prince Edward and party were greeted on this morning at Worsley Hall. A deputation from the workmen's singing classes of Manchester, as well as a further contingent of 1,400 children were there to sing the anthem and cheer the monarch. The excitement continued after the visitors' departure for Windsor, with auctions of the decorations and a grand ball two days later at the Exchange, which received its modern Sobriquet of 'Royal' soon afterwards, in honour of the day.

———•◆•———

1853: Future Prime Minister William Ewert Gladstone, then Chancellor of the Exchequer, visited Manchester on this day.

———•◆•———

2010: Mancunian Jewish novelist Howard Jacobson won the coveted Man Booker Prize on this night, for his comic novel *The Finkler Question*. Despite his long career in literature (he was sixty-eight at the time), this was the first time he had even been nominated. The author joked afterwards that the £50,000 prize might just about cover the price of a new handbag for his wife. (*Guardian*)

OCTOBER 12TH

1840: Claiming to possess the 'gift of tongues', Mormon Elder James Mahon was tested today in Manchester. He failed to understand a word of a Hebrew text, with his own supposed 'Hebrew' determined by an expert to be gobbledegook. Thomas Taylor of the town later published the withering *Account of the Complete Failure of an Ordained Priest of the 'Latter Day Saints' to Establish his Pretension to the Gift of Tongues*, which prompted a battle of polemics with the sect.

1865: Mancunian chemist Sir Arthur Harden was born on this day. Graduating from Owens College and winning the Dalton Scholarship, he received his 1929 Nobel Prize for chemistry, for the fermentation of sugars and the biochemistry of yeast. Knighted in 1926, Harden had played an important role in the British Institute of Preventive Medicine.

1885: On this day, Rochdale Road's Free Library opened a reading-room for boys – girls would have to wait.

2000: Her Majesty the Queen opened the striking new Lowry today. It would become a flagship centrepiece to the redevelopment of the city's old docks, soon to be joined by the Imperial War Museum North (*see* July 5th). Named after the renowned local artist, it holds a permanent exhibition of his work, but also serves as a theatre and venue for other cultural activities. £106 million was invested into the project, a quarter coming from the Lottery fund.

OCTOBER 13TH

1245: On this day, King Henry III gave twenty deer to his loyal vassal Lord Grelley of Manchester. Hunt's Bank may preserve the memory of an old deer park adjoining the residence of the lord in his manor house in the present day Chetham's Library.

— ◆ —

1857: Manchester's answer to London's Great Exhibition, The Art Treasures of Great Britain, celebrated its highest daily attendance today – an astronomical 30,000 people. Crowded into the glass and steel exhibition hall, on occasion the crush was such that the police had to be called in to preserve order. One of the artworks still shown bears a permanent reminder of this great event – a recently identified Michelangelo of the Virgin and Child became known as the 'Manchester Madonna'. Having gathered together an orchestra to play for Prince Albert's opening ceremony, Charles Hallé decided to keep this group of musicians together, as it has remained ever since. American author Nathaniel Hawthorne wrote that 'There John Bull and his female may be seen in full gulp and guzzle, swallowing vast quantities of cold boiled beef, thoroughly moistened with porter or bitter.' (William E.A. Axon, *Annals of Manchester*, John Heywood, Manchester, 1886)

— ◆ —

1894: On this day, four years after construction began, the Cumbrian reservoir at Thirlmere sent its first supplies of drinking water down the 100-mile aqueduct to Manchester.

OCTOBER 14TH

1863: On this day, Owen recognised Roman mortar in the base of the tower of the parish church, then undergoing replacement. Workers, impressed with the hardness of it and its peculiar composition, took bits as curiosities and the rest was reinterred into the new walls. Parts of mullions, walls and door jambs of apparent fourteenth-century work also unearthed, all from the old church that had preceded the Warden Huntington's 1400s refurbishment.

1881: On this day, a terrible storm brought torrential rains, causing the River Irwell to rise 15ft, flooding the cellars of Lower Broughton (some of which were still, at this time, people's homes).

1965: Comedian Steve Coogan was born in Middleton on this day, and thereby such Mancunian (anti-)icons as the foul-mouthed Paul Calf and his loose-moralled sister Pauline, and Alan Partridge. Starting out in stand-up, Coogan did voices for *Spitting Image*, and eventually became a well-known television comic. He has appeared in numerous films, some concerning his native Manchester such as his first big screen appearance in *The Parole Officer*, or the more serious *24 Hour Party People* in which he played Tony Wilson in a film chronicle of the Madchester period. Recent years have seen him in Hollywood blockbusters, most notably playing Phileas Fog in Disney's *Around the World in 80 Days*.

OCTOBER 15TH

1651: James, 'the Great Stanley', Earl of Derby was beheaded in Bolton on this day. At the very time of inheriting his father's title, James had been besieging Manchester to seize its munitions for the King. After failing to take Manchester for the Royalists, the earl made various attempts to retake Lancashire for the King, including the notorious Bolton Massacre of May 28th 1644, a sudden night-time attack on the town in which almost 2,000 defenders and innocents perished in the chaos. Convicted at Chester for aiding the King against his own people, Derby was taken to the scene of the massacre and beheaded by the market cross.

2011: The Manchester Quakers held a silent protest on this day. An often-overlooked community, they had a Central Manchester meeting house right on Mount Street facing the Central Library. Taking advantage of their prominent positioning within the town, they mounted the silent protest against growing economic inequality. According to their leaflet; '[We] are Quakers [and] say that everyone suffers when we have millionaires on the one hand and homeless have-nots on the other ... More equal countries have better health, less stress, less violence, more contentment'. Quakers had long played a role in philanthropy in the town, as well as in such fields as science and education, as in the case of their most prominent Mancunian, John Dalton (*see* October 31st).

OCTOBER 16TH

1824: An iron beam fell from its place today at Nathan Gough's factory on Oldfield Lane, killing nineteen millworkers and injuring nineteen others.

———◆———

1838: On this day, a flash flood threatened to tear down the unfinished centres of the arch of the new Victoria Bridge. Its builder did his utmost to save the centres, breaking his leg in the process.

———◆———

1943: Hyde Road, home of Manchester City's previous incarnation Ardwick Athletic FC, was home to a wartime international between England and Scotland on this day. The Jocks were hammered 8–0.

OCTOBER 17TH

1857: On this day, Manchester, England, and quite possibly the world's largest art exhibition ever held, The Art Treasures of Great Britain, closed. The exhibition had been held in a specially constructed temporary Crystal-Palace-style glass and steel venue at Old Trafford. In the 142 days it had been open, more than 1.3 million visitors (four times the population of the city) had inspected the incredible 16,272 artworks on display – it was estimated to be one third of all the artworks found in the country at the time. Queen Victoria and Albert opened the event, which was visited by Charles Dickens, Nathaniel Hawthorne, Napoleon III, and Disraeli too, but the most novel of visitors were the coach-loads of millworkers paying a shilling a piece to view Old Masters and listen to the symphonies of Mr Hallé's orchestra. Coming only four years after Manchester's official elevation to the rank of 'city', the event well and truly put the city on the cultural map of the world. The costs of putting up the pavilion amounted to a huge £25,000 (a ten-figure sum in modern terms) but, amazingly, a profit of £304 was made, thanks to the record-breaking admissions.

OCTOBER 18TH

1746: Reverend Thomas Cappock, was hanged, drawn and quartered for high treason on this day. A Manchester preacher, he had followed Bonnie Prince Charlie up to the border, where the Young Chevalier made him 'Bishop of Carlisle'. Educated at Manchester's free grammar school, he was tried whilst wearing his gown and cassock, in his 'Diocese'. In his final speech, he asked, 'And could it be engraven on my tombstone: Underneath are deposited the ashes of the only English Protestant clergyman whose honour, courage, loyalty and zeal are conspicuous in his royal master's cause. *Dulce et decorum est pro patria mori* (It is a sweet and prober thing to die for one's country)'. (jacobite.ca)

1872: Radical writer Elijah Ridings died at the age of seventy on this day. The tenth of fifteen children, he knew early nineteenth-century poverty well, and took part in much political activity, including the Peterloo Massacre. His works include *The Village Muse* and *Streams from an Old Fountain*. The *Manchester Literary Times* described him as, 'One of the Lancashire poets who had made for themselves a wide celebrity as self educated poets. Ridings has always been true to the rational political opinions which he early commenced his career.'

1893: On this day, Manchester College at Oxford was founded. In 1786, it had been opened in Manchester by Dissenters, but had later moved to York, back to Manchester, then to London, before finally settling for good in Oxford.

OCTOBER 19TH

1746: On this day, a celebration was held in honour of the victories of the House of Hannover over the Jacobites and Bonnie Prince Charlie.

———◆———

1839: Pendleton-born engraver, printer and Quaker George Bradshaw published his groundbreaking *Bradshaw's Railway Timetables and Assistant to Railway Travelling* on this day. It included train fares and travel descriptions to help the Victorian traveller negotiate the labyrinth of different rail companies and timetables of the time. *Punch* magazine did not hold back in its praise, stating, 'Seldom has the gigantic intellect of man been employed upon a work of greater utility.' Bradshaw's works remained relevant well into the twentieth century, and set the standard for much longer, with 1,521 editions of the guide being released. They have recently been celebrated in a television series devoted to the way in which they opened up the country.

———◆———

1871: The Reform Club on King Street opened this day. Two hundred and forty gentlemen were served dinner at the clubhouse, with many more attending a banquet in the club's honour in the Free Trade Hall, including several of the higher nobility, parliamentarians and regional men of influence. An attractive Victorian building in the Venetian Gothic style, its façade holds several allegorical sculpted figures, including architecture, the arts, and weaving. The building itself was the work of the local architectural firm Salomons and Jones.

OCTOBER 20TH

1561: On this day, the Court Leet spoke out against pollution and fly tipping: 'No manner of persons shall not from henceforth cast any dung, filth or muck upon or over the Hanging Bridge', as well as 'The jury presents one Joane Marler, spinster, and Elizabeth Lorde, that they two came to the house of George Proudlove in the Denis-gate, and there did take away certain chippes without license, contrary to honesty, civil order, and to the evil ensample of all good people. We order, therefore, that the said Joan and Elizabeth shall have condign punishment for the same, at the discretion of the Mr Steward [Edward, Earl of Derby, presiding]; after which punishment the said persons shall kneel down, knowledge their fault, and ask mercy at God's hands and the said George.'

———◆———

1694: Today saw the Manchester Sessions House deal with a high-profile trial – that of Sir Roland Stanley and Sir Thomas Clifton, on charges of high treason. Two of the most illustrious families in the North being so represented implied a 'Lancashire Plot' of serious scale. The witnesses, however, were found to have committed perjury and the accused were acquitted, though a bad taste was left in the mouths of the local gentry about the whole affair.

OCTOBER 21ST

1740: On this day, Sir Oswald Mosley leased 'the mine and mines, vein and veins, seam and beds of coal ... in the land around [the Mancunian suburb of] Bradford' to John Seddon, for the annual sum of £50. Seddon employed ten 'gotters' to hew the coal in question, and a branch of the Ashton Canal was later built to connect these workings with the town centre. Extraction had not reached the lower seams yet, but had already reached 67ft deep by the Tudor times. (pittdixon.go-plus.net)

———— • ◆ • ————

1884: Today, H.M. Stanley gave a talk at the Chamber of Commerce on opening up the 'vast tribes' of millions of Africans on the banks of the Congo to free trade. Citing £138,000 worth of cottons and flannel sold at a single Congo trading house in 1879, three-quarters of which came from England, he reckoned that £26 million might be sold if his plans were carried out, stating 'Your own imaginations will no doubt carry you to the limbo of immeasurable and incalculable millions.' He proposed that the Royal Navy and diplomacy be used to ensure Free Trade, that money was to be invested in railways and to support King Leopold of Belgium's proposed International Association government of the region. Back in the height of Imperialist fervour, his speech was met with immense applause.

October 22nd

1761: On this day, Manchester erudite Dr Samuel Ogden (1716-78), who was educated at Manchester's free grammar school and Cambridge, published verses to mark the coronation of George III in Latin, English and Arabic. To which some wit responded:

> When Ogden his prosaic verse In Latin numbers drest
> The Roman language prov'd too weak
> To stand the critic's test
> The English rhyme he next essayed,
> To show he'd some pretence;
> But, ah ! rhyme only would not do
> They still expected sense.
> Enraged, the Doctor swore he'd place
> On critics no reliance;
> So wrapt his thoughts in Arabic,
> And bade them all defiance.

(W.H. Thomson, *History of Manchester to 1852*, John Sherratt & Son Ltd, Altrincham, 1967)

———◆———

1885: Bishop Fraser of Manchester died at the age of sixty-three on this day. He had sat on several Royal Commissions to improve education before he came to Manchester, and continued to work for social progress in his new diocese after his appointment in 1869, where he presided over the Social Science Congress in 1879. Co-operating with other sects earned him the nickname 'Bishop of all Denominations.' News of his death caused the city's busy stock exchange to call it off for the day (*see* April 14th).

OCTOBER 23RD

1838: Manchester, already one of the most populous and industrious towns in the realm, is finally recognised as a Municipal Borough on this day, receiving its Royal Charter on November 1st.

———— ◆ ————

1940: On this day, Arkwright's first cotton mill in Manchester was utterly destroyed in the Blitz. The site of this pioneer, between Miller Street and Angel Street, has lain derelict ever since, apart from its use as a car park and *Time Team* investigated it in September 2005.

———— ◆ ————

1949: Oldham-born J.R. Clynes died at the age of eighty on this day. He had been Labour MP for Manchester, as well as leader of the Labour Party and Home Secretary from 1929-31. A cotton mill worker from the age of ten, he wrote about his experience as a child labourer when sixteen years old, and at the age of seventeen he became involved in Trade unionism. Clynes was present at the 1900 conference where the Labour Representation Committee was launched, which would soon become the parliamentary Labour Party. In 1906 he was elected as MP for Manchester north East, and made a strong impression for the cause of organised labour in Parliament. Supporting the war effort under Lloyd George, he was made Minister of Food Control. From 1921-2 he served as Labour's Chairman, and ran the Home Office from 1929-1931. He remained in Parliament until his retirement in 1945.

OCTOBER 24TH

1572: Edward, Third Earl of Derby and King of the Isle of Man, died on this day. He had long presided over the town's Court Leet. Termed 'essentially the Manchester Earl', he had waited on all monarchs since Henry VIII, was present at the Field of the Cloth of Gold, as well as the coronation of Queen Anne Boleyn. Lord High Steward of England under Queen Mary I, he had led Lancashire and Cheshire forces to crush the Pilgrimage of Grace. 'How liberall was he to his men how carefull for his friende, How good unto his tenante still euen unto his latter ende ... Our noble Queene bewayleth the losse of suche a precious perle, A thousande times (no dowte she sayth) he was a worthye Erle ... The heauens nowe doe possesse his soule the earth his corps retaynes, His passed lyfe a spectacle for others yet remaynes. (Richard Wright Procter, *Memorials of Manchester Streets*, T. Sutcliffe, Manchester, 1874)

1809: On this day, the Ladies' Jubilee School at Strangeways foundations were laid, and the building was named in honour of George III's Golden Jubilee (*see* October 25th). A house was purchased in Broughton Lane with the funds of the philanthropically minded local ladies, and a specially built school was erected in 1810. It was here that thirty young girls were taught literacy, knitting, sewing and the skills needed in domestic service.

OCTOBER 25TH

1798: The Manchester and Salford Light Horse and Volunteers assembled today, opposite the home of Thomas Johnson in High Street. Mrs Ford presented them with their colours, which were a gift from Mr Johnson.

———— • ◆ • ————

1809: On this day, the Golden Jubilee of George III was marked with reluctance by townsfolk, who were still angered over the recent conviction of Colonel Hanson. Nevertheless, some took advantage of the excuse for processions, feasting, dancing and firework displays.

———— • ◆ • ————

1838: A.W. Paulton gave his first lecture on behalf of the recently founded Anti-Corn Law League on this day.

———— • ◆ • ————

1879: On this day, the Marquis of Hartington and John Bright spoke at a great Liberal Party rally at Pomona Gardens, countering the Conservative one at which Lord Salisbury had spoken on the 18th.

OCTOBER 26TH

1868: The mayor, Mr Robert Neill, laid the foundation stone of the New Town Hall at Albert Square on this day. Nearly the whole of the Corporation were present, and at the close of the proceedings 170 guests had a *dejeuner* in the Town Hall. (William E.A. Axon, *Annals of Manchester*, John Heywood, Manchester, 1886)

———— ◆ • ————

1884: World famous angler and Pisciculturist Robert Ramsbottom died at his son's home in Manchester on this day. Born in Darwen seventy-four years previously, he was the author of the important work *The Salmon and its Artificial Propagation*.

———— ◆ • ————

2009: On this day, ITV closed its subsidiary company Cosgrove Hall. They had already closed the Chorlton studios and made all but four core staff members redundant the previous year, robbing the British public of any future counterparts of *Count Duckula*, *Dangermouse*, or *The Wind in the Willows*.

OCTOBER 27TH

1865: Queen Emma of the Sandwich Islands, or rather Kaleleonalani of Hawaii, visited Manchester today, not long after meeting fellow widowed monarch Queen Victoria.

———— • ◆ • ————

1894: Billy Meredith, 'the Welsh Wizard', made his football debut near Chirk in Wales on this day. At the age of twelve he was working in the pits, before he was spotted as a young amateur by Chirk and then Northwich Victoria, where he came to attention of Manchester City. Signing up for the big club, he still kept his mining job and for a while would commute from the pit to Manchester! The Welsh Wizard would go on to score a total of 150 goals for City in his first twelve years with them, and 36 for United in the next fifteen, as well as 11 for Wales from 1895-1920. On retiring he bought a pub, and legend has it that a nearby bomb in the Blitz caused a sudden burst of Welsh international caps into the street. It took a long time to clean up; after all, there were fifty-one of them! He died in Withington, and his previously unmarked grave was provided with a headstone by both Manchester clubs in 2001.

OCTOBER 28TH

1798: Manchester-born John Chesshyre, captain of the sloop *Plover*, captured the ten-gun French privateer Erin-go-Bragh in battle in the North Sea on this day. He later rose to the position of vice-admiral.

———◆———

1835: Through the combined efforts of Richard Cobden, William Langton and James Heywood, the Manchester Athenaeum was established today. It opened on the same day four years later, in a building designed by the architect Barry, through which its founders could claim a connection to the most prestigious architecture of the day – the Houses of Parliament, stressing to the world that Manchester had indeed 'arrived'. Fifty years on to the day it held its jubilee celebration in 1885, with many a self-congratulatory speech from the members and their guests; including MP John Slagg, who ceremonially inaugurated the event. (William E.A. Axon, *Annals of Manchester*, John Heywood, Manchester, 1886; John J. Parkinson-Bailey, *Manchester: An Architectural History*, Manchester University Press, 2000)

OCTOBER 29TH

1820: Withy Grove-born saddler Thomas Barritt died on this day. Barritt's restless mind was not content with leatherwork, and he became a learned and well-read antiquarian and collector of archaeological remains. He was given the special honour of a torch-lit funeral, his coffin escorted by the most respected and prominent citizens. Unofficial town poet laureate Joseph Aston composed a fitting memorial: 'In Mancunium lived a man who knew much of old time, and much of ancient lore. He was vers'd in heraldry, and could tell how all the thanes, and all the knights, and squires, within his shire, had sprung from times remote. And famed too, was he, for his industry.' (William E.A. Axon, *Annals of Manchester*, John Heywood, Manchester, 1886)

————— • ◆ • —————

1867: Following the 'Manchester Outrages' of September 18th, five 'principal offenders' were brought to trial today. Standing before a grand jury, they were charged for taking part in the rescue of two convicted Irish-Americans who had planned to launch a violent uprising in Ireland. The two rescued men had made their way to Liverpool and overseas to safety, while twenty-six Irishmen had been gathered by the local authorities and implicated in the murder of Police Sergeant Charles Brett, of which the present five were singled out as the ringleaders. The verdict would be given on November 1st.

OCTOBER 30TH

1217: Baron Robert Grelley was restored to his fief of Manchester on this day, on the death of King John and the accession of his infant son Henry III (whose regent de Burgh was anxious for support in the country).

1808: Local historian Revd John Whitaker died on this day. His chief monument is his 1771-5 *History of Manchester*, which, in Axon's estimation, 'If disfigured by dogmatism and untenable theories, is a work of great importance and erudition.' Somewhat astoundingly he managed to compile several volumes for Manchester's earliest periods – times for which a more cautious historian would be hard pressed to find evidence!

1855: On this day, John Kennedy, a Kirkcudbright man who had come to Manchester in 1791, died. He had made his fortune by having made some improvements to Crompton's Spinning Mule, and setting up the firm of Sandford, McConnel and Kennedy. He had turned his mind to more theoretical aspects of science as well as the application of technology to industry, and had contributed to the lecturing of the Manchester Literary and Philosophical Society.

OCTOBER 31ST

1794: Gifted scientist John Dalton, a long-term resident of the town, gave his first lecture to the Manchester Literary and Philosophical Society on this day. He took the opportunity to expand upon his own personal experience of colour blindness, and its apparent genetic transmission in his own family, thereby presenting the earliest scientific paper on the subject that has since been known to many around the world as 'Daltonism', in his honour.

———— • ◆ • ————

1836: Thomas Bury, a Manchester fustian shearer and woollen cord finisher, died today. Axon described him as the 'founder' and first ever finisher of moleskin – a heavy cotton fabric sheared on one surface to produce a thick but short furry pile.

———— • ◆ • ————

1963: Johnny Marr was born in Ardwick on this day. He would later go on to become the influential guitarist and co-songwriter of The Smiths. A City supporter, he had once entertained ambitions of a professional football career and even took part in trials, though the fates had other ideas. Many recent performers have cited Marr's guitar style as a big influence on their own music, including Oasis, the Stone Roses and Radiohead. He has most recently been involved in film soundtrack work, including that of the 2010 film *Inception*.

NOVEMBER 1ST

1867: Today, the verdict of 'guilty' was announced for the five alleged Fenians arrested after the 'Manchester Outrages' of September 18th. Anti-Fenian hysteria had surrounded the affair, and there was considerable ground to doubt the evidence – a cause taken up by many across the land, including political philosopher John Stuart Mill and Mancunian politician John Bright. Royal Marine Thomas Maguire figured among the accused, and his subsequent pardon served to demonstrate the perjury involved in the cases against the convicted. US Civil War veteran O'Meagher Condon, who claimed he had organised the attack but had not been present, made no bones about his Fenian sympathies: 'Had I committed anything against the Crown of England, I would have scorned myself had I attempted to deny it. God save Ireland!' Condon's sentence was later commuted, but the others faced the hangman on November 22nd. In court, US citizen Michael O'Brien had railed against the 'Imbecile and tyrannical rulers of Ireland' to the extent that the judge asked him to desist lest he prejudice the jury too much against him. Nineteen-year-old William Allen protested his innocence but stated he would 'Die proudly and triumphantly in defence of republican principles and the liberty of an oppressed and enslaved people.' Michael Larkin was resigned to his fate, and asked God's forgiveness on those 'Who had sworn his life away.' (T.D. and D.B. Sullivan, *Speeches from the Dock*, Dublin, 1867)

NOVEMBER 2ND

1642: On this day, Sir Alexander Radcliffe of Ordsall was arrested. He had been an active participant among the Royalist besiegers of Manchester in September, having held Salford for the King, and was arrested while on the run from the Parliamentarians in Essex, before he was taken to the Tower.

1796: A handbill recorded by Procter on this day, in his *Memories of Manchester Streets*, affords a curious glimpse into the sporting diversions of Manchester men in the late Georgian period: 'At the Circus [a racecourse once sited by Piccadilly] a foot race by Mr Wild (Stump) and another noted runner for ten guineas, twelve times round, making 800yd. Stump is the same who ran on Kersal Moor.' John Wild's feats had been set to rhyme in 1790 (*see* April 15th), and his death was reported in 1840, much to his surprise and speedy refutation.

1884: Mancunian William Harrison, born at Green Bank in Salford, died on this day. A successful Manchester merchant, he retired to the Isle of Man in 1842. While there, he was a member of the Old House of Keys until its dissolution in 1867, and helped found the Manx Society (*see* September 6th), for which he edited fifteen of its thirty-one published volumes on Manx history, language and culture.

NOVEMBER 3RD

1834: On this day, the Northern Lights made a rare appearance over Manchester.

* ◆ *

2005: Prime Minister Tony Blair switched on the CIS Tower's new record-breaking solar panel array today. Covering 3,200sq m of what then, at 122m was still Manchester's tallest building, the new cladding is Europe's largest vertical photovoltaic array, and makes the tower a net contributor to the National Grid.

* ◆ *

2011: It was on this day that local chef Ben Holden announced his innovative Manchester Egg (a pickled egg in a black pudding coating) was to be sold in the City of Manchester Stadium's pre-match gathering area, 'City Square', before and after all future games. The culinary invention is now to be found there alongside the traditional chips, pies and gourmet snacks of Marco Pierre White in the Blue Moon Cafe. (*Manchester Evening News*)

NOVEMBER 4TH

1788: The centenary of the Glorious Revolution was celebrated by an artillery salute in St Ann's Square on this day.

1843: The first Saturday half-day holiday was enjoyed by the mill workers of Manchester on this day. The leisure time provided for would soon stimulate the growth of popular activities, such as attendance of football matches that helped the culmination in growth of professional football as the multi-billion pound industry it is today. Publications such as the 1851 *Half-Holiday Handbook* soon came into existence, as the whole concept of the 'weekend' and its dedication to leisure came into existence.

1875: The new Anglican Diocese of Manchester held its first Diocesan Conference at the Town Hall today. Four hundred and twenty-six delegates attended, comprising 153 clergymen and 273 laymen.

1989: Camper Van Beethoven's cover of the Status Quo track about L.S. Lowry was number one in the US charts for the third week in a row – something rather odd for a song inspired by the factory-scapes of Manchester! Status Quo's original had been their only US hit, though it had only reached number seven in Britain. Brian & Michael were to have more success with a Lowry song later (*see* November 25th).

NOVEMBER 5TH

1627: On this day, Sir John Radcliffe of Ordsall Hall was slain on the French Isle of Ré. An English invasion force of 100 ships and 6,000 soldiers had gained a beachhead, besieging the citadel of St Martin, but was forced to retreat in October. The defending commander was made Marshall of France, little comfort to Sir John's father who had already lost two sons in battle. Ben Jonson set his tragedy to verse; 'How like a column, Radcliffe, left alone, for the great mark of virtue, those being gone.'

* * *

1893: Hundreds gathered on this day for the now regular Anarchist speeches on Ardwick Green. The authorities were mocked in the notices posted at the meeting: 'The sermon will be preached by an Anarchist, the lesson read by Chief Inspector Caminada, and the psalms sung by his crew', referring to the opposition the police and local clergymen had to the meeting. In the event, fireworks disrupted the speeches, and one young mechanic, James Birch, was arrested and fined 40s.

* * *

1947: Herman, of Herman's Hermits, was born today in Davyhulme, as Peter Noone. Schooled at Stretford Grammar, he soon went into acting, playing Stanley Fairclough in *Coronation Street*. He later found success with the Hermits at the early age of fifteen, capitalising on the 'British Invasion' then taking the USA by storm. In 2001 he was elected, by viewers, as 'VH1's Sexiest Artist'!

NOVEMBER 6TH

1874: The Shakespeare Society at Owens College was founded on this day. The group was formed to further the study of the Bard and his language, holding readings, writing papers and encouraging discussion of him and his period.

———◆———

1971: An 'epic' Manchester Derby was played on this day. George Best and Franny Lee battled over Best's dives, Lee giving an especially theatrical demonstration to the referee of his opponent's falls. Other names from the classic age of football included Summerbee and Charlton, and both teams gave it their best at Maine Road, giving the crowd an unforgettably gripping match. 'In twenty-five years I have not seen a more exciting Derby game in Manchester, nor one in which the spectators were better behaved. They must have been too exhausted and absorbed to indulge in private battles,' reported Eric Todd of the *Guardian*. 'We are not likely to see its like again in years. There were handshakes and hugs all round as the players left the field to a great ovation.'

November 7th

1597: On this day, Warden John Dee took a break from his philosophical musings to note in his diary that his young son Arthur had hurt his eye in some boisterous play with 'rapier and daggre of sticks'. Considering himself a latter-day Merlin, and claiming descent from Welsh royalty, his son's name is quite unsurprising. Arthur would follow in the footsteps of his learned father, ending up court physician to Tsar Mikhail of Russia, and later to Charles I.

———— • ◆ • ————

1642: Henry Montagu, First Earl of Manchester, died on this day. As all who have borne this title, he had no other connection with the town – Montagu had received the title from Charles I, but his only involvement with the place was that of 'an occasional present of game'.

———— • ◆ • ————

1831: On this day, landlord John Vandeleur, anxious to keep his tenants from rebellion, invited Manchester socialist Edward Thomas Craig to organise an egalitarian commune on his estates at Ralahine in County Clare. The commune prospered, even introducing a mowing machine – the first employed in Ireland. However, after two years Vandeleur's gambling debts forced him to end the experiment. At their last meeting, the tenants noted down 'the contentment, peace and happiness they had experienced for two years under the arrangements introduced by Mr Vandeleur and Mr Craig, and which, through no fault of the Association, was now at an end.' They were then evicted.

NOVEMBER 8TH

1422: On this day, the Baron of Manchester granted his Hall to the Church. The main chamber, with its huge medieval fireplace, is still much as it was at the time and now forms part of Chetham's School of Music, giving a fine backdrop to their concerts.

———— • ◆ • ————

1865: Today, in honour of William Shakespeare's tercentenary, the Manchester Committee, which was formed to celebrate the event, founded a £40 scholarship for the Owens College, and two £20 scholarships for the free grammar school.

———— • ◆ • ————

1884: The Manchester and Salford Co-operative Society celebrated its silver anniversary with a huge tea party at Belle Vue today. It was certainly an occasion for celebration, as the following figure shows: in the twenty-five years of its existence hitherto it had made total sales of £2,912,984. The headquarters at the Co-operative Hall on Downing Street had set up branches in Great Ancoats, Cheetham Hill, Chapel Street Salford, Oldham Road, Chester Road, Stretford Road, Gorton Moss Lane West, Ashton New Road, Longsight, Hyde Road, Higher Openshaw, Strangeways, Rochdale Road, Regent Road, and Denmark Road.

NOVEMBER 9TH

1841: In honour of the birth of the Prince of Wales, later Edward VII, a subscription was started up on this day, to collect funds for the celebrations. In the event, however, the contemporary backdrop of a trade depression made this seem inappropriate, and so the £2,800 raised was alternatively spent on blankets, coverlets and flannel to be distributed to the most needy – 6,500 households thus benefited from the charity.

1885: Randall H. Alcock, who for many years had been involved in Bury's cotton industry, and a committed amateur botanist, died on this day. He founded and served as president of the Bury Natural History Society, and was elected a fellow of the National Linnaean Society.

1823: The New Quay Company was formed on this day, with John Brettargh and two others stumping up the necessary initial capital of £30,000 to facilitate traffic on the Irwell, much expanded since the days of the first 'kay' dating to the 1730s .

November 10th

1665: Charles II granted Chetham's Hospital its Charter, making its feoffees a legal body corporate.

———— • ◆ • ————

1994: Manchester City were at a low ebb, humiliated by United's 5–0 victory at Old Trafford today. City's fourth-choice goalkeeper, the beleaguered Tracey, was hard pressed, and Andrei Kanchelskis completed his first hat-trick for the Red Devils, thanks to the 'deceptively languid' Cantona's return to form after a less than inspiring recent match with Barcelona. (*Guardian*)

NOVEMBER 11TH

1331: 'In the Fifth year of Edward III, Henry, son of Robert de Ancotes, to farm lets, &c. to Sir R. de Burun, knight, and his heirs, messuages, lands, and tenements, in the hamlet of Annecotes, in the vill of Mamecestre, for the term of forty years, from the feast of St Martin, 1331. To have, &c., yielding one rose.' Such curious rents were a feature of the age, and the same plot at Ancoats had earlier been let by Simon Tinctore (the dyer) to Alexander de Mamecestre for 'one pair of white gloves at the Nativity of the Lord.' (John Harland, *Collectanea Relating to Manchester and its Neighbourhood at Various Periods*, Chetham Society, Manchester, 1866)

———◆———

1656: Richard Hollinworth, Fellow of the town's Collegiate Church, died today. He was one of Manchester's earliest historians, as well as author of *Mancuniensis*, a book that probably played some role in giving the term 'Mancunian' its modern currency.

———◆———

1821: Cheadle Hulme-born Joshua Brookes, a cobbler's son and chaplain of the Collegiate Church, died on this day. Throughout his life, he is believed to have baptised, married and buried more persons than any clergyman in England before or since. Being a rather eccentric figure, he even found his way into literature, most notably in Banks's *Manchester Man*.

———◆———

1887: Work began on the great Victorian industrial project of the Manchester Ship Canal today, with ground being broken at Eastham.

NOVEMBER 12TH

1612: Manchester's first lord of the manor from the Mosley dynasty died on this day. Sir Nicholas had bought the rights shortly before being elected Lord Mayor of London in 1599 and knighted by Elizabeth I. Born in Didsbury, this successful cloth merchant was the second son of Edward Mosley of Hough End Hall, and served as Sheriff of Lancashire in 1604 at the ripe old age of seventy-seven. He was succeeded by his son Rowland.

1838: Today witnessed the opening of the Carpenters' Hall on Garratt Road. As the name suggests, it was the work of the Manchester journeymen carpenters. Motivated by Chartist ideals, its £4,500 construction fee was paid for by no one but themselves.

1881: The first ever Manchester Derby was played on this day. Neither side knew it at the time however, nor were either of the teams playing under their present names. West Gorton (St Mark's) – a little-known team from which Manchester City would later grow – played host at Hyde Road to Newton Heath – Manchester United's equally obscure ancestor. Described as 'a pleasant game' by the *Ashton Reporter*, the match ended with a 0–3 victory to the 'Heathens'. The next decade would see both teams grow in prominence, monopolising the Manchester Cup between them from 1888-93, eventually emerging as the national sides we have come to know.

NOVEMBER 13TH

1865: On this day, Mancunian author Elizabeth Cleghorn Gaskell died. Mrs Gaskell gave us *Mary Barton*, *Cranford*, *North and South* and several other novels, along with the valuable *Life of Charlotte Brontë*, in which she commemorated her friend – one of many prominent figures in literature to visit her home in Plymouth Grove.

———◆———

1880: So far as the gradual process can be dated, today would see the birth of football club Manchester City, as it is now known. This first match saw City's ancestral club, St Mark's (West Gorton), play against a team fielded by the Baptist church in Macclesfield. Not yet clothed in their familiar sky blue, they played in black shirts with white shorts. Macclesfield won 2–1, but the seed was planted that would grow into the world-famous club known today. Curiously, City can claim to be the only major club founded at the instigation of a woman, Anna Connell, daughter of St Mark's rector, who first came up with the idea of using the wholesome activity of football to help combat the social evils of drink and gang violence in the parish. The church had formed a cricket club five years before, but there was a clear need for a winter alternative. She persuaded churchwardens William Beastow and Thomas Goodbehere to start a football team, and personally visited all residents of the parish to drum up support, whether Protestant or Catholic.

November 14th

1757: The infamous 'Shudehill Fight' broke out today, as rioters demanded affordable prices for basic staples. This was met with opposition from the sheriff and local militia, and, after putting up with much stone throwing, the latter opened fire, killing four men. Troubles continued the next day when a corn mill at Clayton was destroyed. The town authorities then ordered a curfew in response to the unrest and outright revolt of the last three days, and two companies of regular infantry were summoned to crush any further disorders. The total casualties amounted to four dead and fifteen wounded.

———— • ◆ • ————

1825: Manchester-born surgeon George Calvert died on this day. He was awarded the Jacksonian Prize of the Royal College of Surgeons three years in a row, and was the celebrated author of *Diseases of the Rectum*.

———— • ◆ • ————

1936: Freddie Garrity, future Manchester milkman, and later chart-topping leader of Freddie and the Dreamers, was born on this day. Part of the 'Merseybeat' phenomenon, the group would get into the UK Top Ten four times in the early 1960s, appear in a handful of films, and then take part in the 'British Invasion' of the US music scene, where their song 'I'm Telling You Now' would make it to number one in 1965. Freddie's mad 'dancing' on stage was something of a signature of the group. He died in retirement at Bangor, Gwynedd on May 19th 2006.

NOVEMBER 15TH

655: The Christian King, Osweo, defeated the Heathen King, Penda of Mercia, at the Battle of the Winwaed on this day, thus avenging his brother Oswald (*see* August 5th) and reuniting the Manchester region with the Kingdom of Northumbria.

———◆———

1801: On this day, Peter Drinkwater died on a journey to London. He had been the first Manchester mill owner to set steam engines to cotton machinery (Arkwright having only used one to lift water to power a water wheel). Drinkwater had set a Boulton and Watt rotary beam engine directly to his cotton preparation machinery in 1790, increasing productivity thirtyfold at his Piccadilly Mill in Auburn Street. Seeking to emulate this success, Robert Grimshaw had set looms to steam power soon afterwards, but received threats from traditional weavers and saw his mill burnt to the ground after only a matter of weeks. Eight years would pass before any other employer in Manchester's fifty-odd mills dared to eschew manual power. (John J. Parkinson-Bailey, *Manchester: An Architectural History*, Manchester University Press, 2000)

———◆———

1922: Regular broadcasting began today for the pioneering radio station, 2ZY Manchester. From its transmitter on the strikingly futuristic iron water tower at Metrovicks electrical works in Trafford Park, the station proceeded with its public service mission to bring news, music and enlightenment to the masses, under the auspices of the British Broadcasting Company – later to become the British Broadcasting Corporation, in 1926.

NOVEMBER 16TH

1835: The Manchester and Salford Institution for the Treatment of the Skin was opened on this day.

———— • ◆ • ————

1853: The people of Manchester succumbed to jingoistic spirit and gathered in the Corn Exchange today, to express sympathy with the Ottoman Empire in its struggles with the Russians. Much Crimean bloodshed would soon follow.

———— • ◆ • ————

1883: Comte Ferdinand de Lesseps came to Manchester on this day, in order to test the water of mercantile opinion on his Suez Canal project. He was much fêted by the townsfolk and presented with several complimentary addresses in his three-day visit.

———— • ◆ • ————

1885: On this day, the City Art Gallery was first illuminated using electricity. (William E.A. Axon, *Annals of Manchester*, John Heywood, Manchester, 1886)

NOVEMBER 17TH

1829: Young Thomas Foster of Long Millgate was accidentally shot on Blackfriars Bridge today, 'while lingering a moment to witness a quarrel.' The culprit was sent to Lancaster Castle Gaol, but later acquitted. (Richard Wright Procter, *Memorials of Manchester Streets*, T. Sutcliffe, Manchester, 1874)

1868: On this day, Manchester holds its first elections since the extension of the franchise by the Reform Act of 1867. The Conservatives' gamble in passing the act to pre-empt the Liberals paid off, winning them three seats in Manchester and Salford, the Liberals taking the other two. This followed the near doubling of the electorate for Manchester (from 25,130 to 47,911) and for Salford (5,960 to 14,827).

2011: The clock tower of the Town Hall was opened to visitors today. People eager to inspect the surroundings could climb 280ft above Albert Square to look through its lofty windows and inspect the 8 metric tonne bell, called Great Abel – named after Mayor Abel Heywood who opened the building back in 1877.

NOVEMBER 18TH

1782: The bellicose townsfolk raised another corps of men to fight in the Americas, as war continued with the Rebels there. One hundred and fifty volunteers were provided under Lt-Col Thomas B. Bailey and Major George Lloyd. Mrs Lloyd presented the regiment with its colours, and the officers' commissions were presented to them in St Ann's Square on this day.

———— • ◆ • ————

1804: On this day, townsman J. Aston released his *Life of Nelson*, possibly the first biography of the great English naval hero.

———— • ◆ • ————

1847: Ralph Waldo Emerson spoke at an Athenaeum soiree today, in the company of local worthies, such as Cobden and Bright, James Crossley and Charles Swain, sharing his impressions of the England of the day; 'Mr Chairman, in looking at these traits (of conscience and friendship) in the English character, it has given me great pleasure to observe that in this time of commercial disaster, in this time of gloom, of bankruptcy, of affliction, and of beggary in the neighbouring districts, the Athenaeum has chosen to hold, with its usual spirit, this its anniversary. It seemed to me, because of these peculiarities which belong to the English character, a certain duty well becoming the managers of the institution; they seemed to me to say, "For all that has come and gone, yet we shall not abate the spirit or the splendour of our annual feast; no, not by an oak leaf; no, not by a chaplet."' (*Manchester Guardian*)

November 19th

1868: Following a disastrous flood in November, a Mr Hawksley presented a report to the Salford Town Council today, in which he recommended the construction of a 30ft diameter tunnel (2 miles in length) to partially divert the Irwell in times of flooding. The estimated cost was £125,000 and, naturally, the matter was dismissed as it was deemed too expensive.

———— • • ————

1881: Bad luck strikes again for John Owen (*see* January 11th), whose toy-making workshop on Catherine Street in Strangeways fell victim to fire once more on this day. The damages to his stock were estimated to have been in the region of £3,000.

———— • • ————

1884: Reverend William Knox, pastor of Chapel Street Congregationalist Chapel in Salford, died on this day. The evening before he had preached at a funeral, in which the hymn 'Abide With Me' had been sung. On announcing it, he had remarked that 'It had been written by a fellow preacher who had just preached an evening service, and had died that very night'. Reverend Knox then did the same.

November 20th

1820: On this day, as news was received that the Bill of Pains and Penalties had been withdrawn, Manchester celebrated with a partial illumination of the town. The bill had been pushed by the unpopular George IV against his own wife, Queen Caroline, and public opinion sided with the rejected royal consort, who was so ignominiously treated by her husband – the Mancunian public all the more, given that monarch's open siding with the bloodthirsty agents of Reaction in the town (*see* August 27th).

1856: A meeting took place in the Free Trade Hall today, calling for an end to capital punishment.

1866: Today, a reform dinner took place at the Free Trade Hall, chaired by the president of the National Reform Union, George Wilson – a ubiquitous name in the annals of Victorian political activism of the town. More than 1,000 gentlemen took part.

NOVEMBER 21ST

1622: Ffrancis Taylior of Bradford was buried at the collegiate church on this day, following 'a fall to the coale pitte'.

———————◆———————

1805: On this day, Manchester greeted the news of Nelson's victory at Trafalgar with great rejoicing. Ardwick Green was the scene of most organised merriment, and a subscription was made in aid of those bereaved by loss of relatives in the engagement. A thanksgiving was also held on December 5th, attended by the local Volunteers regiment.

———————◆———————

1850: In a good old-fashioned bout of anti-Popery fever that accompanied the newly behatted English Cardinal Wiseman's intention to work for the 'restoration of Catholic England to its orbit in the ecclesiastical firmament', Manchester Protestants met to discuss the 'Papal aggression', which was firmly denounced at their meeting in the Free Trade Hall today. Those present then announced themselves fully behind the government's Ecclesiastical Titles Bill, preventing Roman bishops from taking titles in use by the Anglicans.

NOVEMBER 22ND

1935: William Geddes of Stretford, aged twenty-eight and a roofer, was reported to be 'rather poorly' today after his 30ft fall off a roof in Station Road, Pendlebury. He had slipped and grabbed hold of the guttering, before he plummeted to the ground, injuring his back, head and arms. Clearly, they were built of stern stuff back then! (*Manchester Guardian*)

———•◆•———

1935: As Britain painfully climbed its way out of the Great Depression, the Society of Friends (or Quakers) made a great effort to help furnish the unemployed with allotments, as reported in today's *Guardian*. At a cost of just over £53,000, they stated that they had so far helped 120,641 men this way, providing assistance with seed, tools and fertiliser. They urged all desirous of such a means to help feed their families to apply to the local council for a plot, upon which they would be only to happy to assist them make a start.

NOVEMBER 23RD

1867: The so-called 'Manchester Martyrs' were hanged today in the city, for the murder of a policeman. At 8 o'clock in the morning, 8,000-10,000 people gathered outside New Bailey Prison to witness the execution, for which a special 30ft-high platform had been built on the walls, while the city's Irish gathered for Mass in their churches. The police presence was strong, and the 72nd Highlanders and 8th Hussars represented the military. William Allen's neck was broken immediately on the drop, but hangman William Calcraft botched the hangings of the two others and rushed below to pull on the legs of Michael Larkin. Likewise bungling the third hanging, Father Gadd forbade him from performing the same for Michael O'Brien; the priest then held the hand of the dying man and prayed for a full forty-five minutes till his agonies were over. This was the last public hanging in Manchester.

———◆———

1966: Salford's Russell Watson was born on this day. Completely untrained, he began singing in Working Men's Clubs to supplement his industrial labourer's wage. His break came at the opening of 1999 Rugby League Final. His 2001 debut album reached number five in the charts, and many have followed since, combining opera, musicals and pop, more or less inventing the 'Classical Crossover' genre.

November 24th

1639: On this day, William Crabtree, a prosperous clothier of Broughton, informed of a coming transit of Venus over the sun. Observed in readiness all day, he was frustrated by the overcast sky, but finally saw the semi-eclipse shortly before sunset, at around 3.35 p.m. 'Rapt in contemplation, he stood for some time motionless, scarcely trusting his own sense through excess of joy.' This gentleman amateur was widely renowned for his mathematical and astronomical attainments, and corresponded with many of the learned men of his day. (William E.A. Axon, *Annals of Manchester*, John Heywood, Manchester, 1886)

———— • ◆ • ————

1870: Manchester elected its first School Board today, in order that the terms of the new Education Act might be implemented in the city. Herbert Birley was elected as chairman, and forty-four candidates competed for the remaining fifteen seats.

———— • ◆ • ————

1878: Great Mancunian annalist, W.E.A. Axon spoke on botanical literature at the first visit of the United Field Naturalists at the Reference Library in King Street on this day. The event was 'the first occasion of its sort', as Axon himself put it, deeming it quite memorable enough to include a mention in his own *Annals of Manchester*.

NOVEMBER 25TH

1833: Robert Owen founded the National Regeneration Society at a meeting in town today. The society was dedicated to achieving an eight-hour day by March 1st the following year, which was to be achieved by peaceful and rational co-operation between employers and operatives. However, some of the trade unionists took this in their own understanding of socialism as class war and that a March 1st general strike would 'wrest' the concession from the employers.

1977: Aspiring Manchester band Brian & Michael become one-hit wonders with L.S. Lowry tribute song 'Matchstalk Men and Matchstalk Cats and Dogs', which was released today. It reached number one on April 8th 1978, remaining there for three weeks.

2000: On this day, shortly before its demolition in 2002, the Haçienda nightclub was gutted of it industrial-chic interiors. Everything from emergency exit lights to radiators was snapped up by nostalgic clubbers and collectors at a charity auction. DJ Bobby Langley is said to have purchased the DJ booth that had been mounted on a balcony over the dance floor, albeit for an undisclosed fee, after having organised a 'Stop the Scousers' drive to prevent it going to Liverpool's Cream nightclub. Bricks were on sale for £5, and dance floor tiles for £10. (*Independent*)

NOVEMBER 26TH

1772: On this day, at a town meeting, proposals were made to establish a new road to be called Oldham Street. This is now a principal entrance into the city.

◆

1867: On this day, long before the suffragettes ruffled the feathers of the patriarchal Manchester establishment, the first woman ever to vote in a parliamentary election, Lily Maxwell, voted for Jacob Bright, who won the seat. Her name had only been included in the register due to a clerical error, but nobody stopped her from exercising her apparent right.

◆

1879: The Manchester-designed *Resurgam II* or 'the curate's egg' – a submarine invented and manned by Hulme clergyman George W. Garret (*see* February 26th) – was launched on this day. Its maiden dip was at Birkenhead, in the Wallasey East Float. A peculiar iron contraption costing £1,538, she was shaped somewhat like a short pencil sharpened at both ends, and weighed 30 tons. Her smoke stack was retractable, and though the fumes from the coal fire were unpleasant, she could hold a crew of three for as long as thirty-six hours. The Royal Navy showed some interest and asked that the craft be sailed to Portsmouth. Unfortunately, she had to pull into Rhyl for repairs, and was later lost in Liverpool Bay. (*Diver*, April 1996)

NOVEMBER 27TH

1798: Twenty-one-year-old Ellen Nield, was drowned along with seven companions in the Irwell on this day. The night before, a coach had been dragged downstream from the shallows opposite the Old Church tower. The coachman, whose intent merely to wash the vehicle had gone frightfully awry, managed to jump off, but the horses perished. Coming to see the floating bodies next morning, a small crowd gathered on a dye-works platform by the New Bailey Bridge, only to plunge into the icy waters themselves as the wood gave way under their weight. Three were saved, including a small boy saved by the dyer's dog, but Ellen and seven more were lost. Her body was only recovered eleven weeks later at Barton Bridge, once the ice had thawed.

———◆———

1822: Manchester mourned the passing of Old Billy today, a sixty-two-year-old barge horse. He had worked on the Mersey and Irwell Navigation for fifty-nine years in the keeping of the now sadly bereaved Henry Harrison.

———◆———

1995: On this day, Peter Kay, still a fresh young student at Salford University, gave his first non-college performance at the old Frog and Bucket on Newton Street. Back in the days of £2 entrance fees, before the move to Oldham Street, Kay had to change in the loo – a bit of a contrast to his massive arena audience and box office-busting records of today.

November 28th

1746: Lieutenant James Bradshaw, one of the Manchester recruits of the Stuart invasion, was executed today in London for his pains, at Kensington Common. His gallows speech ended thus: 'I am convinced that these nations are inevitably ruined unless the Royal Family be restored, which I hope will soon happen. For I love my country, and with my parting breath I pray God to bless it. I also beseech Him to bless and preserve my lawful sovereign, King James the Third, the Prince of Wales, and Duke of York, to prosper all my friends, and have mercy on me!' (William E.A. Axon, *Annals of Manchester*, John Heywood, Manchester, 1886)

1815: Charles H. Timperley obtained honourable discharge from the 33rd Regiment of Foot, with a daily pension of 1s for wounds received at Waterloo. He had joined up at only fifteen years of age in 1810, and after defeating Napoleon he tried his hand at engraving. Having been, in his own words, 'Early attached to reading ... all [his] life an ardent inquirer after knowledge', he soon left that vocation for that of letterpress printer, with the view of 'affording me that literary information which I so ardently desired'. He would later become owner of a bookshop on the corner of Old Millgate and wrote several works on the history of his craft, as well as one volume of poetry dedicated to the Press, and his 1830 *Annals of Manchester*. (Richard Wright Procter, *Memorials of Manchester Streets*, T. Sutcliffe, Manchester, 1874)

November 29th

1745: Bonnie Prince Charlie arrived in Manchester on this day. His troops, greeted by the cheers of Manchester Jacobites, billeted down in the newly built and fashionable St Ann's Square, while their prince lodged at John Dickenson's House in Market Street. Known later as 'the Palace', this was succeeded by the Palace Inn, and then the warehouse Palace Buildings. A Manchester Regiment was then formed of local volunteers, with commissions given to Captain 'Jemmy' Dawson – later commemorated in the tragic ballad of the same name – and three sons of the celebrated theologian Dr Deacon.

———•◆•———

1875: Chetham's librarian Thomas Jones died today. He had edited numerous historical publications for Chetham's Society, but sadly died before he could make something of his notes compiled for a biography of Elizabethan esoteric and Manchester College Warden Dr John Dee.

NOVEMBER 30TH

1745: On this day, Charles Edward Stuart attended a special service in the 'Old Church', where Manchester ladies of the Jacobite cause were all dressed in tartan ribbons. He then made a speech in St Ann's Square, proclaiming his father 'James III' and himself as Regent and Prince of Wales. Festivities followed, ending in an evening illumination and fireworks. Local Whigs and Presbyterians maintained a very low profile throughout the celebrations.

1819: William Cobbet, a local politician, had intended to pass through town today, bearing the bones of the radical thinker Tom Paine, author of the *Rights of Man*. He had brought the remains back from a visit to America, where Paine had died in exile (and where many were loathe to bury him, as an atheist and blasphemer). The authorities had different ideas, however, and Cobbet was compelled to take a round about route from Liverpool to London.

1917: Manchester-born Sergeant John Thomas of the 5th Battalion North Staffordshire Regiment won the Victoria Cross today, for his bravery at Fontaine in France. In 1954 he died at the age of sixty-seven in Stockport, and was buried in Stockport Borough Cemetery.

DECEMBER 1ST

1745: On this day, Prince Charles Edward Stuart's Jacobite forces returned to Manchester, demoralised and in retreat from the Hanoverian forces of the Duke of Cumberland. They finally left on the 9th and continued their march north, ultimately to the battlefield of Culloden, and Charles to the bonny boat for Skye.

1856: Manchester poet, Charles Swain (1803-1874) received a place on the Civil List today, as well as a pension of 50s. Born on Every Street to a local father and Dutch-born mother, from the age of fourteen he had worked at his uncle Charles Tavaré's dye works. His first full book of poetry was published in 1827, and his genius was recognised by the *Manchester Guardian* on December 8th 1841, in which Robert Southey's words were quoted: 'If ever man were born to be a poet, he was; and, if Manchester is not proud of him yet, the time will certainly come when it will be so.' Many of his works were set to music, becoming popular songs in their own right. He was made an honorary professor of poetry at the Manchester Royal Institution in 1846.

1983: Today saw the release of Chorlton-made animated film *The Wind in the Willows*, in which latex models enacted Kenneth Grahame's classic children's novel. A further sixty-seven episodes were then written for the characters.

DECEMBER 2ND

1771: On this day, Manchester's first bank opened its doors and vaults. A full century after the capital had opened its first native banking houses, the town followed suit with the firm of Byrom, Sedgwick, Allen and Place, whose premises were on the corner of St Ann's Square and what would later be named Bank Street. Edward Byrom, senior partner and son of renowned Jacobite wit and shorthand inventor John Byrom, soon died, however, and the firm was renamed Allen and Sedgwick.

———————— • ◆ • ————————

1841: Manchester's Glee Club was in its prime, and started proceedings off this evening with a hearty rendition of the National Anthem, in view of the recent birth of the Prince of Wales. More were in attendance than ever in living memory, upwards of 140 gentlemen in full voice and glee. Ballads old and new were sung, and a certain Mr Burnett announced his intentions of teaching the members the ambitious skill of part singing, as well as singing from notation. (*Manchester Guardian*)

DECEMBER 3RD

1582: On this day, Robert Worsley, jailer at the New Fleet Prison on Hunt Bank, must have had his sense of enterprise piqued by the opportunities for pecuniary advancement afforded by the practice of fines applied to occasionally wealthy inmates there. The new gaol house had only been founded two years before, and had already been host to Sir John Southworth and other 'obstinate adherents to Popery'. Worsley proposed that, were he to be allowed to keep the proceeds of a year's 'jail tax', he would erect a workhouse at his own expense 'sufficient to afford employment to all the rogues, vagabonds, and idlers in the county.' At the time, the tax amounted to £1 14s 4d from every parish in the diocese of Chester (then including all of Lancashire). (William E.A. Axon, *Annals of Manchester*, John Heywood, Manchester, 1886)

———— • ◆ • ————

1879: Today saw the end of an era for popular science in the city, as the last of the Manchester Science Lectures was given this evening at Pendleton Town hall by Captain W.D.W. Abney, Fellow of the Royal Society. More than a decade's worth of lectures had been given, including some by such prominent men as Professor T.H. Huxley. Public interest had declined, and so the penny lectures came to an end, though they were later published in eleven volumes as *Science Lectures for the People*.

DECEMBER 4TH

1850: Electrical pioneer William Sturgeon died in Prestwich on this day. He was the inventor of the electro-magnet and the first English electro-motor. He had been a superintendent of Manchester's Royal Victoria Gallery of Practical Science.

— ◆ —

1875: The top stone of the tower of Manchester's new Gothic Town Hall was fixed in place today, completing a project that had been ongoing since October 26th 1868. 1,000 builders had assembled 480,000 cubic feet of stone, 16.5 million bricks, 2.5 acres of roofing, 2 miles of iron girders, and 129 tons of lead, along with 3,000 gas burners to light the 314 rooms within. More masons were employed than had been for the construction of the Houses of Parliament. The peal of twenty-one bells was considered by the bellfounder – Taylors of Loughborough – to have been the greatest single such undertaking in the history of the art. The largest, named Great Abel after the mayor, weighed 6 tons 9 cwt, making it Britain's fourth heaviest and sixteenth heaviest in the world.

— ◆ —

1996: Although it had already hosted its first concert, Bridgewater Hall was officially opened by the Queen on this day. All in all, the state-of-the-art venue had cost some £42 million to build, and seats around 2,400 spectators. Its Marcussen & Son pipe organ cost a further £1.2 million to make, and was the biggest built in the country for over a century.

DECEMBER 5TH

1772: Stockport's Revd J. Watson penned a description of a Roman inscription on this day. Found at the nearby site of Melandra Castle, Watson stated that the inscription names the Centurion Valerius Vitalis of the First Cohort of Frisians – a group of Low Countries soldiers who are known to have been stationed by the Romans in the fort at Manchester. The names of other individuals known from this unit have been preserved in other inscriptions, including Lucius Senecianus Martius, Candidus and Massavo, and are the town's first known residents. As well as Frisians, the town's fort also played host to Norici and Rhaetians – Celtic peoples from the Austrian Alps.

❖

1835: Manchester historian and surgeon William Robert Whatton died on this day. He was the author of Volume III in *The History of the Foundations of Manchester,* along with many other works. He had also served as librarian for the Manchester Literary and Philosophical Society.

❖

1883: The Crown Prince of Portugal, Duke Carlos of Braganza, visited Manchester on this day.

DECEMBER 6TH

1814: Miss Lavinia Robinson of Bridge Street disappeared on this day, the eve of her marriage. Rumours circulated of foul play, implicating her betrothed, the surgeon Holroyd, who was forced to leave the town. Her body was not found until February 8th, having been trapped under the ice of the Irwell for two months. It was conjectured that she had committed suicide after a quarrel with Holroyd, in which he had repeated some slanderous rumours about her.

———•◆•———

1841: The middle-aged Elizabeth Matthews appeared before magistrates today, charged with pick-pocketing the wallet of Thomas Knowles at the White Lion Tap in Deansgate. Wanting to dry off from the rain with a pint of ale, Knowles had been sitting at the fireplace when Matthews came in and tried to get him to read a letter, stating that her husband had died down the pit. She asked for a gill of beer, or 'tuppeny o'rum', but was unsuccessful, and while purporting to take off his wet boots she swiped his wallet, which contained over five sovereigns. He ran after her, regaining the wallet minus one sovereign; this was later found, hidden in her mouth, by the arresting constables. The story of her husband passing was proved to be totally false, and she was 'committed for trial at the next Sessions'. (*Manchester Guardian*)

DECEMBER 7TH

1756: The price of bread had shot up by 20 per cent in three months. Prosecutions were threatened against the manorial officers for failing to stamp out price-rigging by the unscrupulous, but to little avail. A committee was formed today to buy up corn to sell to the poor at cost, and £1,500 had been spent by next April. This was not enough, however, and a spark would soon flare up into the 'Shudehill Fight' (*see* June 7th).

1821: Martha Brotherton published her *Vegetable Cookbook* on this day. She was sister to the Mayor of Salford and second president of the Vegetarian Society, William Harvey (himself father-in-law of the first, James Simpson), and wife to Joseph Brotherton, Salford's first MP.

1862: Lancashire was caught in the grip of a merciless depression in trade, many mill hands being laid off or working reduced hours. The scale of the disaster could be seen in the figures for outdoor relief paid to these and their dependants: £13,734 2s 4d. The Relief Committee registered an outlay of a further £19,157 6s 4d.

December 8th

1720: On this day, George I signed the Act providing for the making of the Irwell and Mersey navigable for Manchester boats (*see* June 6th).

------◆------

1859: Manchester-born man of letters, Thomas de Quincey, died on this say. In Axon's estimations he was the 'Most brilliant magazine writer of the century' and his lasting fame was earnt by his ever-in-print *Confessions of an English Opium Eater*. He died in Edinburgh, where he is buried in Greyfriars Church.

------◆------

1867: On this day, funerals were held in Irish-inhabited areas for the Fenians hanged for the recent 'Manchester Outrages'. The name of 'Martyr' was already being granted to the three men hanged by that community, despite the avowed disapproval of the Catholic hierarchy. A famous song was soon composed in their honour:

> Climbed they up the rugged stair, rang their voices out in prayer,
> Then with England's fatal cord around them cast,
> Close beside the gallows tree kissed like brothers lovingly,
> True to home and faith and freedom to the last.
> 'God save Ireland!' said the heroes;
> 'God save Ireland' said they all.
> Whether on the scaffold high,
> Or the battlefield we die,
> Oh, what matter when for Erin dear we fall!

DECEMBER 9TH

1707: Today, a disturbing entry was recorded in the parish register: 'Buried, James Glassbrook, a soldier, burnt himself in the dungeon.' The exact circumstances of this sorry event – whether it was suicide, accident, or insanity – are unknown.

1745: The occupying force of the Jacobites ordered a levy of £2,500 from the inhabitants of Manchester today, to pay for the forces' upkeep and further expenditure. They would quit the town the following day.

1960: On this day, ITV aired the first ever episode of *Coronation Street*, with the long-serving Ken Barlow and iconic Ena Sharples. Around 8,000 episodes later, the series has stood the test of time and is the flagship product of locally based Granada Television. The soap has kept the good old familiar theme tune by Eric Spear (who only got £6 for his trouble), executed by cornet player Ronnie Hunt. Arriving on screen when the proper 'BBC voice' was still very much in dominance, Tony Warren's creation immediately won viewers over with its mix of local speech and lively drama.

DECEMBER 10TH

1293: The sceptical friar Hugh of Manchester is mentioned in a letter from Archbishop John Romanus of York on this day. Hugh had penned a volume named *De Fanaticorum Deliriis, or Of the Delusions of the Fanatics*, in which he (a likely close relative of Manchester's barons) decried the credulous abuses of his superstitious age.

———— • ✦ • ————

1757: On this day, a sugar plant worker fell to his death in a horrific accident; the cause of death was recorded as scalding.

———— • ✦ • ————

1908: Ernest Rutherford, professor of physics at the Victoria University, Manchester, was awarded his Nobel Prize for chemistry today. This came almost a decade before the achievement he is now principally remembered for – the 1919 'splitting' of the atom, in effect the 'philosopher's stone' of the ancient alchemists, all of which took place at the labs on Bridgeford Street off Oxford Road.

———— • ✦ • ————

2010: Two Russians, Andrei Geim and Kostya Novoselov, made a startling discovery in Manchester – a new form of carbon known as graphene. This new carbon promises to revolutionise nanotechnology, and it is for this discovery that Andrei and Kostya received their Nobel Prize for physics on this day. Graphene is 100 times stronger than steel, and its engineering potential is something to keep an eye open for in the near future.

DECEMBER 11TH

1554: On this day, the Court Leet ordered that, 'The inhabitants of the town of Manchester that doth keep swyne, shall pay unto an officer that shall be paid to keep them upon a common called Colyers [Collyhurst], for every swine quarterly 1*d*; or so to keep them within upon their back side, that they do not go abroad in town or market, nor in church yard, after the Purification of our Lady [February 2nd], 5*s*.' The swine horn was blown at 8 a.m. and the first named swineherd was Thomas Ranshawe in 1570.

———•◆•———

1855: A meeting at the Town Hall today resolved to erect a statue to the memory of the steam pioneer James Watt in front of the Infirmary (now Piccadilly Gardens), which was fast filling up with monuments.

———•◆•———

1962: On this day, Alexander Montagu, the 13th Duke of Manchester, was born in the city of Geelong in Australia. He had been married three times (once bigamously), had fired a spear gun at his wife, and attempted to sell a hire car. He ended up in America, where he was arrested in Las Vegas for writing a very large cheque that bounced. His Grace does not appear to have visited Manchester, which is probably for the best!

DECEMBER 12TH

1745: On this day, the Duke of Cumberland, known as 'The Bloody Butcher' to the Jacobites, arrived in Manchester. He was hot on the heels of the Young Pretender, who he would eventually catch up to at Culloden.

———— ◆ ————

1891: The first edition of the socialist penny weekly, *The Clarion*, was issued today, from a room on Corporation Street. The cheap paper tore during the printing process, and the publicity posters were all washed away in torrential rain. However, Robert Blatchford, the editor, had earned many loyal readers while working at the *Sunday Chronicle* and 40,000 copies were still sold. These figures doubled over the next twenty years, and the paper spawned numerous cycling, rambling, drama and scouting societies, many of which are still going today.

———— ◆ ————

1970: George Best broke Manchester City's Glyn Pardoe's leg in today's Manchester derby match. Having been City's youngest ever player at his sixteen-year-old debut in 1962, and scoring the winning goal of the recent FA Cup Final, Pardoe was now in grave danger of having his leg and livelihood amputated. He recovered, however, and resumed his playing career in 1972, but this proved a struggle, and he retired four years later and joined the club's coaching team, where he remained until 1992. City won the Derby in question, 4–1.

DECEMBER 13TH

1763: The Parish's Owd Church (now the cathedral) received its first tower clock on this day. The work of a Mr Hindley of York, this 'very curious and elegant clock' was 'allowed by all judges to be the best constructed thing of the kind ever seen in this country [region, rather], and gives great satisfaction to the whole parish.' (*Manchester Mercury*)

———— • ◆ • ————

1803: Engineering genius Thomas Highs died at the age of eight-four in Manchester today. He was involved in the intricate and unsolvable question of who exactly invented the Spinning Jenny. Even at the time, the issue was horrendously complicated by various disputes over patents and industrial espionage, but Highs undoubtedly played his role in the perfection of the machines that made Manchester into 'Cottonopolis'. In 1772, he at least received an award of 200 guineas from the cotton barons of the city.

DECEMBER 14TH

1422: Rector of Ashton-under-Lyne, John Huntington, was enfeoffed as first Warden of the Collegiate Church today. As one of the chief persons in the medieval town, he received a rich and prominent tomb in the parish church, which he did much to beautify in his lifetime. The capitals of the columns and the earlier wood carvings there still show the curious rebus that displayed to the illiterate the name of the entombed; on one side, a man with dogs blows his horn, and on the other is carved a barrel – 'hunting' and 'tun', creating 'Huntington'.

———— •◆• ————

1918: The first ever General Election held under a franchise of more or less universal male suffrage (and partial female suffrage) was held today, resulting in a surprising Conservative majority. With Manchester and Salford constituencies electing eight Conservatives to three Labour, the Liberals were fast becoming obsolete in the city.

———— •◆• ————

2010: A sad loss to the Manchester skyline as the 180ft-tall smokestack of the Boddingtons Brewery was demolished today. Demolition was carried out by Rafferty International Ltd of Stoke, and was quite a difficult job, given the structure's proximity to the Manchester Evening News Arena, but it toppled down very neatly.

DECEMBER 15TH

1713: John Barnes, who had been the 'bellman of Manchester' for twenty-three years, was buried on this day.

1838: Following the previous day's landmark first ever municipal elections, the new Manchester Council officially assembled today, appointing Thomas Potter as mayor and Joseph Heron as town clerk.

1875: The National Reform Union met for a private conference at the Free Trade Hall today, to discuss their attitude toward further political change. This was a result of the recent Reform Act of 1867, passed by Disraeli's Conservative administration. The evening was devoted to a public meeting on the matter, with some satisfied at the contemporary settlement and others wishing to push for universal suffrage (perhaps even of women).

DECEMBER 16TH

1651: Humphrey Chetham made his will today. In it he provided for the increase of his school of twenty-two poor boys to forty, and requested that £7,000 of his estate go towards the purchase of property to support Chetham's Hospital. £200 was devoted to the purchase of theological books to be chained to desks in local churches, and a further £1,100 was left to build and stock a public library, to which would go any remainder of his fortune on his death. Chetham's School has since been absorbed into other bodies and charities, but the library is still open to this day, and is housed in the impressive medieval cloisters of the former College.

———◆◆———

1798: On this day, rioting broke out due to the scarcity of corn. With working classes close to starvation, local clergymen publicly swore to cut their use of flour to a third, with many middle-class families forswearing pastries altogether. In order to help, the authorities offered prizes for the largest shipments of flour to the market place. In 1799, the town would see the opening of soup kitchens, as well as a proclamation of a general fast for those able to bear it.

———◆◆———

1850: US Ambassador Abbott Lawrence came to visit Manchester on this day. Born in Grotton Massachusetts, it is unknown whether he paid a visit to Grotton by Oldham.

DECEMBER 17TH

1636: On this day, Manchester obtained the use of the noble Stanley dynasty's private chapel in the Collegiate Church to use as a library. John Prestwich of Hulme later donated his own large collection of books, which were kept chained on bookshelves there.

◆

1855: Margaret Oldham died in the Workhouse on this day. She had been the town's first ever Sunday Scholar in 1780, having got up especially early with the full intention of being the first. She did this, knowing that a slice of currant bread rested on the matter, as had been promised by Molly Scholes, keeper of a dame's school at Press Houses Steps near Blackfriars. Scholes announced the opening of her school on the following Sunday. On the day itself, Margaret was rivalled by Betty Hyde, but put paid to the latter by dragging her back by the hair. Molly then gave both women a slice of bread. William E.A. Axon, *Annals of Manchester*, John Heywood, Manchester, 1886)

DECEMBER 18TH

1856: Joseph John Thomson was born in Cheetham Hill on this day. Fourteen years later, he would begin his academic career at the Owens College. Later working at many universities in Europe and America, he was awarded a Nobel Prize for his work in the conductivity of electricity in 1906 and knighted two years later. Discovering the electron, he paved the way for Rutherford's coming Nobel Prize (*see* December 10th).

1910: John Edward Sutton, a 'checkweighman' at Bradford Colliery, was elected Independent Labour MP for Manchester East on this day. He had joined the colliery at the age of fourteen, and was elected councillor in 1894. In his maiden speech, he reminded the House of the stark economic inequalities of the day: 'Practically 30 per cent of our population live below the poverty line … these people are already taxed enough. The aggregate wages of the working classes are going down at the rate of nearly £2m per annum, while the profits of the rich classes who pay Income Tax are going up at the rate of nearly £20m per annum.' (Hansard)

1885: On this day, the mayor opened the new premises of the Schiller Anstalt in Nelson Street. By this time, the association was the main society of the large German element in the city, numbering some 2,000 individuals engaged in trade and commerce, including a young Friedrich Engels.

DECEMBER 19TH

1873: On this day, the RNLI's Seaton Carew lifeboat was drawn through the streets in honour of its £500 benefactor, one-armed butcher Job Hindley of Red Bank. He had previously donated another £1,000 of his fortune to Manchester Royal Infirmary, in gratitude for the work they had done on his remaining limb.

———◆◆◆———

1890: Today's *Birmingham Daily Post* reported that several Brummies, having seen the Manchester Cinderella Club in action, decided to set up one in their own city. The brainchild of local socialist Robert Blatchford, these clubs were an effort to brighten the lives of the poorest children, arranging visits to the countryside or simply putting on the pantomimes for which they were named, all while ensuring they received at least one square meal that week; typically a bowl of hot soup with a bun.

———◆◆◆———

2010: Today, Manchester United's manager Sir Alex Ferguson became the club's longest serving manager. He took over the position from Sir Matt Busby in November 1986 and has been manager ever since. His predecessor held the previous record, and as of today (2012) Sir Alex has over twenty-five years under his belt. He has also broken records for the number of times he has been awarded Manager of the Year, and there are rumours of a future appointment to the House of Lords, no doubt facilitated by his major donations to New Labour.

DECEMBER 20TH

1712: Edmond Harrold's diary entry for this day; 'I had a very midering day.' Perhaps the most distinct word in the Manchester dialect, mider, or rather mither, is still going strong today, despite its absence from most dictionaries. It is gratifying to see it in this early document. Curiously, the Oxford English Dictionary suggests a link to Irish *modartha* (dark, murky, morose) and Welsh *moedro* (to bewilder, perplex), though both might as likely come from the English term, chiefly used in Lancashire and the West Midlands, perhaps ultimately connected with 'murder' in the sense of something arduous or tiring.

1804: Today saw the grand opening of the Rochdale and Halifax Canal at Knott Mill. The committee in charge sailed down from Rochdale on two narrowboats, to the accompaniment of the regimental band of the Manchester and Salford Volunteers. With the festivities out of the way, the new waterway got down to business, and a barge laden with goods from the Pennines came into Manchester that very evening and sailed on to Liverpool the next morning.

1840: The Union Carrying Company's warehouses at Piccadilly burned down today, with a record-breaking £30,000 worth of damage.

DECEMBER 21ST

1790: A large cotton mill by Hanover Street, containing twenty-two people, collapsed today. Many of the people inside lost their lives and others were grievously injured. A poorly built arch in the foundations had sprung, bringing the whole building tumbling down.

———◆·———

1803: One of Manchester's greatest engineers, manufacturers and municipal benefactors, Joseph Whitworth was born in Stockport on this day. In his workshop at No. 44 Chorlton Street, he was the first to produce accurate screws and bolts, and thus there is barely a mechanical device in existence that does not bear witness to his work. Where the human eye and dexterity could produce accuracy at a level of one sixteenth of an inch, his machines introduced a whole new level of precision – one ten-thousandth of an inch in 1850, and one two-millionth in 1859. Whitworth left his fortune to the city, providing for Manchester's Whitworth Art Gallery and Christie Hospital (a globally important cancer research centre).

———◆·———

1844: Taking their lead from Rochdale Pioneers, Owenites formed a Co-operative grocer today, on the ground floor of a warehouse on Toad Lane. Following the collapse of earlier such ventures elsewhere, this shop was under strict rules not to give credit and soon expanded, adding meat sections and others with time.

DECEMBER 22ND

1730: The first issue of Henry Whitworth's *Manchester Gazette* rolled off the presses on this day. By 1737 it had become the three ha'penny *Manchester Magazine*, and later, under Henry's son Robert, *The Advertiser and Weekly Magazine*. The last issue was released on March 25th 1760.

1940: The Luftwaffe bombed the industrial estate of Trafford Park today, including Old Trafford football stadium. Forthcoming matches were called off, but the stadium reopened on March 8th, only to be hit again on the 11th. Subsequently it would remain out of action until 1949.

1949: Twin brothers Robin Hugh and Maurice Ernest Gibb, the two younger members of the phenomenally successful Bee Gees, were born on this day. Only their younger brother Andy (*see* March 5th) was actually born in Manchester, the elder three being born on the Isle of Man (albeit to a Salford mother). But, as Robin himself stated, 'It was in Manchester when we started our career really. It really was here where our interest in music first began, simple as that.' The brothers lived on Keppel Street in Chorlton-cum-Hardy from 1953-8, after which they sailed for Australia. They returned to England in 1967 as fully-fledged professional musicians. The rest, of course, is history. (*Manchester Evening News*)

DECEMBER 23RD

1873: Mark Philips, Manchester's first MP since the 1832 Reform Act, died today. Chairman of the New Quay Company, his political debut saw him speak out in 1826 on the suffering of the workers, the evils of the Corn Laws, and the cowardice of the 'liberals' who forbore to see these realities. Together with his colleague C.P. Thomson, he beat both the Radicals and the traditional Liberals at the first borough election, not to mention the Conservatives. He retired from politics in 1847, returning to the town one last time in October 1871 to join the celebrations at the opening of the Reform Club. His name lives on in Philips Park, and his portrait hangs in the mayor's chambers at the Town Hall.

———◆———

1940: The previous night's bombing continued on into this day. A major seaport and a centre of munitions and weapon production, Manchester was a perfect Luftwaffe target and received its full share of the Blitz. The 22nd and 23rd of December saw a bombardment of 500 tons of explosives and almost 2,000 incendiary bombs, in which over 1,000 lives were lost. Iconic symbols of Manchester – the Royal Exchange, Free Trade Hall, cathedral and Piccadilly Gardens – were specially targeted. The Town Hall and Central Library were luckier, as was the Midland Hotel (it is rumoured that Hitler had planned to make it his regional HQ). Thirteen newly manufactured Manchester Bombers being housed at Metrovicks in Trafford Park were also targeted.

DECEMBER 24TH

1642: Having previously been defeated by Royalist forces at Wigan, the Parliamentarian Manchester Regiment was cheered out of its despondency today. Colonel Roswurm, an early German incomer to Manchester, inspired them to take the field once more, whereupon they won 'a splendid victory' over the SE Lancashire Royalists at the Battle of Chowbent (now swallowed up by Atherton).

1745: On this day, Bonnie Prince Charlie's Jacobite forces holding Carlisle Castle surrender to the Duke of Cumberland after a siege. Among the officers were many Manchester men, including Colonel Francis Townley; Captains Dawson, Fletcher, Sanderson, Moss, Blood, Morgan; Lieutenants Deacon, Deacon, Chadwick, Beswick, Holker, Furnival; Ensigns Deacon, Maddock, Gaylor, Wilding, Hunter, Brettargh, Adjutant Syddall, and ninety-four NCOs and privates.

1893: Despite months of Anarchist scuffles with the police at Ardwick Green on Sundays, nobody turned out to speak today. Detective Superintendent Caminada wryly commented that few of these supposedly committed adherents of Revolution were 'inclined to eat their Christmas dinner in the police station'. (Jerome Caminada, *Twenty-Five Years of Detective Life*, Kensington Publishers, London, 1895)

DECEMBER 25TH

1749: The well-known hymn 'Christians Awake' was penned today. John Byrom presented it as a Christmas present to his daughter, and John Wainwright, who was appointed organist in the Collegiate Church May 12th 1767, then composed a suitably triumphant melody. Less known in recent decades, it was once a staunch favourite and is well worth finding a recording of.

———•◆•———

1788: An 'enumeration' of the town today found it to contain 48,821 persons in 5,916 houses. Salford contained a further 7,566 souls.

———•◆•———

1792: The new St Clement's Church on Lever Street held its first service on this day. It seems that this day was a favoured day for the opening of churches, as Trent Methodists' Chapel on Canal Street was opened in 1821, and the Unitarian Chapel at Greengate in Salford opened in 1824, on the same date.

DECEMBER 26TH

1726: On this day, Whiggish Bishop Peploe tore up a petition presented by the local Tories in church today. Three hundred and forty-one parishioners had signed a document in support of one of their faction, who had been appointed by his Tory predecessor bishop Gastrell while Peploe had been Warden in Manchester. Unpopular in Manchester, Peploe had taken the previous Bishop to court to have his rights to the wardenship confirmed. He may have owed his preferment to his boldness in 1715 when, being forced to hold Divine Service before the Jacobite Pretender at Preston, he had prayed for the ruling House of Hanover.

◆

1847: On this day, Manchester sculptor J.H. Nelson died at Mary Street in Strangeways. He was famous in his day for his sculpture 'Venus Attiring', which was deemed 'anatomically correct' by leading Dublin surgeons, and for which he won the prize of £15 from the Royal Irish Art Union. He left a widow and four children. (William E.A. Axon, *Annals of Manchester*, John Heywood, Manchester, 1886; Walter G. Strickland, *Dictionary of Irish Artists*, Maunsel and Company, Dublin and London, 1913)

DECEMBER 27TH

1832: On this day, a public dinner was hosted at the Theatre Royal, celebrating the election of Mark Philips and Charles P. Thomson – Manchester's first two MPs since the 1600s.

———•◆•———

1913: The great Dr William Edward Armytage Axon, died at his home in Victoria Park in Manchester on this day. A journalist and bibliographer first and foremost, as witnessed by his obituary in *The Times*, he was also an antiquary, whose *Annals of Manchester* have been of immense use in compiling the present work. He worked for three decades at the *Manchester Guardian* and was intimately involved in the questions of political and social reform of the day, recording the life of the great Reformist inspiration Cobden. He was particularly interested in public enlightenment, and in dialect literature and folklore. A contributor to many organs of enlightenment, such as the *Encyclopaedia Britannica* and *Dictionary of National Biography*, he was also involved in the rather more radical movements against tobacco, and for vegetarianism. He was granted an honorary Master of Arts degree by Manchester University, just two months before his death. (*The Times*)

DECEMBER 28TH

1795: In protest against the banning of political gatherings, a Thinking Club had its first meeting today in the Coopers' Arms, at which 300 people sat in silence for a full hour.

———◆———

1830: The last issue of Manchester's journalistic pioneer, the *Mercury*, was printed on this day. Issue no. 3,672 brought to an end the period of seventy-eight years since Joseph Harrop printed its first edition in 1752.

———◆———

1875: Today, the Town Hall's bell and clock tower received its lightning conductor: a great copper ball with 7-in spikes protruding from its surface in all directions. Measuring 2ft 8in in diameter it weighs over 17 stone. Mayor Curtis set it in place.

———◆———

1998: On this day, a supposed gypsy curse is removed from Manchester City's home ground. When the team bought the land at Maine Road in the early 1920s, it is said that a forced removal of a gypsy encampment took place, which was, naturally, accompanied by a curse.

DECEMBER 29TH

1800: Manchester publican and bare-knuckle prize fighter cum engineer, Isaac Perrins was granted an annual £20 pension today. The town awarded him for his 'meritorious services', rescuing people trapped in a huge blazing fire at warehouses in Hodson Square. Unfortunately, he perished just a few days later, on January 6th. According to the Annual Register, he had, 'Possessed most astonishing muscular power, which rendered him well calculated for a bruiser, to which was united a disposition the most placid and amiable. His death was occasioned by too violently exerting himself in assisting to save life and property at a fire in Manchester.' Axon has another anecdote of the gentle giant: 'When challenged to fisticuffs by G.F. Cooke, he calmly picked him up in his arms like a child and carried him into the street.'

1870: The seemingly unstoppable George Wilson died at the age of sixty-two today, whilst on a train to Liverpool. From his humble beginnings as a corn merchant's apprentice, he rose to the position of chairman of the Lancashire and Yorkshire Railway Company, and became one of the most active public men in Manchester, playing a great role in winning the town its Royal Charter. As chairman of the Anti-Corn Law League he led it to success in 1846, and is stated to have taken part in more than 1,361 meetings in the process.

DECEMBER 30TH

1862: On this day, a meeting was held for the county of Cheshire. The people who were of 'means and inclination' were summoned in to response to many months of economic distress that Manchester had been suffering. The meeting collected £30,000 for the relief fund.

———◆◆———

1885: Dr William Roberts FRS received a knighthood today. Born in Anglesey, he joined Manchester's Royal Infirmary at the age of twenty-four and enjoyed a speedy promotion. He served there for three decades before becoming Professor of Medicine at the Owens College. A great contributor to urinary and dietary medicine, he had turned his own home into a mini-laboratory to continue his work when not on the wards.

———◆◆———

1945: Davy Jones, soon to become a teenage heartthrob in The Monkees, was born in Openshaw on this day. He would first appear as a child actor on *Coronation Street*, and then as the Artful Dodger in *Oliver!* (after a brief flirtation with a jockeying career). From the London stage he went to New York's Broadway and appeared, by chance, on the same television show as the Beatles, which inspired him to take up a career in music: 'I saw the girls going crazy, and I said to myself, this is it, I want a piece of that.' (*New York Times*, February 29th 2012)

DECEMBER 31ST

1755: The people of Manchester awoke this morning to scenes of surprising vandalism. A gate from the Collegiate Church had been thrown into the river, and one end of the Market Place Stocks had been wrenched up. A twenty guineas reward offered for information on the culprits remains uncollected.

— ◆ —

1830: This evening, the *Manchester Guardian* reported that 'the Society of Change Ringers of the Collegiate Church rang a true and complete peal of Grandsire Caters, consisting of 10,043 harmonious changes which they completed and brought round in excellent style in six hours and thirty-five minutes, being the longest peal ever rung in this country.' (*Manchester Guardian*)

— ◆ —

1862: On this day, when America was in the midst of the American Civil War, workers from Manchester drafted this letter to President Lincoln: '[We] hope that every stain on your freedom will shortly be removed, and that the erasure of that foul blot on civilisation and Christianity – chattel slavery – during your presidency, will cause the name of Abraham Lincoln to be honoured and revered by posterity.' (*See* January 19th)

— ◆ —

1968: Today, Manchester's Royal Exchange closed its doors for the final time. The values of the stocks at that moment in time are still to be seen on the boards, high on the wall inside.